# BETWEEN THE TIDES
## in California

RYAN P. KELLY, TERRIE KLINGER,
PATRICK J. KRUG & JOHN J. MEYER

# BETWEEN THE TIDES

## in California

EXPLORING BEACHES
AND TIDEPOOLS

UNIVERSITY OF WASHINGTON PRESS

SEATTLE

Design by Derek George
Composed in Ashbury, typeface designed by Dieter Hofrichter

28   27   26   25   24      5   4   3   2   1

Printed and bound in the United States of America

Frontispiece: A tidepool at Partington Cove in Big Sur showcases a
striking array of life forms and colors.

Photographs by the authors unless otherwise noted.

UNIVERSITY OF WASHINGTON PRESS
uwapress.uw.edu

LIBRARY OF CONGRESS CATALOGING-IN-PUBLICATION DATA

Names: Kelly, Ryan P. (Ryan Patrick), author. | Klinger, Terrie, 1956-,
    author. | Krug, Patrick J., author. | Meyer, John J., 1976-, author.
Title: Between the tides in California : exploring beaches and tidepools /
    Ryan P. Kelly, Terrie Klinger, Patrick J. Krug, and John J. Meyer.
Description: Seattle : University of Washington Press, [2024] | Includes
    bibliographical references and index.
Identifiers: LCCN 2023031759 | ISBN 9780295752372 (paperback) |
    ISBN 9780295752389 (ebook)
Subjects: LCSH: Natural history–California–Guidebooks. |
    Coastal ecology–California–Guidebooks.
Classification: LCC QH105.C2 K48 2023 | DDC 508.794–dc23/eng/20231026
LC record available at https://lccn.loc.gov/2023031759

♾ This paper meets the requirements of
ANSI/NISO Z39.48-1992 (Permanence of Paper).

To the many people who have
taught me, intentionally or otherwise.
—RYAN P. KELLY

For Nan and Ed, who first inspired
my exploration of watery worlds.
—TERRIE KLINGER

To Nick, for a lifetime together, and to
everyone I've gone tidepooling with.
—PATRICK J. KRUG

For Mary and Derin, who teach us all to
care for and be curious about the sea.
—JOHN J. MEYER

Large and small spiny lobsters (*Panulirus interruptus*) take refuge under rocks and glower at intruders from shallow pools. Remarkable intertidal hijinks ensue: a moray eel (*Gymnothorax mordax*—"naked biting trunk") writhes out of a hidden cave to pursue a small octopus but loses its target in the surfgrass; returning to its former hideout, the eel finds a large lobster has taken up residence. The belligerent crustacean dismisses the eel's claim to its home with the flick of a pincher. Twice defeated this day, the eel slides off into the surfgrass. Deeper pools witness a tidepool flash mob: schooling fish swim in a frenzied circle; suddenly a large octopus darts to the center, whipping its tentacles to unheard rhythms and strobing its colors like a living disco ball.

# CONTENTS

# BETWEEN THE TIDES
## in California

Point Arena Lighthouse sits on a marine terrace planed flat by the waves of a past era.

# INTRODUCTION

You can tell what people love by what they do in their free time: musicians, after hours, playing together in empty rooms; chefs cooking for one another; artists continually sketching the world around them. Those drawn to the shore are the same. Break time at a meeting of marine biologists will find many facedown on the rocks, surveying and exclaiming—a busman's holiday.

We hope to capture that sense of bottomless curiosity, aesthetic and scientific attraction, and even adventure. This is an easy sell; the US West Coast is visited by millions of people each year, and coastal California is the major draw. But like many things, the shoreline becomes far more interesting as you learn more about it, uncovering its hidden workings and starting to grasp why life between the tides is different in Mendocino versus Santa Barbara or San Luis Obispo versus San Diego. Creating a sense of how coastal ecologies work—which creatures live where and why— deepens our sense of wonder and gives us reasons to keep coming back.

What draws us to the coast? A sense of dynamism and forces larger than us, perhaps. Or a human urge to see the edge of things. The coast gives us a chance to peek under the rug of a different world in which strangely different rules apply—where buoyancy can mitigate gravity's pull, for example, and where animals tend to breathe water rather than air.

Life between the tides is captivating, in part, because it hints at very different ways of being alive on this planet. And yet, the coast is easily accessible. Power, beauty, mystery, and enchantment is an intoxicating mix for locals and the most casual visitor alike.

No two stretches of California's remarkable coastline have exactly the same character, and no beach is ever quite the same on different days. Our goal is to explain *why* different regions have developed distinctive characters, as well as the dynamic forces that make the same beach a slightly different experience on each visit. The physical setting of California's coast is a product of geology, oceanography, and hydrology. Tectonic plates slide by or crash into one another at global scales over tens of millions of years. Rocks form, then get chiseled by waves and carved by glaciers; sediment pours downstream, shifting and accumulating over eons. Remnant effects of the last ice age impact your experience at the beach today—as well as influencing which species live where. The shape of the coastline in turn affects how waves break and tides rise, while rivers exert a powerful influence on the shore and what lives there. Understanding a bit about the forces that have shaped the bluffs and beach offers a handle on *why* there are sea caves here but not there; black sand or coarse cobble underfoot; to the south a sandbar, to the north a mudflat. In turn, these physical features drive how we experience and use the coast, and they dictate the organisms that occupy each location.

Ecology is the study of what lives where, and why. It is the search to uncover the processes behind the patterns we see in the living world. Of course, this undertaking assumes that we have noticed patterns in the living world in the first place. Some of these are obvious: desert floras differ from alpine floras, and freshwater fish communities are distinct from marine fish communities. But many more subtle patterns surround us, providing ample fodder for ecologists to explore the forces driving these patterns. It's not trivial to ask why a particular snail lives under a rock, but a limpet lives on top of the same rock. Or why barnacles may be out of water even at high tide, but only the lowest tide exposes many sea stars, anemones, and other animals. We can ask the same question at a larger scale as well: why does one species of fish live north of Point Conception, while a close relative lives only to the south? These are some of the questions that have fascinated ecologists since before the discipline had a name.

This book is about *why* a certain beach has its features, or a tidepool holds its species of interest, rather than merely listing *what* you might expect to see. The goal is to give the reader a sense of process (*why* you see a thing), not just the patterns those processes create (*what* you see in a place). Viewed this way, a day at the shore becomes a detective's adventure, with each species signifying something about the local environmental conditions, including the other species present. A mussel shell lying on the sand isn't just scenery—it's a clue. Mussels live here or nearby, but which mussel species? Identifying the species could tell you whether conditions tend to be calm or rough. Is the shell whole or fragmented? This may tell you if the former inhabitant was dislodged or eaten, depending on the shell's markings. If the shell is whole but has a small hole drilled into it, that's usually the mark of a predatory snail (which also must live nearby; the shape of that hole could tell you the species of snail). Is anything growing on the mussel shell—barnacles, tube worms, algae? These offer more clues about the conditions at the site.

In writing this book, we follow in the footsteps of many others who have studied marine life along California's shores. Perhaps most foundational is the work of Ed Ricketts and his collaborators, who in 1939 published the first edition of *Between Pacific Tides*. That book has stood the test of time, inspiring generations of marine scientists in ways that Ricketts could not have imagined. This book might be considered a complement to *Between Pacific Tides*, something that honors the importance of natural history—and natural historians—to our appreciation of this half-watery realm.

It is great fun to recognize living creatures as one walks through the world. For many, this can be like seeing old friends, and it lends a sense of place and belonging and connection. But even more deeply, if each living element in a place is a clue about the inner workings of the world, learning about just a few species can spark a lifelong inquisitive flame. This kind of inquiry, this worldview, is what ecology is all about.

So ecologists hope to uncover relatively simple rules by which the riotous complexity of life takes shape. Evolution by natural selection generates the species in existence, generally over long time spans. Then, at shorter timescales, these species arrange themselves in space and time according to the rules of ecology.

Comparing adjacent sites along the shore is therefore an opportunity for ecological inference; environmentally similar sites presumably have similar communities of species, and patterns of communities can tell us something about the underlying ecological forces driving those patterns. Ecologists have long argued over how best to split the world into floristic provinces—geographic areas with distinctive species complements. By anyone's measure, California encompasses a great number of these provinces—from the redwood forests to the great Central Valley; from the cold, wet north to the Mojave Desert. But life in the marine environment tends to play by somewhat different rules than does life on the land. Gone, for example, are the mountain passes and rivers dividing one area from another. In the sea, the analogous borders are changes in currents and temperature and salinity, but these are usually more subtle and diffuse than are terrestrial landmarks. Consequently, species assemblages tend to sprawl and blend into one another, making it hard to draw lines between distinctive faunas. Nevertheless, California has at least two distinguishable intertidal faunas—north and south of Point Conception, in colder and warmer waters, respectively—and arguably more, with the substantial change in sea-surface currents and upwelling at Cape Mendocino as another prominent borderland.

Given what we suppose are the same starting conditions and species, what forces yield different communities at adjacent sites? We cannot know for certain; we are observing a work in progress and inferring its machinations. Just as a baker might infer both the ingredients and the process resulting in a loaf of bread, ecologists propose and test possible explanations regarding how today's species assemblages came to exist.

But bread has just a few ingredients, while an ecological community may have thousands of contributing factors, each one affecting the whole. We therefore look for ways to reduce this complexity to something more manageable or more easily communicated. In this book, we often do so by lumping closely related species together: "limpets," which might be ten or more distinct species, each with a similar, but not identical, ecological role; or "kelp," which can refer to a number of different species. Other common simplifying techniques include grouping seaweeds or animals by ecological guilds that reflect their role or position in the ecosystem (grazer, filter feeder, etc.) or by trophic level (primary producer, primary consumer, etc.).

But whether species are lumped together or identified with particularity, ecologists find great beauty and intriguing complexity in ecological systems, and those attributes can be shared with and appreciated by others.

Spotting animals and seaweeds in the intertidal can challenge even the most astute observer. The key is to find the right habitat for the species of interest. The marine realm is rife with specialized ecological associations, and sometimes a more obvious species will point to less obvious companions. These associations can reveal reliable ecological interactions, and once learned they provide both clues and shortcuts for locating organisms of interest.

## EXPERIMENTS AND TIME SERIES

Observing patterns in nature can suggest an underlying process that produced what you see, but how would you choose among possible explanations for, say, a consistent association between species? For instance, if you regularly find a species of limpet—a snail with a cap-like shell—sitting on kelp at low tide, you might suppose the limpet eats kelp. Maybe, but perhaps the limpet has a brown shell and evolved to hang out on kelp for camouflage from predators, leaving during the safety of high tide to scrape food from rocks. Or does the limpet scrape tiny algae and animals off the kelp, actually helping the seaweed in a happy symbiosis?

Faced with competing possibilities, ecologists perform experiments to manipulate the environmental factors that are under suspicion out in nature. You can imagine the logistical challenges of trying to confine, remove, or track tiny snails, hungry sea stars, or foraging octopuses in a wave-swept inter-tidal zone. Marine ecologists have developed a range of techniques to dissect and manipulate the possible forces acting within an ecosystem: there's a lot of slipping and swearing, drilling bolts into rock, counting between waves, sore knees, and sandy cars. The goal is to rule out ideas that don't correctly predict the outcome of experiments. Only the best explanation is kept, a kind of "last person standing" approach to studying the natural world. For example, if limpets eat kelp, you would predict that removing limpets should make kelp grow better and survive longer, whereas if limpets keep the kelp clean from organisms that weigh it down or block photosynthesis, the kelp should do worse when the limpets are removed. To test the "high-tide foraging" idea, you might cage some limpets, confining them to their kelp host, then compare the growth of algae on nearby rocks against rocks next to uncaged limpets. By ruling out poor explanations, scientists end up with one hypothesis or perhaps a few contenders that account for the observed patterns. Ecologists go to great lengths to repeat their manipulations on many individuals, across locations and even seasons; such replication ensures that results are repeatable and consistent and don't reflect idiosyncrasies of a particular individual, tidepool, or time. In this way, general principles can be divined about how species interact and function as a community.

Scientists also make extensive use of time-series data to understand long-term trends in the ocean and atmosphere and how coastal species respond to fluctuating conditions. Long-term data provide a critical baseline against which we can evaluate recent events, such as the disappearance of kelp forests or loss of sea stars to wasting disease. Are these recurring events that happen periodically and predictably, and can they be linked to specific environmental conditions? Does the system typically return to "normal," and if so, how long does that take? Alternatively, does such an event reflect a departure from historical trends, perhaps meaning the duration and consequences will be unpredictable—that is, have we seen this all before, or are we in uncharted territory? Such data series tell us, for example, that bull kelp forests (see Species of Interest in chapter 3, Far Northern California) in central California historically died back during strong El Niño years, but quickly recovered. In contrast, prolonged ocean warming from 2014 to 2017 coupled with explosive growth of purple sea urchins was associated with dramatic loss of bull kelp for over five years, a troubling deviation from trends going back at least to the 1980s.

Great effort goes into sustained monitoring efforts. For example, a network of marine protected areas dotting the coastline is closely monitored by scientists working with the state of California. Increasingly, remote sensing technology using satellites and drones allows accurate measurement of ocean conditions and marine communities (microalgal growth, kelp cover), enhancing the power of time-series measurements. Together, experimental and time-series studies allow scientists to predict how ecosystems will respond to short-term "pokes" (e.g., a severe storm), recurring events (El Niño cycles), or long-term stresses (fifty years of ocean warming).

This book is a compact tool for better understanding and appreciating the beauty of the California coast and the living things found on a visit to the shore. We write for the nonexpert, drawing together ideas from oceanography, ecology, and geology; we highlight human history, stretching from the densely populated shores of Southern California to the desolate and rarely visited beaches of the state's far north. Despite our focus here on California, the general principles of why coastal communities are the way they are apply to shorelines worldwide.

Accordingly, we set out general information in the first two chapters, describing the backdrop against which coastal ecology plays out, first describing the nonliving parts and then the living ones. We apply these concepts by featuring selected coastal sites in subsequent chapters. We organize these latter chapters geographically, working systematically from north to south. In highlighting particular sites and species, we attempt to provide interesting or distinctive examples of broader ecological concepts. We could have chosen other sites to make the same points, and there are plenty of wonderful sites along California's coast that are not included here. We encourage readers to explore widely and at whim—no need to be constrained to the set of locations described here.

To avoid giving redundant information, we cross-reference chapters to point out ideas or places or species discussed elsewhere, and we refer back to the first two chapters for explanation and context where the connection is not readily apparent. We've included helpful references in Further Reading at the back of the book and have prepared an exhaustive index to provide many points of access for the book itself.

For a few reasons, we have not set out to write a definitive guide to every beach, headland, and mudflat along the California coast. First, such a book would be impossibly large and detailed, heftier than anyone would want to lug around, and hopelessly repetitious. Second, the book would be out of date the moment we finished it; as we show in the chapters that follow, the ecology of the West Coast is dynamic and scientific understanding is constantly growing. Third, many good books already exist to give readers specific guidance on how best to reach the local shoreline and which species they might see once they arrive. We have listed some of these in Further Reading.

Similarly, this book is not an exhaustive guide to every species one might find along the shore. Here again, many such books already exist and several are included in Further Reading. More broadly, though, we have tried to focus on the *why* of coastal ecology, rather than on the *what*. We have given our attention to the most common, compelling, or illustrative species at different sites, knowing full well that far more diversity exists than we can cover here.

This book focuses on California, part of a larger marine ecosystem that includes the coasts of Washington, Oregon, and California. A companion book covers Washington and Oregon, a geographic region in which the shoreline flora and fauna remain fairly consistent by comparison. California offers a remarkable contrast, with substantial ecological transitions from north to south: much of the habitat in Del Norte and Humboldt Counties has more in common with Oregon and Washington than with the rest of California, while San Diego's climate supports warm-water species not found in the north.

In starting to think about what lives where, and why, it might be helpful to think about where you live, and why. Perhaps you were born where you presently live; maybe you came from elsewhere. Perhaps you arrived as a young child, or maybe as an adult. How did you get from your old home to your new? And why did you move, or choose to stay put if that's what you did? Maybe you moved because you have a particular way of making a living, and you needed a place that would let you do that. Perhaps you simply liked the weather in the new place or stayed put in the old place for the same reason. Maybe you couldn't get along with your old neighbors (or their pets). Maybe you have children, and there is some difference between what is good for you and what is good for them. In the end, there are trade-offs between all of these choices—and many others—but each is intimately tied to place and time: where you live is inextricably a product of your personal history and your social and ecological situation. The trade-offs would be different if you lived in another place or time.

And so it is with every living creature. Each faces a variety of constraints; each is the product of history and happenstance. It's because of this that developing an appreciation for ecology requires developing a sense of place and time. What makes this place different from that one is both a cause and an effect of the species that live there and of the processes leading up to this point in time.

Change is a recurring theme of this book. Coastlines are some of the

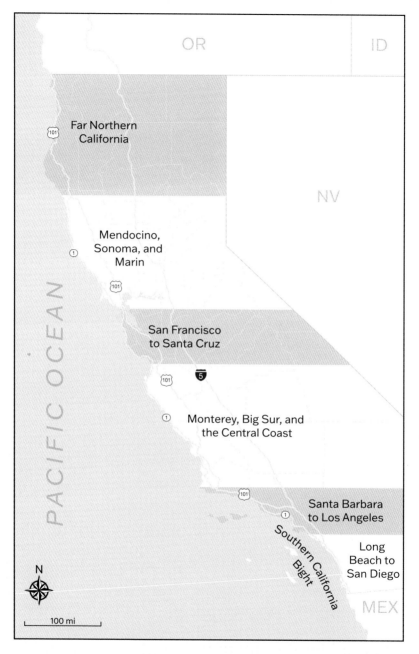

Geographic regions covered by chapters 3 through 7: Far Northern California; Mendocino, Sonoma, and Marin; San Francisco to Santa Cruz; Monterey, Big Sur, and the Central Coast; Santa Barbara to Los Angeles; and Long Beach to San Diego.

more dynamic environments on the planet, changing over timescales ranging from hours to millions of years. Any beach you see will be different from how we experienced the same site, in subtle or overt ways, and by tomorrow that beach will be different for the next visitor. Time and tide will influence the species you see, species abundance will wax and wane over a season or year, ocean conditions will vary, and a warming planet will shift the tenuous balances that now exist, perhaps precipitously.

When we started out to write this book, we asked ourselves, Might we be doing more harm than good, encouraging people to visit beautiful habitats that could be damaged by growing visitation? Our answer is that, by helping visitors understand and appreciate the natural world, we can both encourage and protect. We hope to inspire a sense of collective responsibility to preserve these habitats for future generations and for the sake of their own intrinsic worth.

## BEACH ACCESS AND THE PUBLIC TRUST DOCTRINE

Shorelines have an open, public quality to them. You have very likely spent time at the water's edge even if you don't own waterfront property. Many beaches you've visited may have been public parks of some kind, but interestingly, many states recognize a right to access the shore even if it appears to be on private property.

This public-ness is a legal distinction that stretches back beyond the Magna Carta to Roman law (and perhaps earlier). These ancient legal authorities recognized some things "common to all [hu]mankind," including the air, running water, sea, and shores. Through the formation of the US and via a variety of court cases, the present version of this idea comes down to us as the public trust doctrine: that each state holds some land and waters in trust for the benefit of its citizens. The rights to

Visitors enjoy a public shore at Sea Ranch on the Sonoma coast.

use and enjoy these places can't be sold off or privatized, and hence you are allowed to paddle along the shore or wade in the water, even if you don't own the property you're in front of.

Along the West Coast, Washington, Oregon, and California all recognize some version of these use and access rights.

The California Coastal Act (1976) is an overarching legal infrastructure for the state's coastal management that set up mechanisms to balance development and public use of some of the more valuable shorelines in the world. In general, California recognizes a broad public trust doctrine with public rights to wet sand (that is, beaches below the mean high-tide line), although dry sand is less obviously public. The California Coastal Commission, consistent with its goal of maximizing public access to the beaches, works to improve access from coastal roadways by marking public stairs and paths leading to the beach. Detailed descriptions of public access points and facilities are provided in the *California Coastal Access Guide*.

Between Point Arena and Dodoga Bay sits Sea Ranch, an important footnote in the struggle to reconcile the human goals of development and conservation in the state of California. Sea Ranch is a dispersed housing development grounded in a design/arts/land aesthetic that emerged in the 1960s. The project led to a degree of soul-searching for coastal Californians over the degree to which coastal property should be public versus private; ultimately, Sea Ranch included public-access trails linking the highway to the sea, and—much more far-reaching—led to a statewide initiative creating the California Coastal Commission, the state agency with broad authority over coastal land-use decisions.

As far as we are aware, the first detailed English-language narrative of life along the shore is Philip Henry Gosse's *A Naturalist's Rambles on the Devonshire Coast*, from 1853. Even then, with the world population less than one-sixth of today's, Gosse encountered the English shore in the wake of the industrial revolution, subject to human pressures of all sorts. And half a century later, Gosse's son referred (in his 1907 *Father and Son*) to the English shore as having been "ravaged" by collectors, "crushed under the rough paw of well-meaning, idle-minded curiosity" in the intervening years. The classic book *Between Pacific Tides* recounts the Gosses' experience as a lesson for readers of the mid-twentieth century, its message no less relevant today.

Perhaps people are always inclined to view ecosystems of the past as unspoiled relative to today's, but we have good evidence to the contrary. Environmental stewardship has grown over the past half century, with clear results. In the western US, air and water quality have generally improved over the past couple of generations. Whales and pinnipeds have returned in significant numbers to the West Coast. Bald eagles and brown pelicans are once again common, and California sea otters have reoccupied part of their historical range. These and many other examples are great and important successes. If we do not appreciate them as such every day, it is because humans quickly adjust to changing surroundings and, in many cases, quickly forget how things were in the past. Ecologists sometimes refer to this as the *shifting baseline* problem: because the world is always changing under us, we tend to keep resetting our idea of "normal" to match present conditions.

In sum, naturalists of every era encounter a world changed by their predecessors. But this need not mean a constant decline in the state of the world's ecosystems. Indeed, we hope and believe that better understanding the places one visits is a means of improving stewardship of those places.

## TIPS FOR BEING A RESPONSIBLE STEWARD

- Walk gently, and avoid stepping on living things.
- Leave living things in place where they can survive and grow.
- Take and share photographs to help others appreciate the environment.
- Use care when turning over rocks, and always turn them back over when done looking.

1

Waves crash against a sedimentary shore, giving shape to the land over geologic time.

# THE
# TUMULTUOUS
# EARTH

P late tectonics, ice ages, climate variability, and other processes directly influence the species you see at the shore today, but they act over timescales varying from millions of years (tectonics) to just several years (El Niño). Although not always obvious in everyday life, longer-term processes tend to be more evident in California than in some other places: earthquakes remind us of the tectonic forces at work, and a serious El Niño can flood the streets of Los Angeles and remodel Malibu's coastline. These forces hint at the planet's history and inner workings, and they often go a long way toward explaining what lives where, and why.

Another example is less obvious: during the last ice age, more of the planet's surface water was locked up in the form of ice, resulting in a sea level that was about 350–400 feet lower than it is now (indeed, this is true of all glacial periods). As a result, shorelines worldwide were farther seaward than they are today, with important consequences for tides and currents and for all manner of marine life. The habitats of many marine species were fragmented by newly emerged land bridges, while these same bridges created new habitat for land-based species.

A well-known example of coastal ice-age differences in the United States comes from Alaska, where humans migrated from Asia to North America by traversing a land bridge that separated the North Pacific from the Bering Sea. In Southern California the same ice age combined the northern Channel Islands into a single larger island and brought its coastline within a few miles of the mainland. Large mammals and other

## LONGER-TERM EARTH PROCESSES

What caused the glaciers to expand and contract?

Periodic changes in the way the earth revolves around the sun mean that some millennia are cooler than others. Ice builds up in the cooler millennia and breaks down as the climate warms. These cycles are excellent examples of how small changes at cosmic scales (who knew the tilt of the earth, the wobble of the earth on its axis, and the earth's orbit around the sun could change over time?) can have enormous effects at ecological scales—for instance, by burying large parts of continents under massive slabs of ice. And of course these changes can affect humans directly, too, determining where we live and how we disperse over time.

The planetary counterpoint to glaciation is melting, with the consequent fall and rise of sea level as ice sheets wax and wane. During past glacial periods, the ice that formed glaciers and ice sheets originated from enormous amounts of precipitation that failed to reach the sea, temporarily reducing the volume of the ocean. During these periods, there was a lot less water in the ocean—about ten million cubic miles less—and as a consequence, sea level dropped by hundreds of vertical feet. What we see as islands today may have been headlands and peninsulas during a former ice age. What is a strait today earlier may have been a valley. When sea levels were lower, New Guinea was joined to Australia, and Russia and Alaska actually held hands, separating the Bering Sea from the North Pacific for thousands of years at a stretch.

vertebrates—previously excluded by miles of ocean—invaded the island and were subsequently isolated from mainland populations as the ice age receded and waters returned. Over time, the isolation resulted in the evolution of a species of miniature mammoth called the "exiled elephant" (pygmy mammoth, *Mammuthus exilis*, sadly now extinct), the island fox (*Urocyon littoralis*, with its six distinct subspecies, one for each island, and happily still extant), and a variety of other species unique to the islands.

Thus, life along the Pacific teaches us that nature is dynamic: movement along faults reshapes the coast over geological timescales; new species arise, interact with others, and eventually disappear; and changing patterns of weather and climate shift the windows of temperature and habitat that individual species find tolerable. And this is to say nothing of the humans that have come to dominate the coast over the past 20,000 years, whether hunting and gathering along the waterfront, exploiting the nearshore mammals for their fur, or raising skyscrapers at the shore.

With our comparatively short life spans, we get to see only a small slice of the continuing drama that defines life along the Pacific coast. That's why we often think of the natural world as constant, enduring, even monolithic. We tend to assume that the plants and animals we see on the shore today are the ones that have always been there and that they've always been in about the same place. It turns out this isn't true at all. On the contrary, rocks and plants and animals and ecosystems are mere samples plucked from an ongoing narrative, telling a story of their origins and peregrinations. Every scene is a product of ancient forces still in progress.

This is what we call developing a sense of place and time: with each visit to the shore grows the knowledge that today is a consequence of an ocean's worth of yesterdays—the idea that *here and now* is inseparable from *there and then*.

## BINS OF TIME

Because our personal experiences span relatively limited time frames, it is difficult to think in terms of deeper time. It's easy to let a thousand years and a million years seem like similar, vaguely abstract numbers: our brains tend to round them off to something approximating "far longer than I've been around."

A useful way of learning to zoom in and out through different time-scales while looking at, say, a beach is to create "bins" of time as mental shortcuts. Biologists do this as a matter of course, using terms like *ecological time* (which might encompass weeks to seasons to decades to perhaps thousands of years), *evolutionary time* (hundreds of thousands to millions of years), and *geological time* (anything longer than that). This kind of shorthand allows one to ignore particular dates or counts of years and instead focus on rough estimates of time in a way that remains quite helpful for appreciating the different processes that have led up to the present day.

The rocks, the sand, the rivers of the West Coast have stories to tell, and all along the California coastline, those stories are spectacular. We need not get bogged down by specific dates, or even a decimal place or two. Simply understanding the changes that have occurred over time, and how one change was followed by another and another, helps to deepen our sense of both time and place.

## DEEP HISTORY: SHAPING CALIFORNIA'S COASTS

Looking back in deep geological time, hundreds of millions of years ago, most of today's West Coast simply didn't exist. The landmasses today that are home to most of the region's people—those of western Washington, Oregon, and California—were for millions of years Pacific seabed on a collision course with North America. Over mind-bendingly long periods of time, blocks of rock accumulated along the West Coast as tectonic plates collided with one another, eventually shaping the landmass as we currently know it. By a few tens of millions of years ago, still squarely in the bin of geological time, the major pieces of California were in place. But this merely set the stage for more recent dramas to play out.

Earthquakes can lift the coastal zone in places, thrusting formerly submerged habitat above sea level, resetting the intertidal zone, and likely killing the previous residents. Subsidence—that is, sinking—can happen, too, when uplifted blocks shift and settle. Both occur with some regularity around the entire Pacific Rim: examples come from Chile, Mexico, Northern California, Alaska, Japan, New Zealand, and other places where one tectonic plate is being forced beneath another.

So in a very real way, the past is not truly past. Ongoing planetary-scale changes shape life along the coast for humans and for every other species that lives here. And developing the most basic sense of the sequence of geological events gives visitors to the coast a powerful lens through which to appreciate the goings-on. That is, the visitor will have developed a sense of place and time that will reveal the coast to be an even more fascinating place than it had seemed at first.

## OCEANOGRAPHIC AND EARTH PROCESSES

Key aspects of the planet's behavior can help to identify common causes behind an astonishingly broad set of patterns. For example, things as different as coastal fog and fish abundance are both linked to ocean processes, which in turn are shaped by earth processes that have forged the landscape and seascape before us.

### Tectonics and Subduction

Much of North America's Pacific coast is an active margin where tectonic plates collide or grind against one another, creating earthquakes and raising mountains in the process. The region that we now call California was formed over the past roughly 250 million years, first by subduction—one plate diving beneath another, in the process remodeling ocean-floor rock into the modern-day Coast Ranges—and later by horizontal faulting as the San Andreas Fault System became active, forming a transform margin between tectonic plates. The resulting mountains influence regional weather patterns and affect life along the shore, and the narrow continental shelf allows deep, cold water to pool close to shore.

By contrast, the Atlantic coast is a passive margin, consisting of a broad, sandy shelf stretching for miles out to sea. And here, *passive* is the correct word: for half a billion years, the Appalachian Mountains have been eroding into sand, silt, and clay and transported to the coast by rivers.

# SEA STACKS

Photographs of the Northern California coast often showcase sea stacks, fragments of coast that seem the very embodiments of durability in the face of adversity. And in many respects, this symbolism is fitting: what we see as sea stacks are surviving pieces of earlier coastlines, bits of more-resistant rock that are left behind as less-durable surrounding rock erodes into the waves.

There is a feedback loop to this process: as a resistant chunk of rock begins to emerge out of a cliff side, it forms a headland. Headlands, in turn, are magnets for wave energy as refraction focuses energy along their length, accelerating erosion of the land connecting headland and cliff side. The result, after a time, is a sea stack. The timeline for this process can be quite short, both underscoring the dynamic nature of ocean shores and somewhat undercutting sea stacks as symbols of durability.

Sea stacks—remnant rocks once connected to the mainland—are common in parts of California, underscoring the dynamic nature of the coast.

# TYPES OF CONTINENTAL MARGINS

**ACTIVE MARGIN — US WEST COAST**

- subduction zones where plates collide and one dips below the other
- transform boundaries where plates move past one another

**PASSIVE MARGIN — US EAST COAST**

- no plate boundaries nearby; seafloor spreading areas far offshore

The arrangement of tectonic plates influences everything from mountains to weather to biodiversity. Plate boundaries along the West Coast of North America make this an active margin, with a subduction zone in Northern California (top) and a transform fault (middle) along much of the rest of the state. These stand in contrast to the passive margin on the continent's East Coast (bottom).

These geological contrasts provide the setting in which coastal life arises and persists. While the West Coast has many and varied habitats, the habitats of the East Coast are fairly consistent between Cape Cod, Massachusetts, and Florida: mainly sand and mainly flat. Over evolutionary time, more diverse habitats trigger the evolution of more diverse suites of species. It's quite likely, then, that the ecology of the West Coast has been considerably more diverse than that of the East Coast for millions of years.

Continental plates move great distances over geologic time, but average only inches per year in human lifetimes. This is why we think of landmasses most of the time as being static. But the dynamic nature of tectonic plates over very long periods of time has created the conditions that we observe, and live in, every day.

The deep ocean water just off the West Coast's shores causes big differences in temperature between land and sea during the daytime, which in turn creates predictable local wind patterns and coastal fog. At a larger scale, prevailing winds tend to blow toward the south along the West Coast, causing coastal upwelling (see below) and in turn fueling entire food webs. Differential heating drives global wind patterns and surface current patterns, while seasonal variations due to the earth's tilt on its axis have profound effects on life on the shore. Without these and other forces, we would lack the diversity of intertidal species that has evolved in place over tens of millions of years.

## The Coriolis Effect: As the World Turns

Under just about all normal circumstances, it is perfectly safe to ignore the fact that we all live on a giant rotating ball. The earth rotates at an essentially constant speed, so there is no acceleration, and we don't feel as if we're moving. Instead, the sun appears to be moving. This is reflected in how we talk about these events ("the sun sets . . .") and in the fact that it took centuries to convince the average person that we—and not the sun—are in motion relative to the rest of the solar system.

However, in some contexts our existence on a rotating ball becomes highly relevant. An airplane leaving San Francisco and aiming at Miami,

Florida, for example, would land in the Gulf of Mexico if the flight path weren't adjusted for the fact that the earth rotates under the airplane while the plane is in the air. Atmospheric and ocean currents, too, are subject to the same dynamic: physics dictates they move in a straight line, but the earth is continually rotating beneath these currents. To an outside observer, the result is that the paths of these currents appear to curve (to the right in the northern hemisphere, to the left in the southern hemisphere).

This apparent curvature of the paths of things in motion is called the Coriolis effect. And because air and water are in constant motion across

## CORIOLIS EFFECT

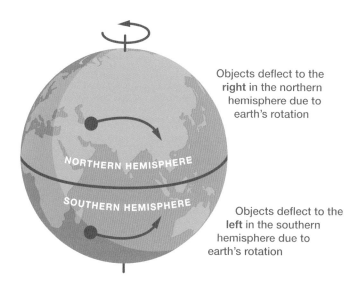

Objects deflect to the **right** in the northern hemisphere due to earth's rotation

Objects deflect to the **left** in the southern hemisphere due to earth's rotation

The Coriolis effect is a feature of life on a rotating globe. Throwing a ball while on a moving merry-go-round is a good small-scale approximation of the same idea. Moving objects appear to deflect to the right in the northern hemisphere and to the left in the southern hemisphere, with profound consequences for ocean circulation, weather, and climate.

the surface of the spinning earth, we need to account for Coriolis effect when we think about air and ocean currents.

Most notably for our purposes, Coriolis effect plays a role in coastal upwelling and in wind and weather patterns.

## Coastal Upwelling

Strong seasonal winds blowing from north to south along the California coast, combined with the earth's rotation, cause surface waters to move offshore. As they do so, deeper water is drawn upward to replace the water that's been moved offshore. This is coastal upwelling.

# UPWELLING

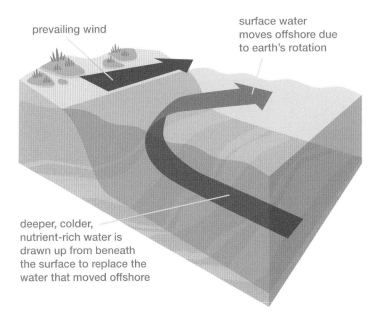

Along the West Coast, prevailing winds blowing toward the equator combined with the rotation of the earth cause surface water to move offshore, drawing nutrient-rich deeper water toward the surface to replace it. Along most of California's coast, the prevailing winds blow southward down the shore.

Because this upwelling draws nutrient-rich deeper water up into the surface zone where sunlight is available, the result is a big boost in productivity. It's recycling on a grand scale, in which the food scraps of the marine environment—dead cells and other organic matter—are composted and transported back to the surface, where they are used to fuel new algal growth. At the same time, the cross-shore movement of water carries animal larvae and other zooplankton away from shore (during upwelling, when winds are strong) or toward shore (as winds relax), influencing where and when animals might feed, settle, and grow. Because coastal upwelling is driven by prevailing winds, its strength is seasonal, occurring in spring, summer, and fall along the Pacific coast.

## Wind, Weather, and Climate Patterns

Water deals with heat like a herd of elephants changes directions. It takes an enormous amount of energy to change the temperature of water. The larger the body of water, the more energy required to change its temperature and, hence, the more stable its temperature. Larger, more stable bodies of water have proportionately more influence on the temperatures around them. A small pond, for example, might slightly influence the conditions along its edges—after all, that is one good reason to sit near a pond on a hot summer day. But the Pacific Ocean is a much larger pond and correspondingly has a much larger effect: it drives weather and climate at regional and planetary scales.

An active continental margin with deep submarine canyons just offshore, the West Coast owes its weather directly to the adjacent vast reservoir of Pacific Ocean water. As land and air temperatures rise and fall over the course of a day—their temperatures perhaps changing by 20 degrees Fahrenheit or more—the Pacific remains unmoved, its temperature changing by only a degree or two. Different rates of heating and cooling between land and ocean result in predictable winds—onshore in the afternoons, offshore at night—and only moderate differences between seasons along the Pacific coast. For example, compare San Francisco (on the Pacific) with Lexington, Kentucky (inland), and Ocean City, Maryland (on the Atlantic), all of which sit at roughly the same latitude. The average high temperature in San Francisco, strongly moderated by its proximity to the Pacific, varies from 58 degrees Fahrenheit (January) to 76 degrees Fahrenheit (September), a mere 18 degrees difference over the year. With no ocean nearby, temperatures in Lexington vary more than twice as much between seasons (about 45 degrees difference in average highs, from 42 to 87 degrees Fahrenheit). And temperatures in Ocean City, on the Atlantic's shallow, passive margin, behave much more like Lexington than San Francisco (about 39 degrees difference, from 46 to 85 degrees Fahrenheit). The moderating force of ocean water plays a big part in creating these differences between locations.

Coastal fog and upwelling, described above, are also closely tied to an active margin and its associated offshore water. And at a local scale, even real-estate prices are affected: there are many reasons coastal real estate is more expensive than real estate elsewhere, but climate is surely one of them. Weather patterns, fog, and sun—not to mention the coastal views that tectonics have ultimately created—all are likely to be wrapped up in the price of a house or apartment.

## Waves and Beach Shapes

Wind energy creates the waves you see at the beach, although the wave that's breaking right now could be a product of stormy conditions far out at sea days ago. Such waves capture energy from the wind, organize themselves, and can travel great distances before they reach shore. As the wave approaches land and the water grows shallower, friction between the wave and the sea bottom causes the wave to slow down and eventually break. Larger waves will break in deeper water. If it were otherwise, with very large waves breaking only in very shallow water, surfing would be a lot less fun and a whole lot more dangerous.

The depth and shape of the sea bottom therefore influence the shape of the waves. But the converse is also true: the nature of waves shapes the beach. Large, powerful waves can erode a shoreline, while gentler surf will deposit sand and broaden the beach. In places where sandbars shift with tides and currents, the size, shape, and location of waves can change radically over the course of days, as surfers and boat skippers well know. The frequency of waves and their timing, the direction from which waves approach, and the configuration of the ocean bottom all influence changes in wave height and direction as waves reach the shore, with consequent changes in wave energy from place to place. Because of refraction, wave energy tends to concentrate on headlands and dissipate in bays.

Generally, the longer the stretch of uninterrupted water over which the wind blows—a measure known as *fetch*—the larger the swell. This is why waves are much larger in Pacifica than in, say, Oakland. Pacifica and other towns in coastal San Mateo County face the open expanse of the Pacific and are exposed to a long fetch, while Oakland (and the rest of the East Bay) is exposed only to the relatively small fetch within San Francisco Bay—a good location, indeed, for a large commercial port.

Waves also influence both the beach slope and the size of sand grains that make up the beach. Finer-grained beaches tend to have shallower slopes because both the swash (movement of water up the beach after a wave breaks) and the backwash (the surf receding back to the ocean) have about the same amount of energy, distributing the grains relatively evenly across the beach. On beaches consisting of coarse sand or pebbles, where grain size is large, the swash carries sediment up the beach, but wave energy is lost as the water percolates between the grains, and so the backwash is proportionately weaker. The result is a steeper beach—that is, the beach face generally grows steeper as the average grain size increases, though this relationship becomes more complicated on cobble beaches.

## El Niño and the Pacific Decadal Oscillation

Because environmental conditions along the West Coast depend so strongly on the Pacific Ocean, relatively small changes in ocean conditions can have large consequences for coastal systems. On top of unpredictable year-to-year variation in ocean conditions, some of the most important shifts in ocean conditions are recurring, or oscillating, phenomena. Over the past decades, scientists have described multiple large-scale climate oscillations in the Pacific. Two of these are prominent and help us understand year-on-year variability in ocean conditions.

El Niño (or more properly, the El Niño–Southern Oscillation, ENSO) is perhaps the better known of these recurring climate patterns—indeed, it is one of the most significant climate phenomena on earth. ENSO is driven by a weakening of winds and warming of surface waters in the eastern tropical Pacific. This leads to an array of changes around the Pacific, including warmer waters along the US West Coast, weaker upwelling, and reduced productivity along the coast of California. The ecological effects are dramatic and wide ranging, including poor fisheries catches, declines in kelp abundance, and decreased pupping success among marine mammals due to reduced food supplies. El Niño events occur at approximately three- to seven-year intervals, though this can vary substantially, and some events are much stronger than others. An alternate phase of the oscillation is known as La Niña, which brings periods of cooler-than-average water temperatures and strong winter storms to far Northern California. A third phase—the neutral phase—also exists, during which weather conditions are less extreme than in either the El Niño or the La Niña phase.

The Pacific Decadal Oscillation (PDO) is a climate cycle alternating between "warm" and "cool" phases in the North Pacific in which each phase can last a decade or more. The mechanism behind these oscillations is linked to large-scale changes in patterns of sea-surface temperature and sea-level pressure in the North Pacific. The difference between warm and cool phases of the PDO is dramatic; those few degrees' change in sea-surface temperature can mean the difference between high and low levels of ocean productivity. In California, for example, shifts from cool-to-warm phase PDO have been shown to influence the health and abundance of seabirds and marine mammals and may influence recruitment strength in fish populations. The effects of the PDO extend to terrestrial ecosystems too. In some cases, the phase of the PDO can be detected in the rings of oak trees miles from the coast, illustrating the importance of ocean temperature and offering a useful tool for reconstructing historical climate cycles.

## Geology As Destiny: Everyday Effects for the Shoreline Visitor

At the most basic level, life along an active tectonic margin means more miles of rocky shoreline, more habitat for crabs and snails and kelp and other hard-substrate species, and less habitat for clams and sand dollars and other soft-substrate dwellers. The deep water just offshore can moderate temperature swings over the course of a day or a year, causing fairly consistent winds that switch daily between onshore and offshore directions. Fog often follows, to the benefit of land plants in the coastal zone. Upwelling causes an increase in primary production, which in turn fuels larger and more diverse suites of species living in these areas and, consequently, more complex food webs.

The ecological effects of these factors are dramatic. For example, the West Coast has about a hundred different species of chitons, while there is just one species along most of the East Coast, a passive coastal margin. Similarly, kelps, limpets, and other rocky habitat groups exhibit greater diversity along the West Coast than the East Coast. This diversity can be traced to the geological history of the region combined with high biological productivity and high habitat complexity. Over long periods of time, these processes have favored speciation, ultimately creating the biological diversity we see on the shores of California today.

The view across Monterey Bay hides the complex geology lying below the surface.

2

Sun, wind, and waves powerfully shape life along the shore.

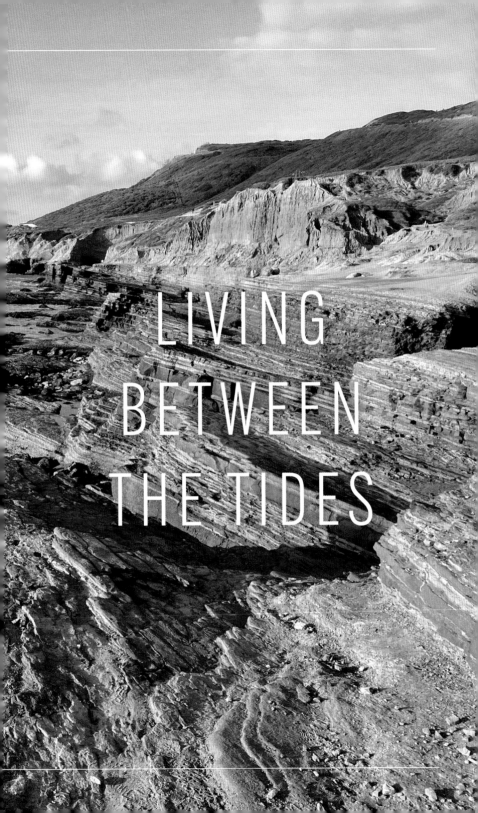

LIVING

BETWEEN

THE TIDES

W hat lives where, and why? It's a complicated question with more than one answer, and this is what keeps ecologists interested in their jobs. Layered on top of earth-history factors (chapter 1), modern forces are constantly shaping and reshaping life along the shore.

Where a species is reliably found, we can assume that the conditions there are favorable for its survival: food is available, water and air temperatures are tolerable, and so on. Other populations of that species may occur nearby, and its prey and predators are likely to be found as well. Groups of species that share space and inhabit similar conditions form ecological communities, which become integral parts of an ecosystem.

And what is an ecosystem, exactly? An ecosystem is the sum of elements and interactions among the elements at a given time and place, both living (like animals and plants) and nonliving (like sunlight, rocks, and water). The term therefore grows and shrinks to encompass an area of interest or a place to study, et cetera. A sandy beach can be an ecosystem, as can an estuary or mudflat. At larger scales, the entire West Coast with all its varied habitats and processes is often considered a single large marine ecosystem.

More than simply being a handy term for a set of places and things, the word *ecosystem* has a deeper sense that suggests the importance of interactions. By analogy, just as the global economy is a product of billions of market interactions among people with diverse goals, ecosystems are a product of a multitude of interactions among organisms and their environment. An ecosystem rich in species tends to be resilient, resisting change (such as invasion by nonnative species); indeed, organisms stabilize their own physical environment—think about how the trees of a forest create shade, dampen wind, and hold soil in place. However, just as many kinds of political and social instability can roil economic markets, environmental changes may tip an ecosystem out of balance. Often the system will bounce back, but sometimes a stressful event causes an unexpected shift to an alternative community that may persist for long periods, in the same place as what was there before. Economies and ecosystems can behave in unexpected and sometimes dramatic ways, for the same reasons: both are precarious, ever-changing arrangements, with many forces acting upon and shaping them. Both have an inherent capacity to surprise.

Given that shoreline ecology has so many moving parts, one can be forgiven for thinking of it as an incomprehensible consequence of happenstance. But important patterns and processes governing what lives where have been uncovered through decades of study by thousands of people. In short, there are rules by which nature plays. Or perhaps *guidelines* better describes the mix of predictable outcomes and chance events that structure life along the shore.

## NONLIVING ELEMENTS THAT SHAPE ECOSYSTEMS

Tides, temperature, and sunlight are three of the dominant physical factors acting on intertidal habitats, and they interact in complicated ways to influence where plants and animals live on the shore. It is difficult to fully separate the effects of these forces, but it is important to understand the general influence of each and their outsize roles in shaping ecosystems.

### Tides

The rise and fall of the tides creates a habitat like no other on earth. Over a period of several hours, land becomes sea, then sea becomes land, and species living between the two experience a wholesale change of surroundings, threats, and opportunities. Eons of tidal oscillations have shaped a vibrant and diverse set of species that exist nowhere else but this intertidal zone.

Tides are very large waves that slosh around ocean basins; the local crest of such waves creates high tide, and the trough creates low tide. Gravity drives these large waves, as the sun and moon tug on the ocean's

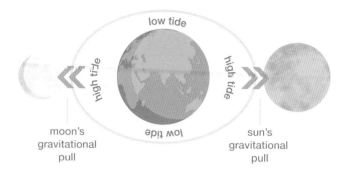

Tides are very large waves created by the gravitational effects of both the sun and the moon. The magnitude of the tide is at its maximum when the sun and the moon are either directly opposite one another (pictured here; a full moon) or when the sun and moon are aligned on the same side of the earth (not pictured; a new moon).

water. The highest of high tides and lowest of low tides occur when the sun and moon line up—that is, every two weeks, when the moon is full, and again when the moon is new.

These semimonthly periods of very high and very low tides are often referred to as spring tides, but don't be fooled: they are unrelated to the season that we call spring. Instead, think of these as periods when the tide "springs forth." Between these periods of spring tides, the moon and sun are positioned at angles to each other. While the sun is much larger than the moon, the moon is closer to earth, and both exert force on the earth, but in this configuration the forces work in different directions, partially canceling each other and reducing the magnitude of the tides. During these periods of more moderate or neap tides, the high tide is neither very high nor the low tide very low.

The US West Coast and many other places experience two high tides each day of unequal height and, similarly, two unequal low tides. The position of continents and landmasses means that some other coasts experience only one daily high and low tide or have two tides of relatively similar height. On the West Coast, the tides are an ever-shifting regime that will keep you on your toes (or tentacles or fins); hour to hour, day by day, the environment is constantly shifting around the inhabitants of this dynamic strip of shoreline. The waves that create tides propagate northward along the California coast, causing high or low tide to be earlier in the day in San Diego than in Arcata. As a general rule, the farther north you go, the bigger the difference between the high and low tides; tides are more extreme in Alaska than in California. In most of California, the difference between the highest and lowest tides of the day can be eight vertical feet or more; this means if the ocean were lapping at the size-20 feet of the tallest basketball player on a spring low tide, the athlete's head would be underwater a few hours later when the high tide peaked. In places with shallow sloping beaches, that change in height can translate to hundreds of horizontal feet of intertidal habitat.

## HOW (AND WHY) TO READ A TIDE TABLE

Any visit to the shore will be shaped by whether the tide is high or low or somewhere in between. When the tide is high, the beach will be comparatively narrow or will disappear completely, limiting access to lower zones, making it impossible to negotiate headlands, and sometimes cutting off access to upland trails. On the other hand, when the tide is low, intertidal habitats will be exposed and accessible. In between these two extremes, mid-tidal heights are fine for beach walks and picnics, but not so good for intertidal exploring.

Enter the tide table. These tools, widely available on the internet, offer predictions of tidal height versus time of day for virtually every location on California's coast for days, weeks, and even years into the future. Because these tables are based on astronomical predictions, the actual tidal height on a given day may vary somewhat due to factors such as wind and weather, as well as offshore water temperature, but the information is likely to be accurate enough to guide visits to the shore, enhancing the experience while adding a margin of safety.

When intertidal invertebrates and seaweeds are the focus of a visit, it's helpful to arrive at the shore an hour or more ahead of the predicted low tide. Tidepool exploration is best done on a falling tide; once the tide turns and the water begins rising, searching becomes less fun and walking becomes more diffi-cult, sometimes dangerously so. In California, tide heights of 0.0 feet or less (that is, negative tides) will expose the greatest amount of habitat.

Tide predictions come in both graphical and tabular forms. Graphical representations show the height of the tide at a particular location on a particular day (or month or year) as an illustration in which the rise and fall of the tide is plotted over the course of a day (or month or year). The predicted height of

## TIDE CHART

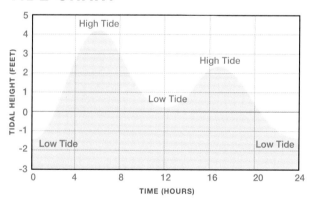

A typical tide table shows daily high and low tides at specific locations and at corresponding times of day. Generally, tides below the 0.0-foot tide level offer a good opportunity to explore tidepools. Tides are inde-pendent of daylight, so low tides may not occur during hours convenient for daytime exploration.

the tide is shown on the vertical axis and the time of day on the horizontal axis. These charts are intuitive, and at a glimpse it becomes clear when the tide will be high or low—and also how these highs and lows cycle over the course of, say, a month.

Tabular forms are a bit less intuitive. They can be found online and in small printed booklets frequently available in places like bait stores and surf shops, listing the time and height of the two high tides and two low tides for any calendar day. To use a tide table of this sort, choose the column with the month and day of interest, then move to the right along consecutive rows to view the times and heights of the tides on that day. Pro tip: make sure the times listed in the table are given in the local time zone, and check the units (metric vs. English) in which tide height is given, to minimize chance of surprise.

## Time, Tide, and Temperature

Species that live between high and low tide marks are tightly tuned to the tides. Some feed at high tide, hiding the rest of the day. Others do the opposite. When the tide is up, animals and seaweeds are covered by seawater and don't have to contend with the stresses of terrestrial life—warm (or cold) air temperatures and desiccation. As the tide moves out, temperature and desiccation stress move in. Warmer temperatures during daylight hours tend to boost metabolism and accelerate growth, to a point, and this can be a good thing. But too much sunshine and heat during a low tide can quickly cause physiological stress and even death. To an extent, intertidal organisms along the California coast are protected from the physiological stress of extreme heat in summertime when low tides occur at night or very early in the morning, when air temperatures are relatively cool. Even so, the intertidal can heat up quickly when the tide recedes in winter and spring; there's a reason people visit California beaches year-round, after all.

## MICROCLIMATES

Overlaid on the temperature effects associated with tidal cycles is the familiar association between temperature and latitude: as a general rule, air, land, and sea temperatures all become cooler as one moves northward toward the pole. This is one reason why San Diego draws more beachgoers than does, say, San Francisco.

But local factors cause both air and water temperatures to vary along the coast, creating a mosaic of habitats that does not follow a strict pattern. You might find cooler water temperatures in Monterey than along the Sonoma coast, for instance; at smaller scales, a deep bay may be cooler than an adjacent shallow bay. And at even smaller scales, you could find cooler temperatures under an overhang or in a shaded place compared with a neighboring area exposed to full sun. For example, shaded surfaces can be 20 degrees Fahrenheit cooler than unshaded surfaces nearby, and as a consequence, a snail sitting in direct sunlight might have more than twice the metabolic rate of—and therefore burn through twice as much energy as—a shaded neighbor.

Temperature tolerance is a major factor that shapes how far up the shoreline a species can survive. Being cold-blooded, invertebrates depend on a range of adaptations to manage their body temperatures, including the evolution of body or shell color or the development of avoidance behaviors like nestling in wet crevices or sticking shell fragments to their bodies like hundreds of tiny hats.

## PHYSICAL EFFECTS OF TEMPERATURE

Temperature isn't just a sensation; it acts at a molecular level, influencing many of the physiological processes that make life possible. This includes everything from photosynthesis (in plants and algae) through metabolism, and even the firing of neurons, which is necessary for every perception and every movement. Each species has a range of body temperatures within which their chemistry works well, and different species have different ranges. Because we find different air and water temperatures along the California coast, we expect to find different communities of species in different places.

## Sunlight

Sunlight warms the intertidal but also supplies the essential energy needed for photosynthesis. In a feat of chemical engineering, algae and plants convert sunlight and carbon dioxide into sugar and water; sugars in turn become the food fueling nearshore food webs. The waste product of photosynthesis is oxygen; indeed, the vast majority of oxygen in the air is the by-product of photosynthesis, and about half the oxygen we breathe comes from photosynthesis in the ocean. If you take two breaths to let this fact sink in, you can thank ocean photosynthesizers for one of those breaths.

The colorful pigments characteristic of seaweeds and seagrasses play an essential role in this process. The patchwork of colors splashed across the intertidal zone, from gold and brown to green, red, and even pink, is an indication of the photosynthetic machinery at work in this system.

## Salinity

Ocean salinity is nearly constant worldwide: 3.5 percent, commonly expressed as thirty-five parts per thousand. If you've ever accidentally swallowed seawater, you have some appreciation for the vast practical difference that 3.5 percent makes. Apart from making seawater undrinkable for humans, salinity changes the fundamental qualities of water. Salt water is more dense than freshwater and conducts electricity thousands of times better than freshwater due to the dissolved salts (solute). To marine organisms, the solute is what keeps the concentration of water inside their cells balanced with the surrounding salt water. Put a kelp frond in freshwater and this balance is immediately thrown off; water will rush into the kelp's cells, which swell and perhaps burst. If you've ever walked on the beach after a rainstorm, you may have seen beach-cast kelps that are bumpy with blisters: this is the effect of freshwater on kelp tissues.

Most species are adapted to either freshwater or salt water, and that's why we think of marine and freshwater species as belonging to different communities. Open-ocean species usually tolerate a narrow range of salinities and quickly become stressed when local circumstances cause salinity to change. However, freshwater runoff from rivers (and from urban engineering) can substantially dilute seawater close to shore. Conversely, evaporation can increase salinity in shallow areas—the Dead Sea is the most famous example, and it is dead for precisely this reason. The same forces act at much smaller scales in tidepools, where salinity can climb high during periods of evaporation or drop after a rainstorm. Thus, because salinity tends to be lower and more variable along the coast, many intertidal species can tolerate substantial changes in salinity.

Life in estuaries requires exceptional flexibility to tolerate unpredictable swings in salinity caused by freshwater from rivers mixing with tidal inputs of seawater. Moreover, in bays and river mouths, less dense freshwater often floats on top of salt water, temporarily forming a freshwater "lens" that can be inches to feet thick. Some species have evolved to move between saltwater and freshwater habitats. Salmon are probably the best-known example of such a lifestyle; they hatch in freshwater, spend one or more years in the ocean, and then return to freshwater to reproduce. Salmon switch worlds in this way using molecular pumps to move excess salt out of their cells while in salt water.

## Energy

What powers an ecosystem? What makes it go?

In the realm of biology, we most often think of chemical energy as the currency of living things, the energy with which cells make sugars, proteins, and lipids to grow and to power the day-to-day functions of life. When one individual eats another, stored energy is transferred from the eaten to the eater; however, this process is notoriously inefficient, with something like 90 percent of energy lost as waste and heat between each link in the food chain. Even so, the food web is a sort of wiring diagram for an ecological community, illustrating where chemical energy comes from and where it goes: from the sun, moving through photosynthesizers to grazing herbivores, and ending up in apex predators—then in humble detritivores, consuming all of our remains.

Perhaps a more familiar form of energy is kinetic energy, which is the kind associated with motion. Kinetic energy comes visibly into play along the shore. Just as you might use a whisk to beat air into a bowl of cream

## WHAT'S THAT SMELL?

The perfume of the shore can be unmistakable—and unforgettable. Many things contribute to this characteristic fragrance, but decaying seaweed is often a big contributor, producing an odor both loved and hated. Phycologists—scientists who study algae—tend to be among those who love the smell of seaweed as it rots on the beach. Some can even identify algal species based on their scent alone.

The distinctive odor of decaying seaweed on a rocky or sandy beach is due in part to bromophenols, a class of compounds containing bromine, an element with similar properties as chlorine and iodine. Those with a keen nose may be able to tease out these smells on a beach full of seaweed wrack. The ecological role of bromophenols is not entirely clear, but they may provide living seaweed with a defense against invertebrate grazers.

A tangle of beach-cast kelp and other seaweed will eventually begin to decay, giving off a characteristic smell that many associate with a visit to the beach.

The smells emanating from mudflats are different, and typically more pungent, than those on a sandy beach. The really objectionable smell coming from mudflats is hydrogen sulfide gas produced as microbes decompose organic matter in the absence of oxygen. Hydrogen sulfide is typically produced in anaerobic sediments or "black mud" that forms a layer beneath the more oxygenated surface sediments. If you churn up the sediments in a mudflat, you'll cause hydrogen sulfide to be released. It's likely that our aversion to the smell of hydrogen sulfide is related to its toxicity, though a visit to a mudflat is unlikely to cause any harm. Decaying algae, too, can give off hydrogen sulfide, sometimes in deadly amounts (see sea lettuce in Species of Interest in chapter 6, Monterey, Big Sur, and the Central Coast).

to make whipped cream, waves along the shore beat air into the surface waters of the ocean, creating bubbles and in the process helping dissolve oxygen and carbon dioxide into the water. Nearly all animals in the ocean breathe oxygen directly from the water, making dissolved oxygen a critical measure of who can live where. For seaweeds and other organisms that take up carbon dioxide, the concentration of carbon dioxide ($CO_2$) has the same importance. Waves mix things up, continually refreshing surface waters, maintaining tight connections between ocean and atmosphere.

When ecologists refer to "high-energy" environments, this sort of wave-beating kinetic energy is generally what springs to mind: a shore being pounded by waves clearly has a lot of kinetic energy. But kinetic energy in nearshore habitats takes many forms: for example, fast currents flowing through narrow passages are a form of kinetic energy. And the amount of kinetic energy in marine habitats varies widely, with consequences for the organisms that live there. For example, in back bays and lazy estuaries, sluggish circulation and lack of wave energy can reduce the availability of nutrients and increase the accumulation of fine particulate matter, creating muddy habitats. Where water flows slowly or not at all, black mud can form. This mud can be entirely devoid of dissolved oxygen, a condition referred to as anoxia, the black color and attendant sulfurous smell resulting from specialized bacteria that have moved in to take advantage of the low-oxygen conditions. All along California's coast, the kinetic energy of a site, be it wave-beaten shore, muddy estuary, or anoxic bay, plays a large role in determining the numbers and sorts of species that live there.

## Wave Action, Exposure, and Disturbance

Wave action is a defining characteristic of any coastal site. Waves can be generated by local winds or they can arise from distant weather systems that are uncoupled from local conditions.

Scientists often describe a site as more or less exposed, which is shorthand for the degree of wave action and kinetic energy we observe

High-energy, wave-exposed shorelines, like this one near Bean Hollow State Beach in San Mateo County, south of San Francisco, define much of California's coastline.

there; more exposed sites are subject to larger and more frequent waves, while less exposed sites tend to be protected from wave forces. More exposed sites typically have a long fetch (the length of water over which the wind has blown before reaching the site): imagine a beach with an uninterrupted view of the horizon. Less exposed sites have shorter fetch lengths—for example, in bays, in coves, or behind islands or headlands. Wave exposure may determine how much wave force an organism routinely experiences, one of many stresses that affects where a species is or is not found.

The energy that comes with wave exposure is a major underlying force that shapes communities along the shore. Some species tolerate battering by waves by being very stiff (e.g., mussels), others are quite flexible (e.g., feather boa kelp, *Egregia menziesii*; see Species of Interest in chapter 7, Santa Barbara to Los Angeles), and still others adopt a streamlined shape (e.g., limpets). Some grow in clumps or clusters that help to shed wave forces. Some seaweeds bend with the waves and have elastic structures that snap back into place once the wave energy has dissipated. Many animals, in addition to having streamlined forms, adapt their behaviors to resist the waves: limpets, chitons, abalone, and others tend to clamp down hard on the rocks or other firm surfaces, resisting the pressure to be dislodged.

Those species that can't tolerate wave forces require calmer conditions, where they maintain their space by being superior competitors in those more protected surroundings. Consequently, a visitor might find one species abundant on a headland, only to find that it disappears around the corner where conditions are more protected—for example, kelp species that occupy the most exposed locations on rocky headlands typically won't be found in calm areas nearby. Likewise, kelp species that favor calmer conditions aren't found in the most exposed locations. The result is a mosaic of species along the shore shaped partly by physical forces and partly by competition and other interactions among species.

Storms can rearrange intertidal communities by creating larger-than-normal waves or turning boulders and logs into deadly projectiles. When waves tear away or crush the previous inhabitants, space opens for new settlers to move in once conditions calm down. In this way, disturbance can be a source of renewal in intertidal communities, akin to a tree falling in an old-growth forest. Its effect is often seasonal, with storm-driven winter waves having the greatest impact.

The sea palm (*Postelsia palmaeformis*; see Species of Interest in chapter 4, Mendocino, Sonoma, and Marin) is a great example of a disturbance-dependent species. In locations north of San Luis Obispo, this kelp lives exclusively on rocky benches exposed to extreme wave action. In these habitats, mussels outcompete the sea palm for space, so mussels generally dominate and suppress the sea palm before it has a chance to grow. But when big waves remove patches of mussels, space becomes available for this kelp to occupy. Sea palms tend to grow in stands consisting of many individuals: this configuration, along with their highly flexible stipes (stems) and very strong holdfasts (root-like masses for attachment), helps them shed wave forces and persist in the most wave-swept locations.

## Nutrients, Oxygen, and Carbon Dioxide

Basic life processes require just a handful of ingredients. For photosynthetic plants and algae, the raw materials required are sunlight, carbon dioxide, water, and a few nutrients (chiefly nitrogen and phosphorus). The creation of organic matter by plants, referred to as primary production, is an outcome of photosynthesis. When the organic matter produced by plants and algae is eaten by consumers (e.g., snails, bugs, your family) to support their growth, secondary production occurs.

In air, $CO_2$ rarely limits plant growth; in caring for a houseplant or garden, ensuring your plants have sufficient sunlight, nutrients, and water is usually sufficient. In the ocean, primary production also depends on the availability of sunlight, nutrients, and $CO_2$. In most locations, the surface ocean has plenty of sunlight and $CO_2$, so primary production is typically limited by the availability of nutrients, especially nitrogen—not too different from the situation in a kitchen garden. Nutrients enter the ocean in river runoff, via deposition from the air, or (most noticeably in areas where human populations are very large) from human sources

Seaweeds and other algae use an array of different-colored pigments to harvest energy from sunlight, creating organic matter that ultimately feeds much of the intertidal community.

such as wastewater treatment facilities. Once in the ocean, nutrients are transported by water motion or moved around by animals as they excrete waste matter or eventually die and decompose. In coastal areas, nutrients that sink out of the surface layers can be resuspended by the process of upwelling. Such mechanisms fertilize the intertidal garden, which in turn supports the diversity of life dependent on this primary production.

Animals, by contrast, don't directly harvest their own energy from the sun. So animals typically eat those species that do, just as garden snails eat growing vegetables. And in addition to food, animals need oxygen to survive and grow. Humans and other land animals, of course, get oxygen from the air, and many marine animals can do the same, at least for limited periods of time. But with the important exception of marine mammals, animals that spend much or all of their lives underwater need some way of obtaining oxygen while submerged. They do so by using gills or gill-like structures to remove oxygen that is dissolved in the water, but there's a catch: dissolved oxygen is in relatively short supply in sea-water. So processes that help replenish dissolved oxygen in seawater—for example, photosynthesis and wave action—are important to the survival of animals.

In brief, marine algae are likely to grow—and produce both biomass and oxygen—wherever there is sunlight and a sufficient supply of nutrients. Where these primary producers are abundant, they provide fuel for animals and help support productive food webs, building complexity and biomass in nearshore systems.

## Wind, Drying, and Cooling

Wind is a persistent force, a fact of life along the California coast. Onshore winds, also known as sea breezes or day breezes, are locally generated winds blowing onto shore from the ocean. They tend to be a daily feature, developing in the afternoon along the West Coast as air rushes from relatively cool high-pressure areas over water to warmer low-pressure areas over land. The pattern relaxes as land cools overnight, resulting in the opposite pattern in the morning, with air moving from land to ocean. These morning offshore winds, or land breezes, are favored by surfers because they produce waves that hold their shape.

Prevailing winds are winds that blow predominantly in one direction. They are caused by larger-scale patterns of movement in the earth's atmosphere. Along the West Coast, prevailing winds tend to blow from the northwest. Prevailing winds generate waves and cause coastal upwelling, both of which are important physical processes along the California coast.

The ecological effects of wind are perhaps less obvious, but they are important, and intertidal organisms must find ways to deal with wind and its effects. For example, as wind passes over an animal or seaweed, it causes evaporation, drawing water from the organism's body into the air. Such wind-driven drying causes rapid cooling, as any swimmer knows; hence, intertidal organisms exposed to wind can experience drying and cooling at the same time.

Evaporative cooling is temporary and usually not sufficient to protect from excessive heat on a hot day; in reality, the combination of

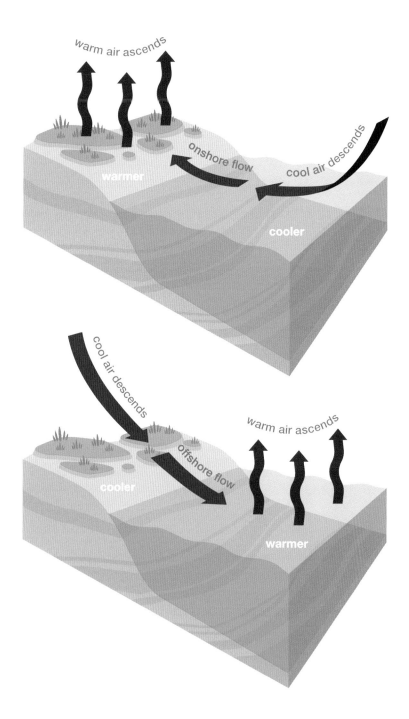

Coastal wind patterns shift between onshore flow during the afternoon (top) and offshore flow during the morning (bottom).

desiccation and heat, not cooling, is typically more stressful for intertidal organisms. Species that cannot move away from harsh conditions have traits that allow them to cope with the one-two punch of desiccation and heat during low tides. Mussels and barnacles tightly close their shells to preserve interior moisture, as do some snails. Other species grow in tight clusters to reduce their combined exposed surface area—for example, a large patch of anemones heats and dries far more slowly than does a lone anemone living in isolation.

Animals often slow their metabolism during stressful periods, reducing both energy requirements and the accumulation of waste products that are difficult to purge under such hermetic conditions. Some seaweeds, on the other hand, have adopted a counterintuitive strategy for dealing with heat and drying: they simply dry out and live to tell about it. Many intertidal seaweeds can lose a remarkable amount of water without lasting damage, then rehydrate when the tide rises again.

## LIVING ELEMENTS THAT SHAPE ECOSYSTEMS

It's clear that physical forces like sun, wind, and tides play a big role in giving any stretch of coast its particular feel and explaining what species live there. But the neighbors matter a lot too. The other species living nearby can mean the difference between a site being habitable and uninhabitable.

Neighbors can be helpful. For example, seaweeds can provide cover for small animals, reducing their exposure to sun, wind, and predators, and their blades can provide surfaces to live on. But neighboring seaweeds and invertebrates often compete for space, and invertebrates compete with each other for space and food. Space especially can be limiting in the intertidal, just as it is in dense urban areas where humans compete for housing. And neighbors can be predators too: the neighbor that doesn't appropriate your space may eat you instead.

A century of ecological research has endeavored to distill the messy, complicated interactions among living things into the kinds of solid, comforting rules that govern the physical world. When we drop an apple, that apple predictably falls with a known acceleration and hits the ground with a known force. But no simple formula predicts the future community if we add a new species of snail to an existing tidepool community or after powerful waves remove a mussel bed and clear space on the rocks.

The range of possible interactions among species seems to preclude the kind of falling-apple rules that physicists enjoy and ecologists envy;

## LARVAL DEVELOPMENT AND TRANSPORT

Seaweeds, mussels, barnacles, tube worms, oysters, anemones, sponges, tunicates . . . many of the most common species in the intertidal are literally stuck in place. Indeed, many make their own glue or cement, relying on its strength to keep them anchored in spite of the oncoming waves. And even those that aren't permanently place-bound are unlikely to transport themselves over any serious distance: it is difficult to imagine a sea star or hermit crab moving from one rocky outcrop to the next, and yet these species cover our shores. How did they get there?

Most coastal species have a life cycle quite different from our own. Invertebrates and fish typically start out as microscopic larvae, passing through at least one (and up to twelve!) larval stages, each with its own shape and name, before reaching a recognizable adult form. Just as a butterfly begins life as a caterpillar, a barnacle is first a nauplius, a clam is first a veliger, and a sea urchin is first a pluteus. If you are a person who enjoys extremely specific, arcane vocabulary, larval biology might be the field for you.

Seaweeds are even stranger than animals in their life cycles (and the terminology even more arcane). Rather than sequential larval stages, many seaweeds pass through unrecognizably different growth forms (microscopic spores and gametes, and larger forms that are crustose, upright, or bladed) that have differing numbers of chromosomes. Those giant kelps growing just offshore? They alternate with a microscopic form that produces eggs and sperm from which the behemoths spring forth. And the red seaweed known as Turkish washcloth (*Mastocarpus papillatus*) has two alternating forms so different that one was originally described as an entirely different genus (see Species of Interest in chapter 6, Monterey, Big Sur, and the Central Coast).

For many intertidal species, the larval, spore, or gamete phase is the chance to disperse, or move around. Free from the constraints of the adult form, these tiny stages swim or drift, surfing ocean currents often long distances away from their parents to colonize new territory. This behavior makes marine invertebrates and seaweeds similar to wind-dispersed land plants: essentially stuck in one place as adults, relying on currents, wind, and water to ferry offspring toward parts unknown. And as in land plants that spew seeds far and wide, a spawning marine organism's success rate is similarly low. Generally, marine species make thousands to millions of microscopic offspring for every one that survives to adulthood. A few drops of seawater may contain larvae from many species, a soup of marine miniatures; if you've ever accidentally swallowed seawater, you've ingested an invisible raw bar of larval snails, worms, sea stars, oysters, and other animals all in the same mouthful.

Larval behavior explains in part why empty space is at a premium in the intertidal: every wave sloshes countless thousands of larvae and spores over any bare patch of rock the minute that space opens up. To complete their life cycle, those tiny propagules must settle, attach, and metamorphose into a miniature adult; chances are good that at least one will choose to settle on any given surface, and quickly. Hence, barnacles have forever been the bane of both sailors and whales, attaching to their boats and backs alike—a drag, literally, for the swimming and sailing bodies slowed by such unwelcome settlers.

however, biologists recognize a few critical ecological interactions as key to regulating communities and predicting outcomes, notably competition, predation, and facilitation. Parasitism is another. Recognizing these interactions in the field helps the observer understand what's happening at a site and make good guesses about what might happen next.

## Competition: Striving for Real Estate and Food

Competition is largely what it sounds like. Imagine two siblings given a cookie to share. Each might ungenerously compete to monopolize this common resource (the cookie), spending time and energy to ward off the other only to end up with less than either would enjoy as an only child (the whole cookie—the ultimate win).

Ecological competition plays out continuously even if we don't see it quite as directly as a cookie squabble; individuals of the same and of different species compete, but the idea is the same: everyone loses a bit, and some (often the smaller competitors) lose big. On every rock or patch of sand along the shore, every individual of each species struggles to maximize its share of common resources, which include food, space, sunlight, and other necessities. Species that are less suited to a particular setting tend to get outcompeted and locally displaced by dominant competitors, creating an artificially static appearance amid a dynamic and never-ending battle for turf and snacks. We see only the winners that remain in a spot on the shore, but trace the tide line down a rocky wall, or walk a shore from high to low wave action: the results of competition may start to reveal themselves as one species replaces another.

Competition for space can be particularly intense in the intertidal realm, given the narrow sliver of real estate between land and sea. Seawater is teeming with the spores of algae and with larvae and juveniles of all sorts of invertebrates. Under the right conditions, these early life stages will settle and grow into adult forms, but many require a suitable landing pad or attachment spot to make their permanent home. Consequently, the race to occupy bare space is quickly won; where space is limited, species often grow right on top of one another. Photosynthesizers need light, other organisms need food and shelter from pounding waves and baking

A crowded tidepool is filled with invertebrates and seaweeds at Partington Cove, Big Sur. Different life forms and modes of feeding mean that the inhabitants don't all compete for the same food resources, but each does require space for attachment.

sun, and so every species constantly has to compete for space that meets its needs. Invertebrate larvae use chemical cues to sniff out favorable places to settle, ensuring they grow up near a suitable source of light, food, or friends, depending on the habitat needs of that species. Where to settle down is a make-or-break decision in the life of a marine organism—and it has to be made while the organism is a microscopic vagabond.

If you see a patch of bare rock between the tides, look around for the explanation. You may see a large limpet hiding along the edge; these snails scrape off algae and use their wedge-like shells to dislodge animals such as barnacles, or even other limpets, from the substrate. Or you might see piles of driftwood or large cobbles on the beach above the high-tide line; big waves could have turned these objects into projectiles that cleared space, offering a physical, rather than biological, explanation for bare rock. You may even, upon close inspection, find evidence of early colonists moving in—tiny barnacles or small tufts of algae.

## ALGAE AND SEAWEEDS

The term *algae* (singular alga) sometimes conjures green scum growing on ponds or maybe even in your swimming pool. But algae are much more diverse and perplexing than that. The term refers to a varied group of taxa from multiple distinct lineages that tend to live in marine and freshwater environments. Many algae exist as single cells (microalgae), while others are multicellular (macroalgae). The marine macroalgae commonly are referred to as seaweeds and include species of red, brown, and green algae. These three groups are distinct from each other, having evolved from different ancestors. With only a few exceptions, seaweeds are anchored to the substrate by holdfasts (seaweeds have no roots). Seaweeds use their blades to take up nutrients directly from the surrounding seawater, and the blades are also used for both photosynthesis and reproduction.

Kelps are a special group of brown seaweeds, meaning that not every large seaweed is a kelp. Kelps belong to a single order (the Laminariales) in the brown algae and are among the largest of the seaweeds. Some kelps play important ecological roles, forming extensive underwater forests, while others grow in intertidal areas, typically low on the shore where they provide habitat for a host of invertebrate species.

## Predation: Eating One Another

Life is stressful enough; imagine if when your neighbors got hungry, they could choose to eat you. Marine animals have evolved an impressive array of ways to consume one another. The first image of an ocean predator that springs to mind is likely one of sharks or large marine mammals, predators that can tear prey into pieces using a muscular body and a mouth full of teeth. Indeed, such rapacious species stalk hunting grounds along the West Coast, but thankfully not typically in the intertidal.

To biologists, predation is a far broader concept that applies any time one living thing eats another, regardless of whether the prey is an animal, plant, or any living thing. Indeed, picking and eating berries on a lovely summer day would qualify you as a predator. Predation can be challenging to observe among some of the smaller organisms on the shore; you have to look pretty closely to see the action as tiny animals endeavor to eat without being eaten. And while we often think of predators as pursuing their prey, many acts of predation at the shore are carried out by organisms stuck in place. All those barnacles and mussels and anemones need to eat too.

## SO MANY WAYS OF EATING

For example, barnacles cement themselves to the rock, essentially landing on their heads as larvae and then building their volcano-shaped shells around themselves. From there, they use modified legs that look like tiny feathers to reach into the water and pull out minuscule bits of suspended food that includes plankton and detritus. This is called suspension feeding, and it is used in various forms by many intertidal invertebrates. Clams, oysters, mussels, and the like also feed by capturing small particles. They do this by extending a siphon to draw water in, filtering out the food particles, and spitting out the remaining water. And a technical aside is needed here: the term filter feeding, which is perhaps more familiar than the term suspension feeding, is really just a special type of suspension feeding, most appropriately applied to animals that use active behaviors (pumping water, secreting and ingesting mucus nets, etc.) to capture suspended food particles.

A wide variety of animals from worms to sea cucumbers ingest sediment, eating sand or mud and digesting the organic matter, leaving behind a trail of clean sediment as their waste, like nature's vacuum cleaners. Deposit feeding (as this is known) is a lifestyle that works on land too: it has followed our earthworms out of the sea and into our fields and lawns.

A gooseneck barnacle (*Pollicipes polymerus*) uses its feather-like appendages to pull small bits of food from the water, while a black limpet (*Lottia asmi*) finds purchase on the barnacle's plates.

Anemones use a far different strategy to capture prey. With their bodies fixed on the substrate, they spread their tentacles and lie in wait for potential prey to make contact. The tentacles contain specialized stinging cells that are used to immobilize and cling to small prey. Once the prey is immobilized, the tentacles move it to the mouth, where it is eaten.

Some anemones hedge their nutritional bets by also maintaining single-celled algae in their outer layers. These algae contain light-harvesting pigments and carry out photosynthesis while living within the host animal. The anemone benefits from its houseguests, collecting some of the compounds the algae produce via photosynthesis. The anemones' relatives, the tropical reef-building corals, employ the same strategy.

Animals that can move about have developed different means of feeding. Snails and their allies use specialized feeding structures called radulae (singular radula), which resemble Lilliputian belt sanders, to scrape algae from rocks or bore into the shells of their prey. For good measure, some limpets and chitons coat their teeth with iron, creating rows of metal dentition that can rasp against rock without being quickly worn to nubs. Intertidal crabs use prominent claws to crush the shells of their prey and complicated mouthparts to slice and tear the prey into manageable bits. Fish, too, feed in the intertidal when the tide is up, many with jaws quite similar to our own.

The group called echinoderms has evolved many radically different feeding strategies. Urchins use a radially symmetrical array of five tooth-like structures to graze kelp and other fleshy seaweeds, in places feeding insatiably, leaving barren zones like underwater deserts. Sand dollars can stand themselves on edge like self-stacking plates in a dishwasher and use hydraulic tube feet to snare small food particles from seawater in the zone of breaking waves—or, lying down on the sand, they can pluck up food grains like a roaming dust buster. Sea stars famously turn their stomachs inside out through their mouths to digest prey outside of their bodies, while their relatives the sea cucumbers use tentacles to scoop in suspended particles or detritus (dead organic matter) and will readily spew out their guts when annoyed.

The above examples are by no means exhaustive. Several hundred million years of evolution has produced a kaleidoscope of predatory strategies among animal lineages, and new ways of eating among intertidal organisms are still being discovered today.

## OFFENSE AND DEFENSE

The dual needs to eat and avoid being eaten have shaped evolution in the sea for over 500 million years, resulting in an arms race: predators with slightly stronger claws or teeth survived to pass their traits along to their even more terrifying offspring; the prey that survived passed on their own thicker shells and longer spines to offspring that grew up better protected than the previous generation. Thus both offensive and defensive traits intensified over time through natural selection, seen as successive waves of traits in the fossil record. Today's species are only the most recent products of this long process.

Shells, jaws, and other hard parts of marine creatures are made from compounds found in seawater. Most commonly, these parts are of calcium carbonate—familiar as classroom chalk, which is itself formed by the accumulation of tiny shells of marine creatures. Calcium carbonate is readily formed from seawater, and hence it is both ubiquitous and critically important for both predation and defense from predators. Other hard parts, such as the tiny spines inside most sponges and the intricate pillbox-shaped shells of microscopic diatoms that fill the sunlit ocean, are generated from silica, or silicon dioxide, familiar to us as glass.

Plants and seaweeds, too, have evolved mechanisms to deter grazing. Similar to invertebrates, some seaweeds deposit calcium carbonate in their cell walls, protecting their tissues from grazers and wave force—the pinkish coralline algae are masters of this (see Species of Interest in chapter 5, San Francisco to Santa Cruz). Other seaweeds have developed elaborate chemical defenses to dissuade predators; although antipredator compounds are more common in tropical seaweeds than in temperate species, local algal species nevertheless produce a suite of chemical compounds. One such species, the dark sea lettuce (*Ulvaria obscura*), even produces dopamine—which we know as a human hormone and neurotransmitter and which also deters growth in rival algal species.

## LAND-SEA LINKAGES

If the shoreline is a boundary between land and water, it is a porous one. Fish forage among rocks inundated by a rising tide. Seals haul out to sun themselves on the same rocks exposed at low tide. Rain washes soil downhill and into the sea, recycling sediment and nutrients. Tangled masses of kelp break loose and wash up on beaches, creating new habitat for a community of terrestrial insects.

Terrestrial mammals often use the shoreline at mealtime, although we typically don't think of them as beachgoers. Racoons and deer pick their way among the boulders at low tide, hunting for meals. River otters and mink and foxes sneak shoreward in broad daylight. Of course, these examples all are in addition to humans: we routinely eat shoreline species without thinking twice about being a linkage between land and sea.

These (nonhuman) mammals serve coastal ecosystems by moving nutrients out of the ocean and uphill onto land. Their droppings (and ultimately their bodies) fertilize the plants of the coastal zone. Birds such as ospreys and eagles and cormorants perform a similar function, hunting and eating sea life but making a home on land. And where they still occur, Pacific salmon move nutrients far inland as they run up rivers. So the sea feeds the land, just as the land feeds the sea, with rivers carrying away mountains bit by bit.

Perhaps, then, it's better to think of the shore as a border region—having some width, some content of its own—in which elements of land and sea overlap.

Land-sea linkages are created by species that traverse this boundary, such as terrestrial animals that forage in the intertidal or marine species that frequent terrestrial habitats. Cormorants, for instance, feed at sea and roost in trees, depositing marine-derived nutrients in the process.

## Facilitation: Benefitting One at No Cost to the Other

In competition, two organisms fight over a resource; in predation, one organism *is* the other's resource. Ecologists increasingly recognize the positive effects one species can have on another as important, especially for survival in stressful environments where a go-it-alone approach could prove fatal. Facilitation is the ecological term used when one or both interacting organisms benefit and neither is harmed—the flip side of competition, or what we might call "helping" if it's a one-way benefit and "cooperating" if both parties win as a result. Some species do best when individuals live in groups, and larvae of these species may be triggered to settle nearby as adults release chemical attractants. In the high intertidal, groups often tolerate desiccation and wave stress better than lone individuals, while the same crowding can lead to competitive jousting (tentacle-throwing?) in the low-intertidal zone where conditions are less severe. Mussel beds readily show the benefits of group living, as do clumps of gooseneck barnacles, swaths of clonal anemones, swards of high-intertidal seaweeds, or gangs of tiny periwinkle snails clustered in wet crevices high on the rocks.

Facilitation also works when different species provide resources or services to one another in the form of habitat, food, or refuge from stress or predators. By creating a more favorable environment, facilitation can increase species diversity in a given location, enriching the community through mutual benefits. Such positive effects can occur when the excretions of one species fertilize another or when the canopy of one species provides shade for another. Many species create physical habitat with their shells, tubes, or bodies. For instance, mussel beds create tiny spaces that smaller animals can live in, hiding from predators and wave action, while mussel shells provide hard surfaces for barnacles to grow on. Mussel beds offer opportunities for hundreds of other invertebrates to make a home and a living, even if the mussels gain nothing in return. Similarly, many organisms that burrow into soft sediment habitats oxygenate the surrounding mud, preventing the buildup of otherwise toxic hydrogen sulfide and allowing other organisms to survive beneath the surface.

Likewise, facilitation can be a two-way street. In estuaries, eelgrass

(*Zostera marina*; see Species of Interest in chapter 3, Far Northern California) and suspension-feeding bivalves (clams, oysters) can provide mutual benefits. eelgrass creates physical structure and stabilizes the sediment while bivalves remove plankton from the water column, ultimately improving light penetration and encouraging growth of the eelgrass. Anemones give single-celled algae a safe, sunny home inside their tentacles and are fed by these symbionts in return. Multiple snail species scrape seaweed blades clean of attached invertebrates and algae that otherwise reduce the growth of the seaweed, while the snail custodians gain protection hidden within the seaweed's blades. Such partnerships evoke a gentler image of a natural world, wherein species cooperate as well as compete, rather than nature red in tooth and claw—at least until you try to pick up a crab and get a pinch of harsh reality.

### Parasitism

Although they are often overlooked, parasites and the pathogens that cause disease outbreaks occur in marine systems, too, and can be common in intertidal communities. Parasites need to eat like everything else, and while they are perhaps unlovely, their complex life cycles are some of the most extraordinary examples of adaptive evolution. Many parasites progress through multiple larval stages that each colonize a distinct host species before entering their final host, in which the parasite becomes an adult and gets to finally have sex and reproduce—fun for them, less so for the many infected organisms it took to complete their journey.

Many Californian shorebirds are infected by parasitic trematode flatworms and pass fertilized eggs out with their waste. A larva will first parasitize the California horn snail (*Cerithideopsis [Cerithidia] californica*) in a marsh, castrating the snail and pumping out hundreds of clone offspring on every high tide. A more dominant parasite species can move in and kick out the previous parasite, but otherwise there is no hope for that snail to resume a normal life; it is a parasite incubator now. The swimming trematode larvae next infect a crab or fish and alter this secondary host's behavior, such as making fish swim near the surface and twitch to flash light off their scales, so a shorebird will be sure to spot and

# INTERTIDAL ZONATION

It's generally held that the lower limits of a particular species are set by competition and predation, while upper limits are set by environmental factors such as temperature and desiccation. Mussels, for example, could tolerate environmental conditions lower on the shore, but in lower zones they are more vulnerable to being eaten by sea stars and other predators. Conversely, mussels can't tolerate the heat and desiccation much higher on the shore, although facilitation helps as their dense beds stay damp and cool compared to a lone mussel on a hot, bare rock. So mussels are where they are—restricted to a narrow band at mid-tidal height, neither the highest of rock dwellers nor venturing down to a permanently submerged position, underwater

Distinctive bands of organisms become clearly visible at low tide. The most striking ecological pattern in many coastal habitats is intertidal zonation—the arrangement of species in consistent bands moving from high to low elevation on the shore. This pattern is most obvious on vertical or steeply sloping faces, neatly summarizing many of the ecological forces that determine who lives where.

long enough to feed, but not too long lest they be fed upon. Above the mussels, a band of barnacles encrusts the rock, able to seal themselves inside their shells and survive longer, drier, hotter periods out of water. Below the mussel bed, anemones and sea stars arrange themselves along the low water mark. Thus, the concerted effect of tides and waves and temperature, plus competition and predation, yields a surprisingly consistent pattern that can be seen all along the California coast.

The height—that is, the vertical extent—of these intertidal bands depends on tidal amplitude, increasing from south to north as that amplitude increases. Other factors such as the slope or angle of the rock, and exposure to waves and sun, also play a role. And patterns occur even within an intertidal band: species with similar habitat requirements often partition space depending on who moved in first, who can hold space longest, and the vagaries of chance in the ongoing lottery for intertidal real estate.

eat the infected fish, thus returning the parasite to the bird, where it may encounter other equally successful flatworms and mate.

Crabs can be infected by trematodes but also play host to bizarre barnacles called rhizocephalans. So modified by evolution for a parasitic life that you would scarcely recognize them as barnacles, rhizocephalans eschew the suspension-feeding ways of their rock-bound relatives and live almost entirely inside their crab hosts; they are major pests of commercial crab fisheries in some parts of the world. Have sympathy for that crab that tried to pinch you in the previous section; its life may have been harder than you knew.

Disease outbreaks can reshape intertidal communities, sweeping along a shoreline much as human pandemics spread across the globe. Bacteria or viruses that cause marine diseases occur naturally, but may be increasingly spread by human activity, their effects worsened in populations already stressed by climate change. Pathogens have reduced populations of important organisms along the California coast, including abalone and sea stars in recent years, and in other parts of the ocean seagrass, sea urchins, and corals have been decimated by disease.

## LIVING BETWEEN THE TIDES

Given the physical and biological challenges of intertidal life, why live between the tides at all? For starters, the edge of the ocean that lies against the coast is one of the most productive areas on the planet: the marriage of nutrient-rich water and sunlight provides fuel for phytoplankton and seaweeds that sustain small animals. Those small animals filter, graze, or otherwise consume the productivity fed by the sun, in turn supporting entire food webs. And the intertidal offers space to settle, grow, and reproduce: rocks and cobbles, for example, create lots of places for species to attach or hide, and sandy habitats are ideal for burrowing. The diversity of intertidal habitats supports an assortment of life that is weird and wonderful, tailored to this highly variable environment.

## WHAT'S IN A NAME?

Shakespeare famously asked "What's in a name?" Perhaps to his credit, the brilliant bard was no scientist. Since the time of Linnaeus in the mid-1700s, scientists naming living things have followed a convention called binomial nomenclature. Each species is identified using two words that either come from Latin or are modified to look Latinate, because Latin was the international language of science for centuries. The result is a formal system of naming that is subject to humor and occasional ridicule but that remains firmly in place.

Take, for example, the purple-ringed top snail, *Calliostoma annulatum*. *Calliostoma* is the genus, a group of closely related snail species, and it is a noun. The species name is an adjective describing that noun: *annulatum* refers to the particular species of *Calliostoma* in question. The underlying idea is that scientific names reflect evolutionary relationships like a family tree: the species within a genus are more closely related to one another than they are to species outside that genus. And each combination of genus and species names is unique, so those two words alone identify any species unambiguously: there is only one kind of animal called *Calliostoma annulatum*. Stylistically, scientists always capitalize genus names, never capitalize species names, and always italicize both.

Latin names are descriptive by design; if you can read some Latin, they tell you something about the species itself. *Calliostoma* is a mash of Greek and Latin roots meaning "beautiful mouth" (referring to the opening), and *annulatum* is straight-ahead Latin meaning "ringed." Hence, any species with the name *Calliostoma annulatum* had better be one good-looking

The Latin name of the blue-ringed top snail—*Calliostoma ligatum*—aptly describes this common intertidal resident.

snail, and indeed it is. Its close relative the blue-ringed top snail, *Calliostoma ligatum*, is not quite so ornate, but its species name *ligatum*—meaning "banded"—still perfectly describes its appearance.

Latin names often describe the location where a species was first discovered or commonly lives (e.g., *Mytilus californianus*, the California mussel; see Species of Interest in chapter 6, Monterey, Big Sur, and the Central Coast), something about its appearance (e.g., *Halosaccion glandiforme*, "salt sac" "shaped like an acorn"), or sometimes the name of a person (e.g., *Laminaria setchellii*, named in honor of the prominent phycologist William Albert Setchell). These names can even be inside jokes: the blue whale, for example, is the largest animal on earth yet bears the scientific name *Balaenoptera musculus*, where *musculus* means either "mouse-like" or "well-muscled," depending on whether Linnaeus was in a jocular or serious mood on the day he chose the name. Giant kelp has one of the more interesting names: *Macrocystis pyrifera*—"great flaming balls"—referring to the flame-like blade emerging from each of its ball-like pneumatocysts. And where scientists aren't sure what species they're referring to, they'll either abbreviate *species* as "sp." (or plural "spp.") or just use the genus name, as in "I slipped on some *Laminaria* and fell into a tidepool."

Scientific names can change for a few reasons. First, as new evidence comes to light, perhaps what had previously been classified as a single species becomes split into two or more. This happened commonly, for instance, once it became possible to compare DNA sequences between populations, revealing genetic differences that were not superficially apparent but that usually aligned with subtle distinctions in anatomy or appearance. Most often, this "splitting" introduces new species names into a genus without removing older names. "Lumping" can occur instead when scientists realize two or more names refer to the same species; younger names are subsumed under older names per a talmudic series of rules maintained by the governing bodies of taxonomic nomenclature, which are as much fun as they sound.

Second, occasionally researchers will review the organization of names for a whole group of species. The organization of names should reflect the relatedness of species, like Russian nesting dolls. When the understanding of the evolutionary relationships within a group changes, names may need to be changed accordingly. Such reorganization might move a species into a different genus. For example, the red sea urchin was renamed from *Strongylocentrotus franciscanus* to *Mesocentrotus franciscanus* during one such review, moved out of the genus it used to share with the common purple sea urchin (*Strongylocentrotus purpuratus*) after research revealed the two were not very closely related (see Species of Interest in chapter 4, Mendocino, Sonoma, and Marin).

Common names, in contrast to scientific names, don't follow strict rules and are almost always descriptive, though sometimes in ways that stretch the imagination. The purple sea urchin is a good descriptive name: the urchin is clearly purple, unlike its cousins the red and green urchins. Rockweed is a descriptive, but somewhat less helpful, common name: lots and lots of seaweeds grow on rocks, so choosing just one genus (*Fucus*) to call rockweed is a bit arbitrary (see Species of Interest in chapter 4). Other common names are applied to more than one species, often totally unrelated. For example, dead man's fingers refers both to the green seaweed *Codium fragile* (see Species of Interest in chapter 5, San Francisco to Santa Cruz) and to a terrestrial fungus that grows on decaying wood. And fat innkeeper (*Urechis caupo*) is one of those common names that stretches the imagination, though this worm does tend to be pudgy and does create burrows that host other species.

3

White sea foam runs up a black sand beach on California's Lost Coast.

FAR
NORTHERN
CALIFORNIA

The view to the sea from the northernmost part of California is open and alluring on a clear day. Near the state border, the shore is hard to distinguish from the beaches of southern Oregon; the terrain is dominated by sand deposited by sometimes-distant rivers and sculpted into dunes by the constant wind. This system of dunes and the freshwater Lake Earl behind it are, in fact, the northernmost remnants of the region's coastal lagoons, the others being a few dozen miles to the south in Humboldt County, where the largest, Humboldt Bay, forms an estuary around which the region's economy revolves.

Between the Oregon border and the Lost Coast, coastal California has an almost forlorn feel; it is rural and exposed, with rough edges. Fishing, crabbing, and timber remain important industries in the twenty-first century. Dense forests paint the cragged inland areas of the Klamath Mountains and their associated river drainages—the Rogue, Smith, Klamath, Trinity, Eel, and others—span southern Oregon and Northern California. Commercial fishing vessels fill the region's harbors, and US Highway 101 links the population centers of Crescent City, Arcata, and Eureka with points north and south.

Tectonic plates move and shape the shoreline here in ways that may not be intuitive. Situated along the southern end of the Cascadia subduction zone, the land around Crescent City is rising faster than average rates of sea level rise, leading to an apparent drop in local sea levels. On the other hand, a comparatively short distance south in Humboldt Bay, sea level is rising two to three times faster than average because the land

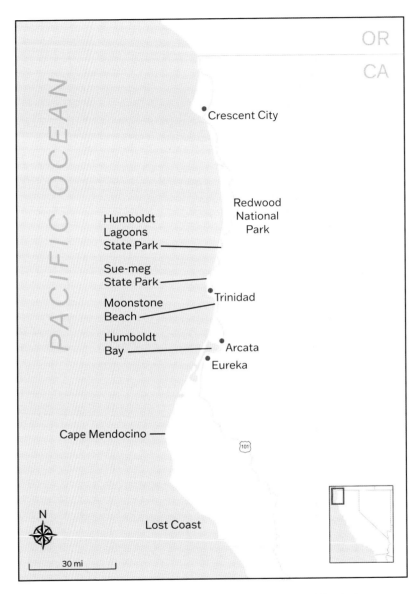

OR

CA

PACIFIC OCEAN

Crescent City

Redwood
National
Park

Humboldt
Lagoons
State Park

Sue-meg
State Park

Moonstone
Beach

Trinidad

Humboldt
Bay

Arcata

Eureka

Cape Mendocino

101

N

Lost Coast

30 mi

The Northern California coast, from the Oregon state line to Cape Mendocino.

Dunes are common in northernmost California, a conspicuous difference between this region and most of the rest of the state's shoreline. The dunes vary in age and size, with many being stabilized by vegetation, some of it nonnative.

is sinking. These land motions occur over long periods of time compared with the life spans of marine organisms, but even such slow processes can influence life on the shore by creating or destroying intertidal habitat.

The threat of tsunamis is also ever-present along this stretch of coast. Crescent City is particularly vulnerable, and several large tsunamis have been recorded there in the past century alone. An ocean tsunami is a set of waves caused by the sudden movement of water, generally as a result of an undersea earthquake. These waves displace gargantuan volumes of water at speeds of up to 500 miles per hour and can be some of nature's most powerful forces. They are far larger than standard wind-driven waves, and because of their long wavelengths, tsunamis may look more like a fast-rising tide than like a typical breaking wave. Quirks of bathymetry (submarine topography) and the geometry of the coastline contribute to this vulnerability: at Crescent City, an offshore ridge along the seabed can amplify the incoming waves. The 1964 Alaska earthquake triggered one such tsunami, killing at least eleven residents and injuring many others as it destroyed much of the town. Decades later, the 2011 Tohoku earthquake in Japan triggered an eight-foot surge that wrecked the city's harbor. Crescent City bears its scars visibly, with memorials and markers prominent near the shore. Evidence of tsunamis reportedly exists in the shoreline geology too: for example, prior tsunamis are thought to have deposited debris on wave-cut platforms at Pebble Beach, just north of Crescent City.

Directly south of Crescent City, dense coast redwoods quickly swallow the road as US 101 climbs the first big rock of California. The tallest trees in the world—*Sequoia sempervirens*, wholly absent a few dozen miles to the north—abruptly dominate the landscape just inland from the coast.

Coastal geomorphology leaves Crescent City and the wider region prone to tsunamis. Signposts identify tsunami hazard zones along vulnerable parts of the West Coast, and some signs point out routes to the safety of high ground in the event of an earthquake.

# REDWOODS

Coastal regions of Northern California boast forests of the coast redwood (*Sequoia sempervirens*), the tallest trees in the world. Indeed, the three tallest known living trees anywhere in the world reportedly exist in Redwood National Park. The largest of these is named Hyperion, a Titan from Greek mythology said to be the father of the sun, moon, and dawn.

The ancient feel of a redwood forest is in some ways an accurate reflection of the history of the species: redwoods and their close relatives first appear in the fossil record during the Jurassic Period (200 to 145 million years before present). Much more recently, during the last ice age about 12,000 years ago, redwoods grew across much of North America and well south of their present distribution. For example, redwood bark appears in the La Brea tar pits of Los Angeles. As recently as 1850, coast

Coast redwoods are giant fog capture-and-delivery organisms, providing water to sustain the forest ecosystem.

redwoods occupied a couple of million acres between Big Sur and southern Oregon; about 95 percent of these trees have since disappeared.

Coast redwoods rely on marine fog for moisture during the dry season, favoring areas of the coastal mountains where fog is frequent. For redwoods, fog delivers water: their evergreen needles are structured in such a way to scoop fog out of the sky and condense it into droplets that drip down on the forest floor, in some cases contributing more than 30 percent of the annual water supply to the forest system. Moreover, the thin film of water condensed on the surface of needles reduces the amount of water a tree needs to draw from its roots to maintain its water balance, and it simultaneously decreases the amount of water vapor lost to the atmosphere through evaporation. Fog, then, is critical to the persistence of coast redwoods and to the rich forest communities they sustain.

Coast redwoods grow impressively straight, are relatively light and strong, and are resistant to insects and fire, making them a highly desirable product for constructing buildings and other infrastructure. Many Northern California towns were built almost entirely of redwood. The milled wood has a beautiful reddish-brown hue, hence its name. Extensive logging began in the early nineteenth century and went unchecked for decades, leaving what's left protected by a patchwork of national, state, and regional parks. Conservation efforts have long been under-way, removing old and abandoned logging roads, developing new partnerships with landowners and conservation groups, and promoting forest stewardship that aims to coax often unhealthy second-growth forests to their full potential. Some particularly beautiful old-growth redwood forests remain, often in terrain that was too difficult to support commercial logging, and wandering through one of these groves can be a deeply rewarding experience, unique to California.

Coastal California at this point seems to have begun in earnest, although in truth it is only south of Humboldt Bay that the region's characteristic rugged coastline really becomes apparent.

Farther south, cool, still air hangs heavy with fog and time, enveloping the old-growth temperate rain forests of Redwood National Park and nearby state parks. Enormous banana slugs glide across acidic redwood soil, mushrooms abound, and condensation gathers on understory fields of ground-hugging wood sorrel (*Oxalis* sp.) and ferns. The coast redwood so dominates the landscape that it creates its own rain, gathering fog in its formidable upper reaches. Redwoods grow in only a narrow strip of coastal territory, bound to the sea because of the fog that it brings, providing water for the trees even in dry years.

To the south of Humboldt Bay, Cape Mendocino appears as a large and relatively inaccessible knob of land that stands out on any map of the West Coast. Just offshore, the Gorda plate is a geological train wreck in action, dragged under the North American plate on its eastern side, inching past the Pacific plate on its southern side, and pulling away from the Pacific plate on its northern side. This mess results in constant small earthquakes (and an occasional large one), animates the inland Mount Shasta and Lassen Peak volcanoes, and lifts the land here faster than most anywhere else along the West Coast.

## PLACES TO EXPLORE

### Humboldt Lagoons

The lagoons of Humboldt County are a striking coastal feature, the highway weaving around and over them in an attempt to avoid the more rugged terrain inland. These brackish lagoons appear to have been formed by a combination of tectonic uplift and wave-borne sand anchored by drift logs and other debris. The relatively persistent sandbars are high and wide, separating the shallow water bodies from the sea, and are breached by waves a few times each year during storms. Humboldt Lagoons State Park sits between Redwood National Park (to the north) and Sue-meg State Park (to the south), encompassing three discrete lagoons and one wetland whose days as an active lagoon are now past. Comparing these

A sandbar separates Big Lagoon (left) from the Pacific Ocean (right) north of Eureka.

present and former lagoons with others to the north and south—Del Norte County's Lake Earl and the large Humboldt Bay—offers a vivid sense of earth processes in action, a cross section of the dynamics of coastal morphology and the longer-term fate of features on the landscape.

The lagoons are fed by small streams that mix with ocean water to create estuarine conditions. The brackish waters support estuarine copepods (small crustaceans, a type of zooplankton) that in turn are food for many species of fish. Coho salmon (*Oncorhynchus kisutch*) and steelhead trout (*Oncorhynchus mykiss*), plus Pacific herring (*Clupea pallasii*), Pacific tomcod (*Microgadus proximus*), starry flounder (*Platichthys stellatus*), Pacific sanddab (*Citharichthys sordidus*), sculpins (Cottidae), and pipefish (Syngnathidae; straightened-out relatives of seahorses) all have been reported from these lagoons. A long list of bird species, both resident and migratory, use these lagoons too. Loons (*Gavia* spp.), grebes (Podicipedidae), sea ducks, diving ducks, plovers (Charadriidae), sandpipers (Scolopacidae), and turnstones (*Arenaria* spp.) all have been sighted, plus ospreys (*Pandion haliaetus*), bald eagles (*Haliaeetus leucocephalus*), hawks (Accipitridae), and more.

The area's prominent sandbars neatly illustrate a type of ecological facilitation, with terrestrial plants being key players in a process that strengthens the dunes and, over time, fills the lagoons with wind-driven sand. A suite of specialized plants evolved adaptations to grow on sand, taking advantage of seemingly barren real estate. In Humboldt County, dozens of species have developed a toehold on the beach, among them yellow sand verbena (*Abronia latifolia*), beach suncup (*Camissoniopsis cheiranthifolia*), beach strawberry (*Fragaria chiloensis*), coast golden-rod (*Solidago spathulata*), beach silvertop (*Glehnia littoralis*), and dune tansy (*Tanacetum bipinnatum*). By colonizing the beach, the low-lying plants stabilize the sand and, in so doing, facilitate growth of other species nearby as soil accumulates over time. Several nonnative species join these native examples and have similar effects: here and elsewhere, managers struggle to control pampas grass (*Cortaderia* spp.), European beach grass (*Ammophila arenaria*), and ice plant (*Carpobrotus edulis*) that have become established on dunes.

## Sue-meg State Park and Trinidad

The most extensive rocky habitat in the region is a substantial promontory occupied by Sue-meg State Park on its northern side and the town of Trinidad on its southern side. In total, this chunk of rock creates a five-mile-long interlude between Big Lagoon and the much larger Humboldt Bay. Elsewhere, the sparse rocky habitat in the region highlights the abundance of sand, gravel, and cobble in this northernmost corner of California; even in rocky areas, mid-intertidal elevations are subjected to constant sand scour, resulting in smooth rock faces and a reduced diversity of invertebrates and algae. But here at Sue-meg, which now again bears its Indigenous Yurok place-name after having been known for decades as Patrick's Point, the shore is a jumble of giant boulders and sharp edges. Powerful surf surges among slick blades of kelp and the near-total cover of seaweeds and invertebrates on mid-intertidal rocks can make it difficult for visitors to find a foothold.

The flat pompom kelp (*Lessoniopsis littoralis*; center) grows only in the most wave-swept environments and always quite low on the shore. This kelp builds a very tough, rigid woody stipe to withstand wave action, distinguishing it from other kelps that use flexible and stretchy stipes for the same purpose.

Despite the abundance of intertidal life here, the regional diversity of invertebrates is a bit lower than that of southern Oregon and points farther south in California. Simple explanations for this kind of large-scale diversity pattern tend to elude ecologists, although a combination of oceanography and larval ecology seems likely to play an important role in this case. Most intertidal invertebrates live fairly sedentary lives as adults; their opportunity for longer-distance travel comes only during the larval stages of their early life histories. Consequently, such species rely on ocean currents for transport to suitable habitats where young can settle and grow. Unlucky larvae that end up in unsuitable habitats won't survive to adulthood (see "Larval Development and Transport," chapter 2, Living between the Tides).

To the south, at Cape Mendocino, opposing oceanographic currents can converge and drive a jet of surface water—along with all those larvae and spores—far offshore and out of range of any coastal habitat, cutting

A small six-rayed sea star (*Leptasterias hexactis*; left—the sixth ray is partially hidden here) is dwarfed by an ochre sea star (*Pisaster ochraceus*; right). Despite considerable differences in size, the two sea stars compete for many of the same prey species.

off connections between northern and southern populations. That is to say, it's difficult for larvae to travel across the cape in either direction. In fact, this situation appears to be a persistent feature of Cape Mendocino, because genetically distinct populations, long-separated from reproductive mixing, are apparent on either side of the cape across species as different as oysters, rockfish, and red algae. Couple the difficulty of larval transport with a dearth of rocky habitat between southern Oregon and Cape Mendocino—such that good habitat for rocky-intertidal species is relatively rare along this bit of coast—and a plausible explanation for far Northern California's dip in invertebrate diversity begins to emerge, though that dip may not be easily discerned on a casual visit to the shore.

The tidepools of Sue-meg feature many of the species that characterize similar habitats elsewhere along the north coast, illustrating common

Blades of the kelp known as sea cabbage (*Hedophyllum sessile*) are drawn back to reveal an understory world of fleshy red algae (middle right), crustose red algae (center), pinkish coralline algae (lower center and right), and patches of rock (pale green and gray) scraped clean by grazing limpets.

processes at play. The tides recede to reveal kaleidoscopic color, with orange and green sponges splayed among pink coralline algae and the deep-red ribbons of their red-algal relatives. Surfgrass (*Phyllospadix* spp.; see Species of Interest in chapter 8, Long Beach to San Diego) whips around in the waves, at low tide lying limp and shading invertebrates with a layer of leafy protection. California mussels (*Mytilus californianus*) and gooseneck barnacles (*Pollicipes polymerus*) compete for space (for both, see Species of Interest in chapter 6, Monterey, Big Sur, and the Central Coast) on large, exposed boulder surfaces, creating three-dimensional structure and tiny niches within which small crustaceans, worms, and molluscs hide from the waves (and presumably from predators). Limpets and chitons act like mini-Zamboni machines, clearing rock faces of thin layers of algae and lurking at the margins of their private algal gardens until high tide when they emerge to feed.

Offshore, California gray whales (*Eschrichtius robustus*) pass nearby along their great migration route, while onshore black bears (*Ursus amer-*

Sea lemons (*Doris montereyensis*) are speckled, bumpy nudibranchs that feed on sponges and breathe through gill plumes (here, exposed to the air at low tide, the nudibranchs have retracted their gill plumes, forming prominent lumps at the rounder posterior ends of their bodies). The two animals shown here (top left) have deposited pale egg ribbons nearby (lower left, upper right).

Fossil shells are exposed in the cliffs behind Moonstone Beach south of Trinidad.

*icanus*) paw for fruits and berries during the summer months. The bears hibernate in dens for the winter months, their heartbeats dropping to about eight beats per minute, only somewhat slower than the resting heart rate of the migrating whales.

Five miles to the south of Sue-meg at the mouth of the Little River, the fine sand of Moonstone Beach creates deep pools around the site's few intertidal rocks. Much of the beach sand is supplied by local rivers, while the modest cliffs abutting the beach to the north consist in large part of shells, fossil remnants of the intertidal residents nearly a million years ago. Many of these same species remain common in the area today.

## Arcata and Eureka

The Eel River was misnamed for its abundance of lampreys—but "Lamprey River" surely doesn't sound as good. The Eel River drains much of two counties, as dark redwood forests drip into convoluted upland valleys. The river brings far more water to the Pacific in winter months than it does in summer, when the flow nearly stops. Along with all that water in winter comes millions of tons of suspended sediment.

Humboldt Bay dominates the local geography, defining the boundaries of human settlement in the region and drawing the eye from all vantage points. This large estuary—the second largest in California—is an economic engine because it is one of the few natural harbors along the West Coast, sheltering a fishing fleet and industrial docks that are in part the remains of once-thriving lumber mills. But maintaining the harbor has taken a lot of human engineering: locals rebuilt the bay's jetties ten times during the twentieth century due to storm damage—a testament, perhaps, to the power of the Pacific or else human obstreperousness.

Intertidal habitat within Humboldt Bay consists largely of eelgrass (see Species of Interest) and unvegetated areas of mud and fine sand, as one might expect from a sheltered embayment. Rocky habitat is restricted to the engineered jetties that push through the dunes to connect the bay with the open ocean. The bay is a key stop along the Pacific Flyway. Expansive tidal flats and their resident invertebrates support foraging by a host of shorebirds when the tide is out; when the tide is high, the margins of the bay serve as places for the birds to rest. Dunlins (*Calidris alpina*), least and western sandpipers (*Calidris minutilla* and *Calidris mauri*, respectively), and marbled godwits (*Limosa fedoa*) are common visitors in winter. A large number of other bird species also use the bay, including black brant (*Branta bernicla nigricans*; see Species of Interest), ducks, and birds of prey such as ospreys (*Pandion haliaetus*), white-tailed kites (*Elanus leucurus*), red-tailed hawks (*Buteo jamaicensis*), and American kestrels (*Falco sparverius*). Small fishes such as the endangered northern tidewater goby (*Eucyclogobius newberryi*) and the three-spined stickleback (*Gasterosteus aculeatus*)—an evolutionary marvel with a handful of marine, brackish, and freshwater forms—inhabit the shallow waters of the bay. Only a small fraction of the bay's original marsh wetlands remains, and much of this remnant is protected in the Humboldt Bay National Wildlife Refuge. Located near the southern end of the bay, the refuge offers the best access point to the wetland habitat.

# ESTUARIES AND LAGOONS

The California coast is dotted with what seem like small lakes and meandering waterways sitting between the shore and the mainland. These are estuaries and lagoons, highly productive ecosystems essential to sustaining local marine life. San Francisco Bay, the largest estuary on the West Coast, encompasses a massive watershed that drains the state's Central Valley from the west side of the Sierra Nevada out through the Golden Gate. Most estuaries and lagoons are much smaller, are often shallow, and border prime coastal real estate. As a result, many have been filled to create more buildable land for coastal cities and suburbs, resulting in the loss of an estimated 85 percent of the state's estuarine habitat.

Functional estuaries are only partially enclosed and have an open connection to the sea; in this feature they differ from lagoons, which are fully enclosed most of the year, but can be connected to the ocean during storm events. Estuaries and lagoons are highly dynamic habitats, with temperature, salinity, and other variables changing over timescales of hours to years, favoring species that can survive such a range of conditions. For example, during rainy months, an increase in freshwater flow drives salinity down; during drier months where river flow is low, the ocean's dominating influence can drive salt content higher. The plants and animals living in these bodies of water must be able to tolerate such fluctuations.

Estuaries and lagoons are nurseries for all kinds of marine species, including fish such as salmon, steelhead, and other commercially important species. Their calm waters provide habitat for birds, shellfish, and a broad array of invertebrates, many of which eventually make their way out to the open ocean where they grow into adults. Even in their diminished state, estuaries are critically important coastal ecosystems that many plant and animal species depend upon.

## CAPE MENDOCINO AND THE LOST COAST

Heading south along US 101, the road turns sharply away from the coast just south of Eureka. For the next 110 miles, the road passes through redwood groves until reaching Leggett, where State Highway 1 heads west through lowland deciduous forest on its way to the coast (see chapter 4's map). The enormous chunk of coastline carved out by US 101's route from Eureka to Leggett avoids the technical challenges of building roads through the steep coastal mountains and simultaneously defines the region known as the Lost Coast. The area is difficult to reach, nearly undeveloped, subject to rough weather, and rugged under even the best of conditions. Anywhere along this route, coastal travelers could be quickly forgiven for thinking they've reached the edge of civilization—it is perhaps the most remote area of coastline in the contiguous US.

Cape Mendocino is the most prominent headland on the Northern California coast. Despite its name, the cape lies entirely within Humboldt County, geographically divorced from the town and county of

Broad vistas and pastoral settings are defining features of Cape Mendocino.

Steep terrain meets the sea across a narrow band of sand and cobble. A carpet of green seaweed (foreground), opportunistic and fast-growing, is a sure sign of wave-induced disturbance. Early colonizers, green seaweeds like this often are the first to appear on cobbles that have been scoured clean by winter waves.

Mendocino that lie to the south. The cape's prominence changes the region's oceanography substantially, exerting a significant influence on the intertidal flora and fauna: for all its isolation, the Lost Coast's rocky intertidal community is surprisingly spare. In many spots, very little seaweed grows on the rocks visible at low tide, in sharp contrast to the impressive algal assemblages that support hundreds of animal species on beaches to the south. Instead, sandstone cobbles and black-sand beaches can stretch for miles, apparently devoid of algae or animals. Zooplankton, too, can be less abundant here, offering less food for their nearshore predators.

Natural disturbance plays an important role in shaping these intertidal communities, as elsewhere along the exposed coast. Strong storms and big waves can cause frequent and severe disturbances and create inhospitable conditions for many intertidal species. Large waves carry logs and mobilize cobble, both becoming projectiles that batter the shore. It's tough for slow-moving or immobile invertebrates to survive such assault—one wouldn't expect to find a lot of sea stars or urchins among the cobble, for example. Only a subset of hardy species can tolerate such conditions; many of these, such as flatworms, chitons, sea cucumbers, northern clingfish (*Gobiesox maeandricus*; see Species of Interest), and segmented tube worms are small bodied and good at gripping the undersides of rocks. Others, such as amphipods and small crabs, nestle in the shell debris that underlies the more prominent cobble.

Volumes of freshwater add to the challenges that rocky-shore species experience on the Lost Coast. Most denizens of the intertidal prefer ocean waters that are suitably salty. Seasonally, tons of rainwater wash down the mountains of the Lost Coast, spilling into creeks and rivers and onto beaches, temporarily reducing the saltiness of waters along the shore and influencing the species assemblages that can persist in these fluctuating environments.

As a result of these and other forces, the marine biodiversity of the Lost Coast can appear a bit impoverished. But given the relatively few visitors that explore this remote shore, the untrammeled intertidal is an excellent place to see species that may be rare or more reclusive elsewhere. On the shore, river otters (*Lontra canadensis*) stalk crabs prowling among smooth low-intertidal boulders, and the occasional northern elephant seal (*Mirounga angustirostris*) hauls out on the dark sand, while herds of elk (*Cervus canadensis*) roam unencumbered on the bluffs above.

## SPECIES OF INTEREST
### Iridescent Horn-of-Plenty

*Mazzaella parksii*, sometimes called the iridescent horn-of-plenty, isn't noticeably iridescent nor does it very much resemble the folkloric goat's horn of plenty after which it is named. Moreover, it's a red seaweed masquerading as something olive green to golden brown in color. Distributed from the Aleutian Islands to Mendocino County, this species occurs no farther south in California—this is the southernmost extent of its geographic range. Notably, populations of *Mazzaella parksii* to the south of Cape Mendocino are genetically distinct from those to the north. The cape thus creates a biogeographic boundary that limits genetic mixing between populations.

This species favors high intertidal rocks in wave-exposed areas, where

The iridescent horn-of-plenty (*Mazzaella parksii*) grows in dense patches high in the intertidal zone. Although it is classified as a red seaweed, it tends to be golden brown in color. Photo by Mandy Lindeberg.

it forms low-growing swards so dense that they exclude nearly all other seaweeds. These dense patches are created by two quite different forms of reproduction, one clonal, the other sexual. Clonal reproduction in this species results from the production of many blades from a single long-lived crust. The crusts can withstand disturbances that clear the fleshy blades from the substrate, producing new blades once conditions become favorable. The species can also reproduce sexually via spores that are released into the water column to settle on suitable substrates nearby. This bet-hedging strategy may be the key to its persistence in rough environments.

## Eelgrass

Typically found growing on mudflats in intertidal and shallow subtidal areas, eelgrass (*Zostera marina*) leaves splay across the muddy surface at

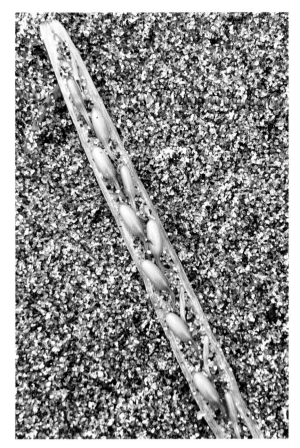

Eelgrass (*Zostera marina*) is a true flowering plant, producing long, linear clusters of flowers on modified leaves. Pollination occurs underwater to produce seeds, shown here still attached within an inflorescence that has broken away from the parent plant. Seeds are released into the water and ultimately grow into new plants. Photo by M. K. Holder.

low tide, lending the mudflat a greenish hue. When the tide is high, the leaves assume a more upright stance owing to tiny air chambers contained within the leaves that add buoyancy, forming underwater meadows that provide habitat for a host of seaweeds and animals—though, interestingly, you won't find eels in an eelgrass meadow.

Neither is eelgrass a true grass, but it is a true flowering plant. It obtains nutrition through its roots, reproducing vegetatively via underground stolons, or runners, and sexually via the production of flowers and seeds. Specially adapted for pollination in a watery setting, eelgrass produces pollen in floating packets that fertilize flowers at the water's surface as well as long strings of pollen that fertilize flowers underwater.

## Bull Kelp

Tangled masses of bull kelp (*Nereocystis luetkeana*) are common among beach wrack from Alaska to central California. Despite the distinctly inelegant appearance of these beach-cast specimens, bull kelp plays important roles in nearshore habitats, both in life and in death.

Although isolated individuals sometimes can be found growing in low-intertidal areas, bull kelp is a subtidal species, forming beds on rocky substrates to depths of around fifty feet. First described from Alaska, bull kelp produces surface canopies composed of individuals that live just twelve to eighteen months. The form of this kelp is unmistakable: a relatively small holdfast of many finger-like branched projections (haptera) gives rise to a single long stipe (stem). In young individuals, the stipe grows until the blades reach the surface; in some specimens, stipes reportedly grow to lengths of one hundred feet or more. The flexible and stretchy stipe is topped by a single orb-shaped float (pneumatocyst) filled with gas that keeps the long blades suspended at the water's surface where

Bull kelp (*Nereocystis luetkeana*) grows in rocky areas to depths of about fifty feet. Their floating canopies tend to be sparser than the canopies of the giant kelp (*Macrocystis pyrifera*) but even so are vital to nearshore ecological communities.

they have access to ample sunlight. The blades release reproductive packets containing microscopic spores that settle on the bottom, forming a sort of seed bank from which the next generation arises.

The underwater forests created by bull kelp are important habitat for a host of species, including fish, invertebrates, and other seaweeds. Several species of seaweeds and invertebrates live directly on the bull kelp tissues, while others make use of the three-dimensional structure, modified light environment, and high productivity of bull kelp forests. Marine mammals and some bird species forage in or at the edges of bull kelp forests. Once dislodged from the rocky substrate, individuals tend to float in twisted mats, carried by tides and currents to places far or near, all the while supporting associated species, including larval or juvenile fishes and birds that choose to hitch a ride. Ultimately these rafts wash up on beaches where their tissue is consumed by beach hoppers (small amphipod crustaceans in the family Talitridae), or they sink, tumbling down submarine canyons where they fuel food webs in deep water.

## Giant Green Anemone

The giant green anemone (*Anthopleura xanthogrammica*) is a standout among the riot of color and texture in intertidal pools. It is common along much of the coast, and the largest of these animals can be nearly ten inches across when fully open, unfurling glowing bright-green tentacles around a broad central oral disc when submerged. As water recedes on a low tide, anemones retract their tentacles, retaining water internally and drooping under the weight. Giant green anemones frequently cover the exterior of their column with shell fragments, thought to protect against sunlight, desiccation, and predation, a behavior they share with aggregating anemones (*Anthopleura elegantissima*).

An effective ambush predator, the giant green anemone consumes mussels, crabs, small fish, and other small animals that might pass by. The tentacles are covered in explosive stinging capsules that, when triggered, launch minute barbed projectiles that immobilize prey. The tentacles then move the prey to the anemone's mouth. Additional nutrients are supplied by endosymbiotic algae that live in the anemone's tissues.

A giant green anemone (*Anthopleura xanthogrammica*), its exterior column covered in shell fragments, waits for the tide to return.

These brilliantly colored anemones can live for many decades, by some estimates up to 150 years. Perhaps relatedly, they have a remarkable power to heal their own wounds and regenerate body parts, including tentacles and even the oral disc.

### Gumboot Chiton

Dubbed the "wandering meatloaf," the gumboot chiton (*Cryptochiton stelleri*) is notable if perhaps not the most charismatic of tidepool fauna. First, there's the name: *Cryptochiton* roughly translates to "hidden frock," a vague reference to the hidden calcareous plates that make up the skeleton of this species, and *stelleri* comes from the prodigious naturalist Georg Wilhelm Steller, after whom species from eagles to jays to sea lions and extinct sea cows are named. Then there's the matter of its

A gumboot chiton (*Cryptochiton stelleri*) wedges itself in a rocky cleft among red seaweeds, its preferred food.

Porcelain crabs (*Petrolisthes* spp.) are small and drab, often sheltering under intertidal rocks and within mussel beds. Despite their large claws, porcelain crabs are filter feeders, subsisting largely on diatoms swept from the surrounding environment.

appearance: big (up to five pounds), bumpy, and reddish, it's the largest chiton on earth, taking on the color of the red seaweeds it prefers to eat. Perhaps most remarkably, its teeth contain magnetite, an iron ore previously known only from rocks. The gumboot's teeth are among the most abrasion-resistant structures in the animal kingdom, superbly adapted to remove tender seaweeds from rocks.

Gumboot chitons can live up to about forty years, during which time they wander only tens of feet from their home. Occupying habitats from the intertidal to depths of about twenty feet, gumboots remain submerged most of the time, using gills to obtain oxygen from seawater, but drawing oxygen directly from air when exposed at low tide. Being poor thermoregulators, they tend to feed at night and take cover during the day.

## Porcelain Crab

Porcelain crabs (*Petrolisthes* spp.) are small-bodied and flat and abundant all along the exposed Pacific coast under rocks and in shell debris. They can occur at very high densities, thanks in part to their habit of gregarious settlement: larvae are likely to settle near an adult of the same species, which is a trait more common among sessile (permanently attached) species than motile ones (capable of movement). This gregarious settlement increases the chances that larvae will settle in habitats that are suitable for survival. For porcelain crabs, though, this behavior comes at a cost: high densities of crabs vying for limited food resources can leave younger, smaller individuals at risk of slower growth and lower egg production.

Porcelain crabs are more closely related to hermit crabs (see Species of Interest in chapter 8, Long Beach to San Diego) than to true crabs such as the red rock crab, though they don't closely resemble either of those relatives. Their broad, compressed claws are large relative to their body size. But despite the size of their claws, porcelain crabs eat tiny diatoms that they filter from seawater using specialized underarm structures that look something like miniature pom-poms. When disturbed, they tend to readily shed legs that appear to shatter as easily as porcelain—hence their common name; the legs grow back after successive molting events.

A sticky, air-breathing fish with no scales, the northern clingfish (*Gobiesox maeandricus*) is often found low in the intertidal, gripping stable rocks with surprising tenacity. Here, the fish's head is exposed, showing its left eye amid a band of yellow, with the rest of its body submerged.

Black brant (*Branta bernicla nigricans*) migrate from Mexico to Alaska each spring. The birds, shown here resting on a rocky shore, use Humboldt Bay as a staging site on their northward migration.

## Northern Clingfish

The northern clingfish (*Gobiesox maeandricus*) inhabits rocky shores in lower intertidal zones between Alaska and Mexico. Typically about three or four inches long, these smooth, scaleless fish feed on amphipods, isopods, snails, limpets, and even other clingfish. They are among more than seventy species of bony fishes worldwide that can breathe air when the tide recedes.

Clingfish are gecko-like in their ability to hold tightly to rocky surfaces. Their grip strength is about 150 times their body weight, strong enough to anchor their body while using their teeth to pry limpets from the rock; their modified fins form a suction cup for attachment to the substrate. They stick better to rough surfaces than to smooth surfaces, and in this they are superior to manufactured suction cups, which work best on smooth surfaces. Their suction cup can hold small amounts of water, allowing the fish to breathe when the tide is out—this trait is in addition to their ability to breathe air when necessary, and no doubt it is handy for a fish living in such a variable environment.

## Black Brant

Black brant (*Branta bernicla nigricans*) are the most marine-dependent members of the goose family. They migrate to Arctic and subarctic breeding grounds in springtime when food in these northern areas is limited. To fuel their journey and the egg laying and incubation that ensues, black brant feed on eelgrass (*Zostera marina*; see Species of Interest) at staging sites along the Pacific Flyway. In California, Humboldt Bay serves as a key staging site for the birds as they make their way northward. The birds feed on attached eelgrass at low tide and at high tide forage for detached eelgrass blades that have washed ashore. It's been suggested that clipping the eelgrass leaves (as brant do) when lots of nutrients (as in lots of goose poop) are present could accelerate the growth of new leaves and induce sexual reproduction in the eelgrass, creating a positive feedback loop between brant foraging and eelgrass growth.

4

Sedimentary bluffs tower above the shore near Point Arena.

# MENDOCINO, SONOMA, AND MARIN

Along the coast from Mendocino County to the Golden Gate, narrow State Highway 1 hugs the shore, with long views out to sea, waves breaking below, and salt spray hanging in the air. The coastline is a tapestry of rural terraces, rolling hills, grass, and stony outcrops. Waves cut these terraces in millennia past, as a series of ice ages raised and lowered the sea. The land, too, has moved over time, as tectonic plates worked—and continue to work—against one another. This roughly hundred-mile stretch holds more rock than sand, more clouds than sun, and more cows than people. Or at least it seems that way.

The stretch of coastline between Point Arena and Point Reyes is part of a conspicuous biogeographic transition zone. On land, for example, this is the southernmost extent of the Sitka spruce (*Picea sitchensis*) that blankets the coast in the wetter climates of the Pacific Northwest and Southeast Alaska. In the intertidal, many warmer-water species have historically reached their northernmost extent here—easily visible examples include barnacles both large (volcano barnacle, *Tetraclita rubescens*) and small (*Chthamalus fissus*). But the geographic ranges of these and other species are changing with the climate, extending poleward as conditions warm, moving north gradually or sometimes in big discrete leaps, creating new ecological communities as northern and southern species mix.

At the same time, the region's complicated ocean circulation influences the movement of species as larvae. Coastal eddies and seasonal upwelling create patchy conditions that influence the distribution of

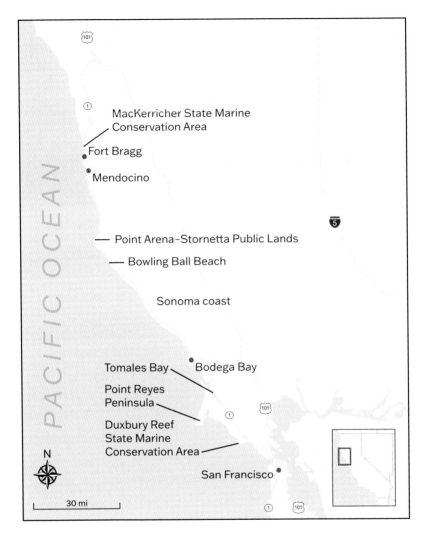

The coastlines of Mendocino, Sonoma, and Marin Counties.

phytoplankton and invertebrate larvae. Among invertebrates, patchy ocean conditions can act a bit like a lottery, determining how many larvae successfully settle on a suitable bit of substrate, and when. Remarkably, the numbers of larvae settling in this region can vary by orders of magnitude across sites or seasons: at Fort Bragg, pulses of recruitment of

## WAVE-CUT TERRACES

In many places along the California coast, there appear to be giant stair steps carved into the landscape—sometimes a single step, sometimes several in a series trending uphill and inland. Erosion caused by wave action creates flat surfaces, or platforms, at sea level, wherever sea level happens to be at that time. As sea level rises and falls due to glacial cycles, wave-cut platforms result, marking past sea levels. Where tectonic forces raise the land with respect to sea level, platforms shift beyond the range of wave action, where they appear as distinct terraces, sometimes hundreds of feet above sea level. And because today's sea level is about as high as it has ever been in recent geological time, today's cliffs represent a temporary victory of uplift over erosion.

Underscoring their marine origins, marine terraces often contain fossilized animals and ocean sediments. For example, clams in the family Pholadidae drill into hard rock in the intertidal zone; fossils of these and other shelled animals found today in terraces well above sea level give a vivid sense of the changeable landscape.

the California mussel (*Mytilus californianus*; see Species of Interest in chapter 6, Monterey, Big Sur, and the Central Coast) can sometimes bring one hundred times more larvae to shore in winter compared with summer. Hence, this region of California vividly illustrates how variability in oceanographic processes can cause substantial shifts in which species are found where, and when.

With a somewhat-denser human population than the Lost Coast to the north, this region remains far more rural than the San Francisco Bay Area to the south. Patterns of coastal settlement could partly reflect geographic and historical factors; the lack of major rivers and large natural harbors between Eureka and San Francisco likely made the area difficult for settlers to access. Ecologically, the lack of major rivers also limits the input of sediment to nearshore areas, exposing the underlying rock that dominates this coastline. Compare, for example, Humboldt Bay's expansive mudflats and protective sandbars versus the almost continuous rocky shore between the Lost Coast and Bodega Bay. The differences between sand and mud, rock and cobble determine the species that occupy these habitats.

## PLACES TO EXPLORE

### Fort Bragg and Mendocino

Fort Bragg is the largest town on the Pacific coast between Eureka and San Francisco, a remnant outpost of the regional timber industry that peaked in the early twentieth century. Intense summer upwelling along this part of the coast, together with the fog it creates, has a cooling effect on the area: Fort Bragg's average daily temperature in August is about 55 degrees Fahrenheit, similar to that of Juneau, Alaska. Fog and cool summer temperatures moderate conditions for intertidal life here, easing the dangers of desiccation and heat stress.

Toward the northern end of Fort Bragg itself lies Glass Beach, which for many years has been a destination of some local renown. Sea glass is scattered among the cobble in the surf zone and in decades past was even a dominant component of the beach in some places, a relic of the beach having served as the town's dump until the middle of the twentieth century. Fort Bragg isn't the only town to have a glass beach of this kind—there's one on the Hawaiian island of Kauai, for example, and Murano, Italy, can brag of handblown glass pieces on the shore—but it is the best known along the West Coast.

Ten miles south of Fort Bragg is Mendocino, hemmed in between forest and sea, perched on the cliffs that dominate much of California's coastline. These remarkably uniform cliffs are eroded into uplifted Pleistocene marine terraces (see "Wave-Cut Terraces" above), interrupted by a headland here or a stretch of beach there. Surrounding the town of

Mendocino at Jug Handle State Natural Reserve, Russian Gulch State Park, and Van Damme State Park, miniature forests of distinctive Bishop pines (*Pinus muricata*) and Mendocino cypress (*Cupressus pigmaea*) grace the tops of these terraces, their growth stunted by nutrient-poor, acidic soils above shallow hardpan. Elsewhere in California, forests growing in serpentine soils (eroded out of the state's official rock, serpentinite) have similarly elfin forms.

Serious and sustained waves pound the bluffs in Mendocino, gradually chipping away at the picturesque town's foundation. The heartiest of the region's invertebrates brave the conditions at Mendocino Headlands State Park, a notable shift from the richer fauna found at nearby coves such as Russian Gulch. In part, the mixture of shifting sandy beach and loose cobble means there is a lot of disturbance in the park's intertidal habitats. But another likely reason for the difference in species composition is significant freshwater input from the imaginatively named Big River, excluding marine species that find low salinities inhospitable. As nearly everywhere along the coast, the California mussel (*Mytilus californianus*; see Species of Interest in chapter 6, Monterey, Big Sur, and the Central Coast) is abundant in the upper intertidal, cheek by jowl with barnacles (*Balanus glandula*, *Chthamalus dalli*, and *Semibalanus cariosus*) and limpets (several species of *Lottia*). In summertime, bull kelp (*Nereocystis luetkeana*; see Species of Interest in chapter 3, Far Northern California) grows just offshore, helping to subsidize the intertidal community by creating habitat and supplying organic carbon—that is, food—to nearshore communities.

The sedimentary sandstone bluffs of the Mendocino Headlands have worn away over the past 100,000 years, leaving impressive caves and sea stacks as evidence of ongoing erosion. The sea stacks just offshore are stranded bits of coastline, remnant markers of the land's past extent (see "Sea Stacks" in chapter 1, The Tumultuous Earth). The storm-cast logs that line the beach most of the year underscore the incredible power of ocean swells along this part of the coast. These former trees may have fallen years ago and many miles away, washed out to sea to parts unknown, only to be beached here temporarily before moving farther down the coast.

The Mendocino Headlands, carved from a jumble of metamorphic and sedimentary rock, form rugged boundaries between land and sea.

Many accessible sites with good rocky intertidal habitat lie within a short distance of Fort Bragg and Mendocino. Cold, clear pools burst with colorful pinks, reds, browns, and greens, the rainbow of seaweeds that are to intertidal life as forests are to the surrounding hills. Sculpins (family Cottidae) hide in plain sight among seaweed-speckled stones, camouflaged in banded or mottled patterns of color, stock-still for long moments but disappearing in a flash when disturbed.

North of Fort Bragg, MacKerricher State Marine Conservation Area sprawls across rocky outcroppings and sandy beaches; the heterogeneous intertidal boulder fields near the park's southern end offers MacKerricher's most biologically diverse habitat. South of Fort Bragg, Caspar Beach—with significant freshwater and sediment input—contrasts neatly with nearby Point Cabrillo, a wave-dominated rocky headland more characteristic of the region. The marine flora and fauna of the rugged, exposed coast is unlikely to be found in the more protected, almost estuarine waters of Caspar.

The seaweed known as Turkish towel (*Chondracanthus exasperatus*) takes on a dark, bumpy appearance quite unlike many of its slippery red algal relatives.

Among the conspicuous seaweeds here—and indeed along this entire stretch of coastline—is the red seaweed known as Turkish towel (*Chondracanthus exasperatus*). Covered in small spines, or papillae, the blade has been likened to a terry-cloth towel, though in a somewhat more rubbery form. The papillae harbor tiny reproductive structures once the blade becomes fertile. *Chondracanthus* and its relatives produce carrageenans, natural gels that are used widely in foods and beauty products, and even reportedly as a thickener in firefighting foam. Deep red in color when alive, this seaweed turns an improbable shade of pink when washed up on shore. Once washed up, the blades decompose relatively quickly, becoming food for detritivores such as beach hoppers.

## Point Arena and the Sonoma Coast

Farther south lies Point Arena, prominent on any map of the California shoreline, and relatively isolated by the lack of direct highway access to

Feather boa kelp (*Egregia menziesii*) drapes across low intertidal boulders covered by seaweeds at Point Arena.

the state's interior. The San Andreas Fault departs the coast for good at Alder Creek just north of Point Arena, heading for the triple junction off Cape Mendocino. Geologically, the shore north of the point belongs to the North American tectonic plate, while to the south, the shore lies on the Pacific plate.

Here the modest Garcia River flows into the Pacific, the Point Arena Lighthouse towering over the landscape. The lighthouse stands on a terrace composed of marine deposits underlain by folded sedimentary rocks from the Miocene. The cliff face and rocks below the lighthouse show evidence of tight folding, deformation, and erosion, visible especially at low tide. In the early 1970s, a proposal to build a nuclear power plant at Point Arena surfaced. The power plant, which would have been sited within a few miles of the San Andreas Fault, never materialized; Bodega Head, farther south in Sonoma County, had a similar brush with the nuclear-power industry.

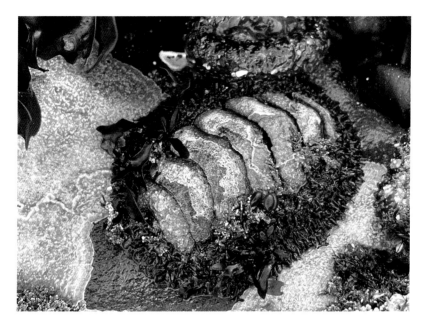

The mossy chiton (*Mopalia muscosa*) grazes an exposed patch of pinkish coralline algae. Patches of the same alga grow on the chiton's calcified plates while small fleshy algae grow at the edges of the chiton's bristly girdle.

The sands of Manchester State Park stretch north of the lighthouse; to the south sit the Stornetta Public Lands, a gateway to the much larger California Coastal National Monument. The monument stretches the entirety of the state's coastline, by presidential proclamation protecting all of the rocky outcrops and islets along the nearly 1,100 miles between Oregon and Mexico.

Public trails lead to tidepools occupied by species similar to those elsewhere along the Mendocino coast. Purple sea urchins (*Strongylocentrotus purpuratus*) burrow into the rocky pavement, chitons wait for nightfall to wander in search of food, and sea palms (*Postelsia palmaeformis*; see Species of Interest) flex and bow under the force of dumping waves. The red seaweed known as salt sacs (*Halosaccion glandiforme*) lends golden hues to the intertidal landscape. Alongside a profusion of gulls and sea ducks, Point Arena attracts a mix of shorebirds and seabirds, including

Golden sacs of *Halosaccion glandiforme* grow amid other species of red algae and partially conceal a sea star. The fluid-filled sacs harbor small zooplankton ranging from worms and crustaceans to the larval forms of bigger species, offering refuge when the tide is out.

plovers, godwits, and sanderlings, as well as common murres, auklets, and shearwaters visible from shore. Nearby sand dunes offer good examples of coastal habitat that is now rare in California.

A few miles south of Point Arena at the north end of Schooner Gulch State Beach lies Bowling Ball Beach, locally renowned for its odd geological formations. Stony orbs, each measuring two to three feet in diameter, are strewn across the beach flat, seemingly the leavings of a giant's bowling tournament. In reality, the formations are concretions, hard bits that form within a sedimentary matrix, bound together with mineral cement. The mineral cement can make the concretion harder than the surrounding sedimentary rock, with the result that, over long periods of time, the surrounding rock wears away and the concretion is left behind. At Bowling Ball Beach, the concretions were formed within and subsequently eroded out of steeply sloping Cenozoic mudstone that can be found nearby.

Spherical rocks, or concretions, are exposed at low tide along Bowling Ball Beach.

The Russian River at Jenner is only intermittently connected to the sea. In fall, a sand-bar (center) closes the mouth of the river entirely, creating a seasonal lagoon (bottom) that becomes home to a diverse suite of species, some of them specialized to make use of this ephemeral habitat. In winter the berm is breached when waves are large and river flows are high, connecting the ocean and river once again (as seen here).

The Russian River, which enters the ocean farther south at Jenner, is largely undammed, allowing much of the river's natural sediment load to reach the coast and feed the beaches of Sonoma County. The river mouth closes seasonally, most often in fall, due to interactions between the river's low flow and ocean wave height, creating a bar-built estuary. Like other such estuaries in California, the seasonal accumulation of sand creates a temporary berm that isolates the river from the ocean, trapping brackish water behind the berm to form a seasonal estuary. In winter, high river flows and large ocean waves breach the berm, allowing the river to again reach the sea, temporarily eliminating this estuarine habitat. While they exist, seasonal estuaries are home to species that have specialized in this narrow ecological niche, such as the endangered northern tidewater goby (*Eucyclogobius newberryi*, a small fish), and also juvenile steelhead (*Oncorhynchus mykiss*) and endangered birds such as the least tern (*Sternula antillarum*) and the snowy plover (*Charadrius nivosus*). At Jenner, in particular, harbor seals (*Phoca vitulina*) use the seasonal sandbar as a rookery, with dozens hauled out on the sand at any given time.

A mudflat-dwelling sea slug endemic to California (*Alderia willowi*) seasonally switches between producing nondispersive offspring in the dry season, when estuaries are closed and swimming larvae have nowhere to go, versus dispersive offspring in the rainy season, when estuaries open and larvae are transported by coastal currents to colonize neighboring bays. This seasonal cycling is distinctively Californian and a feature of the physical environment to which many native species are adapted.

Just south of Jenner is a notable curiosity that vividly bridges millennia. A set of prominent rocks sits on the wave-cut terrace above the sea. These are sections of uplifted marine terrace preserved as sea stacks. At various places the rocks have a distinctive polish to them, extending from about twelve feet high to below the surface of the ground. Available evidence suggests that Columbian mammoths rubbed themselves on these rocks during the last ice age, polishing them to a shine that lasts even today. The species went extinct 10,000 years ago but appears to have left an indelible mark.

## Bodega Bay, Tomales Bay, and the Point Reyes Peninsula

Bodega Bay and Tomales Bay are two of those rare places on earth where tectonic fault lines so obviously sculpt coastal habitats that even a cursory look reveals their dynamic origins. The path of the San Andreas Fault continues south to Bolinas Lagoon and beyond, making the whole region look as if it's been drafted in sand and clay with a handheld stylus. And despite being quite near the urban centers of the San Francisco Bay Area, much of the coast here retains the out-of-the-way feel of places much farther afield.

Bodega Bay and Tomales Bay sit astride the San Andreas Fault, with the North American plate to the east and the Pacific plate to the west. The fault created these embayments—or, rather, the embayments occupy low-lying areas along the fault line. The Great San Francisco Earthquake of 1906 caused some places on the western plate to move more than twenty feet northward relative to the eastern plate, and evidence of such

Patches of olive-green rockweed grow amid a broad swath of red seaweeds at Duxbury Reef. Color patterns in the intertidal can offer clues to the small-scale habitat preferences of seaweeds and invertebrates.

dynamic movement remains visible today. A short distance to the south, Bolinas Lagoon similarly occupies the San Andreas Rift Valley, crossed by two parallel faults, the San Andreas and San Gregorio, which merge to form the San Andreas Fault Zone.

## EARTHQUAKES

A strangely common misconception is that the next big earthquake will send California tumbling into the sea. This simply isn't how California's earthquakes work. Rather than tearing off bits of land, the earthquakes here and elsewhere around the Pacific are merely side effects of tectonic plates moving and hitting one another in different ways. Most of the western part of the state sits near faults that are in the process of sliding past one another, rather than moving apart . . . and hence, California will not be parting ways with the rest of North America.

The earth's molten core powers the tectonic motion itself, sending the plates—that is, the individual elements making

Over many thousands of years, the Point Reyes Peninsula has moved northward along the San Andreas Fault.

up the hardened shell of rock covering the earth's surface—on slow-motion collision courses with one another. Because this process is ongoing, it is certain that California will continue to experience catastrophic earthquakes, although no one can accurately predict just when the Big One will strike.

California's San Andreas Fault is perhaps the most famous fault line in the world, thanks to the 1906 earthquake and subsequent fire that destroyed much of San Francisco and rearranged parts of the nearby landscape. But many other faults and subfaults constantly generate small-bore earthquakes. Processes like this are responsible for the state's iconic and dramatic landscapes, which can come at a high cost for humans and the built environment.

At the northern end of this geologic province, Bodega Head is a solid mass of continental granite that shares origins with rock in the Sierra Nevada mountains. It is tethered to the mainland by a substantial arm of sand forming the northern shore of Bodega Bay. A much slimmer sand spit, Doran Beach, nearly closes off the bay entirely on its southern side, forming a quiet harbor, much of which drains twice daily with the tides to reveal acres of soft-sediment intertidal habitat. Worms and clams of all kinds abound here within the soft substrate of Bodega Bay's intertidal sediments, giant moon snails (*Polinices lewisii*) regally gliding by on the muddy surface. Within the mud, ghost shrimp (*Neotrypaea [Calianassa] californiensis*) and blue mud shrimp (*Upogebia pugettensis*) dig burrows that host small crabs, fish, shrimp, and other animals; the fat innkeeper worm (*Urechis caupo*) similarly hosts multiple species in its U-shaped burrow.

To the south, the Point Reyes Peninsula forms a massive, hook-like feature that for centuries was a landmark for West Coast mariners. Over geologic time, this wayward finger of granite has been transported north from Southern California along the San Andreas Fault. The peninsula now rests on an elevated chunk of ancient rock that was once part of the Tehachapi Mountains, the east-west-trending range perhaps best known to motorists on Interstate 5 as the "Grapevine." East of this block, filling the fault-line rift, is the long inlet of Tomales Bay, which is about twelve miles long and averages less than ten feet deep throughout. Whereas most California estuaries are associated with river mouths, Tomales Bay was formed tectonically by slippage between the Pacific and North American plates; the San Andreas Fault runs down the middle of the bay.

Herring, salmon, harbor seals, and sharks all share Tomales Bay with invertebrates and vegetation typical of shallow soft-sediment habitats. The bay supports an important fraction of California's remaining coho salmon (*Oncorhynchus kisutsch*) and is spawning habitat for Pacific herring (*Clupea pallasii*). Dunlin (*Calidris alpina*) and western sandpiper (*Calidris mauri*) abound, along with other shorebirds and waterbirds such as black brant (*Branta bernicla nigricans*; see Species of Interest in chapter 3, Far Northern California), bufflehead (*Bucephala albeola*), black rails (*Laterallus jamaicensis*), and clapper rails (*Rallus crepitans*).

The south-facing shore of the Point Reyes Peninsula opens to Drake's Estero, a shallow estuary with multiple fingers, or bays. The estuary drains

Drake's Estero on the Point Reyes Peninsula is fed by ocean upwelling in summer when freshwater flows from the land are minimal.

# INVASIVE SPECIES

Invasive species have found a home in Tomales Bay to an extent that is notable along the West Coast. While the much larger San Francisco Bay has accumulated a greater number of invasive species over the past couple of centuries, Tomales Bay is dominated by an international array of nonnative species. The Japanese mudsnail (*Batillaria attramentaria*) reaches very high densities in the bay's calm, muddy reaches, outcompeting the native California horn snail (*Cerithideopsis [Cerithidia] californica*). The European green crab (*Carcinus maenas*), considered one of the world's hundred worst alien invasive species, has taken up residence—a fierce predator that devours clams, oysters, worms, and crustaceans, including other crabs. An ambitious project to remove every green crab from nearby Bolinas Lagoon failed because green crabs eat the developing juveniles of their own species; paradoxically, removing adult green crabs led to a population explosion as uneaten baby green crabs grew up, highlighting the challenge of controlling invasive species while adding a new twist to the phrase "less is more."

Nonnative bivalves also abound in the shallow waters of Tomales Bay, altering benthic communities and removing phytoplankton from the base of the food web. Flourishing invasives include the purple varnish clam (*Nuttallia obscurata*) native to Japan, Korea, and China; the Pacific oyster (*Crassostrea gigas*) from Japan; and the Asian date mussel (*Arcuatula senhousia*), independently introduced to Northern and Southern California from different source populations. And a quite different animal— the small brown sea anemone (*Anthopleura hermaphroditica*) native to Chile and New Zealand—is reportedly spreading in the bay; as its name implies, this species can reproduce on its own, without the help of a mate. Above the water line, invasive ice plant (*Carpobrotus edulis*) from South Africa grows vigorously, and European beach grass (*Ammophila arenaria*) crowns nearby dunes.

The low-lying shale of Duxbury Reef, framed by steep bluffs, creates expansive and varied intertidal habitat.

the surrounding watershed in winter; in summer, ocean upwelling fuels the estuarine food web. Protected from exposure to waves and generally warmer than the ocean waters nearby, the estuary supports eelgrass meadows (see Species of Interest in chapter 3, Far Northern California) and nursery habitat for a broad array of saltwater species and hosts a wealth of birds and mammals. Throughout the Point Reyes National Seashore and the Phillip Burton Wilderness Area, upland trails weave beneath leggy Bishop pines (*Pinus muricata*) slowly climbing skyward, with vultures circling aloft, alert amid the high whistle-whine of elk, the squeak of quail, and the sweet scent of sticky monkeyflowers (*Diplacus auranticus*).

At the southern tip of the Point Reyes Peninsula lies Duxbury Reef State Marine Conservation Area. Named for the ship that foundered here in 1849, this is the largest shale reef in North America, created by erosion of the adjacent mudstone cliffs. Parallel ridges and tidal channels offer clues to the character of the underlying substrate, where ridges are more resistant to erosion than nearby channels, and rocky areas abut those with sand. The habitat complexity here favors a diverse assemblage of seaweed and invertebrate species, consistent with the protected designation of this site.

## SPECIES OF INTEREST

### Dense-Clumped Kelp

Dense-clumped kelp (*Laminaria sinclairii*) is unusual among kelp species on the California coast. Different from the more familiar giant kelp (*Macrocystis pyrifera*) and bull kelp (*Nereocystis luetkeana*; see Species of Interest in chapter 3, Far Northern California), dense-clumped kelp grows in intertidal habitats that are seasonally inundated by sand. Unlike most other kelps that produce a single stipe from each holdfast, this

Strap-like blades of dense-clumped kelp (*Laminaria sinclairii*) emerge from sand that has temporarily buried both stipes and holdfasts. The fringe of blades traces the broad arc of the underlying rock to which the holdfasts are attached.

species produces many narrow, cylindrical stipes from a creeping rhizome that can spread to cover a large area. Each stipe produces a single blade that grows rapidly in the spring and dies back each winter. The basal parts of the kelp are buried as sand accumulates throughout the spring and summer. Storms in autumn and winter remove the sand, once again exposing the stipes and holdfasts. Although this kelp is capable of sexual reproduction, most reproduction appears to be via vegetative spread of the rhizomes.

## Sea Palm

The sea palm (*Postelsia palmaeformis*) is an odd kelp. Living only in the intertidal—never in the subtidal—and only in the very most exposed rocky areas, this seaweed looks more like a small palm tree than like many of its kelp cousins. Anchored by a stout holdfast, the hollow flexible

Found only in the most exposed rocky habitats, sea palms (*Postelsia palmaeformis*) tend to grow in clusters that help them tolerate intense wave forces. They grow quickly and live about one year—here, their golden-green hues mingle among red seaweeds.

Sea palms use short, stout holdfasts to attach to rocky substrates. Their hollow, flexible stipes are adaptations critical for survival in their wave-swept habitat.

stipe is topped by a tangle of blades that, at low tide, hang down like the strands of a mop head. As waves roll in, the stipe flexes, shedding the force of the wave. As the wave passes, the stipe pops upright again, just in time to bow down again for the next wave.

Sea palms typically grow in close association with California mussels (*Mytilus californianus*; see Species of Interest in chapter 6, Monterey, Big Sur, and the Central Coast), constantly competing for space. Mussels tend to grab and hold space in wave-swept areas but occasionally are removed by big waves or logs or some other physical disturbance. When that happens, sea palms can quickly claim the newly opened space, probably because their microscopic forms are waiting on the rocky substrate beneath the mussel bed, ready to germinate when the time is right. Mussels have a hard time encroaching on the sea palms until winter storms remove them—in fact, most sea palms live only one year or less. Once mussels move in, the cycle begins again.

## Rockweed

Rockweed (*Fucus distichus*) is a common brown seaweed found in mid-intertidal areas from the central California coast northward to Alaska. The species is distinguishable by its forked (dichotomous) branches that are flat when young and become inflated with age. Air bladders at the tips of the fronds help the branches to remain upright in the water column when the tide is up, maximizing their exposure to sunlight. Reproductive structures develop on the inflated bladders, appearing as small raised bumps that release eggs and sperm when the time is right.

Often associated with lower-energy environments, rockweed also inhabits some wave-swept shores. It tolerates a wide array of conditions, being equally happy in brackish water and full salt water, and it can survive desiccation during hot low tides and freezing temperatures during cold low tides. Like some other red and brown seaweeds, rockweed produces chemical compounds that deter many—but by no means all—grazers. Where it is abundant, rockweed creates a low-growing canopy that provides valuable cover at low tide to many invertebrate species, helping them avoid desiccation when the tide is out.

Rockweed (*Fucus distichus*) branches become inflated when reproductive, giving rise to the onomatopoeic name "pop-weed" when stepped on.

## Black Katy Chiton

Black katy chitons (*Katharina tunicata*), also known as leather chitons, inhabit exposed rocky intertidal and subtidal habitats from Alaska to Southern California; in the warmer, more southern parts of its range, this species tends to live lower in the intertidal zone, remaining immersed most of the time. Katy chitons, shaped like small leathery footballs, are dark in color with diamond-shaped cream-colored patches of visible shell. They make a living like most other chitons, using mineralized teeth to scrape algae off rocks. They are often associated with pink coralline algae (see Species of Interest in chapter 5, San Francisco to Santa Cruz), a colorful contrast to the chiton's dark form, and can grow to be up to about five inches in length. Katy chitons are eaten by sea urchins, leather stars, black oystercatchers (see below), and gulls. They have historically been an important food source for Indigenous peoples and are still consumed either raw or cooked as part of some traditional diets, especially in British Columbia and Alaska.

Black katy chitons (*Katharina tunicata*) have a dark, leathery girdle on their upper (dorsal) side that is interrupted by eight calcareous plates. Their muscular foot holds them in place on exposed shores.

A shield limpet (*Lottia pelta*; center) waits for the incoming tide, surrounded by red coralline algae (pinkish colors; left), the tar spot alga (Petrocelis; blackish crust at center), and fleshy algae (red and golden hues at right), which they are known to eat.

## Shield Limpet

The shield limpet (*Lottia pelta*) is one of many species of limpets—flat snails, essentially—that occupy rocky intertidal habitats from Alaska to Baja California and are very common along the California coast. Many species of limpets are highly variable in color and pattern, making species difficult to distinguish; shell profile and habitat are more reliable diagnostics. Shield limpets live in a variety of microhabitats, including on rock faces, among mussels, on the fleshy tissues of kelps, or beneath a cover of rockweed. On each of these substrates, shield limpets will develop a distinctive shape and color, with color largely depending on diet—different pigments and minerals are available depending upon whether the limpet is living on a rock or on various algal species, for example. Over their life spans, individuals can move between alternate substrates, and when they do, their shells can slowly change to reflect the change in habitat and diet. During this transition period, individuals appear to be more vulnerable to predation by black oystercatchers (*Haematopus bachmani*; see below), presumably because the mismatch in coloration allows these visual predators to more easily detect their prey.

## Abalone

The role of abalone (*Haliotis* spp.) in the human history of California is far larger than one might expect of a giant snail. Indigenous peoples have long valued abalone for food and cultural purposes. Spanish settlers used abalone shells in trade. Early in the twentieth century, abalone helped sustain Asian immigrants; later, during World War II, abalone were canned as food for soldiers. Throughout coastal California, the appeal

A red abalone (*Haliotis rufescens*) dwells in a tidepool among algal crusts both calcified (pinkish colors) and noncalcified (reddish colors). Crustose algae such as these induce the settlement of larval abalone, helping to ensure that the larvae end up in habitats that support the growth of adults. The animal's epipodial sensory tentacles visibly protrude from the shell's edge.

of abalone meat—their large, muscular foot is the main culinary attraction—grew steadily and the snails' populations declined accordingly, so that some species now exist only at very low numbers. The towering piles of discarded shells that at one time dotted the coast were an indication of the large number of animals harvested.

Worldwide, there are more than fifty species of abalone, all in the genus *Haliotis*. Seven of these are known from California: black (*H. cracherodii*), south of Mendocino county; green (*H. fulgens*), Southern California and Baja California; flat (*H. walallensis*), uncommon, central Oregon to central California; pink (*H. corrugata*), Southern California and Baja California; pinto (*H. kamtschatkana*), Alaska to central California; red (*H. rufescens*), central Oregon to Baja California; and white (*H. sorenseni*), endangered, Southern California to Baja California. Like other gastropod molluscs, abalone cling to rocky substrates using a muscular foot. They feed on living and drift seaweeds using their radula as a rasping tool. Holes along the margin of the shell let water pass through, ventilating the animal even while it remains firmly attached to the rock; this flowing water is crucial for respiration and reproduction. Eggs and sperm are shed through the holes in the shell into the water column where fertilization occurs, ultimately producing planktonic larvae that feed themselves from a yolk sac that they carry with them. And this is where things get interesting, at least from an ecological perspective: the planktonic larvae depend on chemical cues from algal crusts or associated biofilms to induce settlement. One can imagine these chemical signposts guiding larvae like a neon sign to settle in locations that are favorable for their growth and survival.

From the pearly nacre that lines their shells to the flavorful foot muscle that makes abalone a favorite of humans, octopuses, and otters, these large flattened snails are emblematic of California's rugged appeal. Notably, red abalone are the biggest abalone in the world. Five species of abalone—red, black, white, pink, and green—have been the focus of recreational and commercial fisheries in California for 150 years. Once so abundant that the fisheries limit was 1,140 animals per person per day, abalone have since declined precipitously due to overharvesting, disease, introduced parasites, rising ocean temperatures, and loss of kelp cover.

Even so, abalone persist along the California coast and are the subject of efforts to rebuild their populations.

## Unicorn Snail

Unicorn snails (*Acanthinucella* spp.) sport distinctive shells that bear a small spine, or tooth, on the edge of the shell's opening, or aperture. The spine is presumably the source of the common name *unicorn*, and undoubtedly the origin of the genus prefix *Acanth*, which comes from the Greek for "point" or "thorn." Two species (*Acanthinucella spirata* and *A. punctulata*) have been reported from Duxbury Reef. Referred to as the angular unicorn and spotted unicorn, respectively, both are dedicated predators, feeding mainly on barnacles or other snails. Like their kin, these snails can use their mouthparts to drill into the shells of their prey to access the edible bits inside. But these two species have a second mode of predation: using the spine on their underside, they can jab, pry, and fracture the plates of barnacles to gain entry. This second means of predation produces a meal in less time than it takes to drill a hole, meaning that the snails can consume more prey over the course of a tidal cycle.

The angular unicorn (*A. spirata*) was long considered to reach its northern range limit in Tomales Bay. Recently, though, a population of this species was reported more than 250 miles north, at Cape Mendocino, an impressive jump for a species that lacks planktonic larvae. And even the populations around Tomales Bay are relatively recent in a geological context: the species has been steadily working its way northward along the California coast since the Pleistocene; as it has moved north, the species has rapidly evolved a new shell shape relative to its southern ancestors.

## Hilton's Nudibranch

Because of their bright colors and relative rarity, nudibranchs and other sea slugs attract special aficionados (called branchers, pronounced "brankers") who hunt in tidepools the way bird-watchers search for elusive species to complete their life list. Such devotion is scientifically useful, providing data on the geographic ranges of many species going

The angular unicorn snail (*Acanthinucella spirata*; center) lies high and dry in the intertidal. Small black periwinkles (*Littorina scutulata*; upper left) are among its preferred prey.

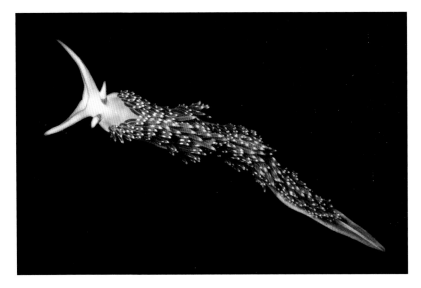

Hilton's nudibranch (*Phidiana hiltoni*) shifted its range northward from Monterey to Duxbury Reef, leading to sharp declines in the abundance of other sea slugs where *Phidiana* is newly present. Photo by Angel Valdes.

back more than fifty years. Such data allow scientists to assess how species have shifted their distributions in response to climate change—and, in turn, how ecological communities are altered by changing arrangements of species.

Aeolid nudibranchs like Hilton's nudibranch (*Phidiana hiltoni*) bear feathery projections, called cerata, on their backs that ripple in moving seawater like grass rustling in a breeze; the group is named for the wind god Aeolus, son of Poseidon. Most aeolids eat cnidarians (anemones, jellyfish, and corals) and store their stinging cells for defense; cerata deliver a painful zap to the mouth of a would-be predator (or a human hand, in the case of some tropical species). *Phidiana hiltoni* eats both hydroids and other nudibranchs. Historically found south of Monterey, *Phidiana*'s population shifted sixty miles northward over fifteen years, to north of San Francisco Bay, leading to sharp declines in the abundance of its prey species in the new habitat. This is merely one small example among many in which a change in the abundance of one species can have cascading effects on a community. Similar range shifts in snails, barnacles, and other species since the 1970s have resulted in subtle but substantial changes to intertidal communities elsewhere in California.

## Lined Shore Crab

Small and quick, lined shore crabs (*Pachygrapsus crassipes*) dart from place to place in the intertidal; turn over any rock, and you're likely to see these crustaceans scatter. Found high in the intertidal in crevices and among boulders, lined shore crabs are well adapted to life in air, equipped with reduced gills that leave them better able to breathe out of the water than in it; they can live several days out of the water, though occasionally they will take short dips to rewet their gills. These diminutive crabs are the scavengers of the shore, feeding on algal films, bits of sea lettuce (*Ulva* spp.; see Species of Interest in chapter 6, Monterey, Big Sur, and the Central Coast), and other algae and generally happy to take meals wherever they might be found, often using their claws to tear their food into tiny pieces before consuming it. In turn, the crabs are eaten by gulls, fish, and even raccoons.

Lined shore crabs (*Pachygrapsus crassipes*) are common throughout California. Their color can vary from green to red to black, all with bright thin lines running side to side across the carapace.

## Red Sea Urchin

The red sea urchin (*Mesocentrotus franciscanus*) is common in low-intertidal and subtidal habitats from Alaska to Baja California. Red urchins are larger than purple urchins and typically—although not always—a deep red color. They grow throughout their long life spans, slowly increasing in size for decades; some individuals may live more than 200 years, as confirmed by radiocarbon analysis of their calcium carbonate jaws.

Red urchins feed mostly on kelp, using specialized mouthparts on their undersides to scrape algae from rocks, while sometimes snagging drift algae carried past on currents by using their long spines like chopsticks, as well as their suction-tipped tube feet. Red urchins reproduce by releasing eggs and sperm into the water column where the eggs are fertilized. The planktonic larvae, once settled, grow into juveniles that sometimes find shelter beneath the spines of the adults.

The red sea urchin (*Mesocentrotus franciscanus*; center left) sits amid a crowd of purple sea urchins (*Strongylocentrotus purpuratus*). Occurring from Alaska to Baja California, red sea urchins can grow to be quite large in subtidal habitats.

Sea otters are the principal predator of red sea urchins, which are also preyed on by crabs, sea stars, and fish. In subtidal areas where red urchins become abundant in the absence of their predators, they can form dense feeding aggregations, or fronts, that quickly decimate kelp beds and cause changes in nearshore community composition.

## Ochre Sea Star

The ochre sea star (*Pisaster ochraceus*) is perhaps the most recognizable star on California's coast. Often colored bright orange, individuals also can be colored purple, red, or brown. Like other echinoderms, ochre stars exhibit radial symmetry, meaning their body plan is organized around a central disc, far different from the left-right symmetry of humans and most other animals. The ochre star doesn't have a brain per se—instead, a nerve ring connects radial nerves to relay impulses across the body. Even

Ochre sea stars (*Pisaster ochraceus*) of several colors aggregate at low tide between a row of giant green anemones (*Anthopleura xanthogrammica*; bottom) and dark patches of red algae (top).

so, these sea stars exhibit complex behaviors that make them one of the most formidable predators on the shore. Both the circulatory and muscular systems are hydraulic, powered by seawater. Thousands of sucking tube feet on the underside utilize the same hydraulic mechanism, allowing the animal to cling to rocks even when exposed to sustained wave action. Specialized connective tissue allows them to be stiff one moment and somewhat floppy the next. Tiny pincers cover their bodies, grabbing and removing particles or would-be parasites. Their stomachs digest food outside of the body instead of inside it. And like other sea stars, ochre stars have good regenerative abilities and can regrow arms once lost.

Ochre stars can have outsize ecological effects on intertidal communities. Their preferred prey is the California mussel (*Mytilus californianus*; see Species of Interest in chapter 6, Monterey, Big Sur, and the Central Coast), and the two species are often found in close association. In the

Sea stars use hydraulic-powered tube feet to cling to rocks and grip prey. The tube feet are strong enough to withstand pounding waves and to pry apart bivalves such as California mussels (*Mytilus californianus*).

absence of ochre stars, ecological theory suggests that mussel beds will expand as mussels outcompete anemones and other soft-bodied animals for space, reducing diversity among large-bodied organisms. At the same time, the tiny interstices formed between adjacent mussel shells offer shelter for small organisms. Hence, in the absence of ochre stars, an expanding mussel bed adds habitat for hundreds of species unable to persist on bare rock, representing a gain in diversity. The loss of a predatory species like the ochre star can thus have varying effects on an intertidal community, resulting in a loss or gain of species diversity, depending on the scale of analysis—one challenge among many for studying this dynamic ecosystem.

## Black Oystercatcher

Black oystercatchers (*Haematopus bachmani*) are unmistakable: with their bright-red bills, yellow eyes, and pink legs set against dark plumage, these birds look a bit clownish. Their loud, ringing whistles only add to their charm. Distributed from Alaska to Baja California, black oystercatchers frequent rocky shorelines where they feed on mussels, limpets, and chitons (though, curiously, not oysters), using their stout bills to strike or pry their prey from the substrate. Often seen in pairs, black oystercatchers are territorial during the breeding season, vigorously defending their foraging and nesting areas from interlopers and would-be predators. The birds are sensitive to disturbance by humans and marine mammals alike, and both can reduce the reproductive success of oystercatchers in California.

A black oystercatcher (*Haematopus bachmani*) hunts for molluscs in the low intertidal. The genus name—*Haematopus*—comes from the Greek word for "blood-footed," a reference to the bird's pink feet.

California mussels (*Mytilus californianus*) carpet Scott Creek Beach north of Santa Cruz.

# SAN FRANCISCO TO SANTA CRUZ

The coast between San Francisco and Santa Cruz feels like a secret hidden in a fog bank. With sleepy beach towns and strawberry farms hard by the breakers, State Highway 1 accompanies the traveler on the way to nowhere in particular.

The spine of the Santa Cruz Mountains divides San Francisco Bay and Silicon Valley from the ocean and its wind and fog, largely containing the Bay Area's human population and protecting the shoreline from urban spillover. This also means that the coast can be 20 degrees Fahrenheit cooler than the Bay-side cities less than a dozen miles away.

The San Andreas Fault runs inland, not quite parallel to the coast. Its furrow delineates the boundary between the North American plate and the Pacific plate, a monumental distinction in terms of the earth's history that is underappreciated by commuters who twice daily make the crossing, no passport required. The fault splinters, creating lines of valleys and ridges, but its main bit slices through the shore in south San Francisco, on its way northward to form Bolinas Lagoon, Tomales Bay, and Bodega Bay. This fault and others mark places where the earth's tectonics have assembled and rearranged California, leaving a mix of rock types and ages to face the waves.

Summer mornings dawn in a blanket of fog; by early afternoon there's not a cloud in the sky. Evenings see the predictable onshore winds returning the moisture that supports coastal redwoods, oaks, and shoreline shrubs, the rhythmic incursion of fog substituting for rain during the summer months. Winter brings nearly all of the region's annual rain, when it comes—typical of the Mediterranean climate for which coastal California is famous.

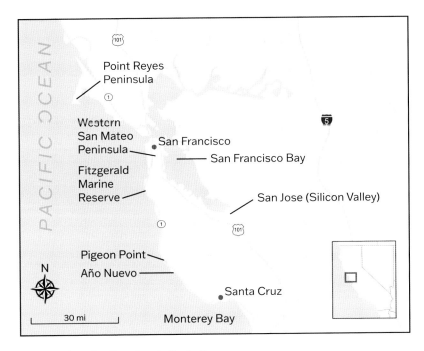

The coast from San Francisco to Santa Cruz.

San Francisco Bay is the largest estuary on the West Coast, a natural harbor connected to the ocean via the Golden Gate's narrow opening. The twin arms of two peninsulas—Marin to the north and the San Mateo Peninsula to the south—envelop more than 1,500 square miles of water. The great rivers of the Central Valley, the Sacramento and San Joaquin, drain water from nearly 40 percent of the state into the shallow bay, battling the tides' saltwater pulse. Occasionally the rivers win this battle, when large rainstorms temporarily lower the salinity of much of the bay.

The San Mateo coast features the largest waves in California, thanks to steep bathymetry that quickly drops away to deep water just offshore, persistent prevailing winds, and a huge stretch of uninterrupted ocean that makes a long runway for these large breakers to develop. Winter storms in the Pacific bring the possibility of forty- to fifty-foot waves, a tantalizing but occasionally fatal prospect for big-wave surfers.

A young male northern elephant seal (*Mirounga angustirostris*) rests onshore. Battles with other males have left visible scars on his neck and chest.

This high-energy pounding erodes seaside bluffs and beaches, making for unstable substrates along the shore—a challenge for highway construction at large scales and for limpets and seaweeds at smaller scales. And just as landslides clear the hillsides on occasion, so too do wave-driven disturbances wipe boulders free of marine life periodically, creating bare patches in which colonizing species gain a toehold.

The coastal waters here are productive, supporting rich food webs that sustain a host of seabirds and marine mammals, most prominent among them the northern elephant seals (*Mirounga angustirostris*) of Año Nuevo. In winter, the seals come ashore to give birth and breed, with the very high metabolic demands of growing pups ultimately met by the upwelling-driven productivity just offshore.

## PLACES TO EXPLORE
### San Francisco Bay

San Francisco Bay is a crossroads, a meeting of fresh- and salt water, surrounded by hills and sheltered from the ocean and its breakers. As a consequence of its protective geography and mild climate, the bay has seen the rise of three major cities—San Francisco, Oakland, and San Jose—and two centuries' worth of modifications and abuses. Astonishingly, even the earliest of these is still with us: the bay is still dealing with the tailings from the hydraulic gold-mining of the nineteenth century, during which miners washed Sierra Nevada hillsides into local tributaries. Wreckage from the 1906 San Francisco earthquake and fire filled in the proximal parts of the bay, creating land for new neighborhoods in the burgeoning city; the 1915 Panama-Pacific International Exposition did the same. The twentieth century saw the bay burdened by airports, artificial islands, salt-evaporation ponds, military installations, and the industrial demands of two world wars, resulting in further habitat loss and contamination of bay water and aquatic life.

And yet San Francisco Bay remains vital estuarine habitat, supporting much of California's remnant wetland acreage and, underwater, a community of estuarine and saltwater species characteristic of low-energy, soft-bottom environments.

The bay is a new feature of the West Coast, geologically speaking. San Francisco Bay is formed by a minor depression in the land between two faults—the San Andreas and the Hayward. It spent the most recent ice age not under a glacier—as did, for example, Washington's Puget Sound—but instead as a grassy, oak-covered valley; the ocean was at the time two dozen miles west of the present coastline, just beyond what are now the Farallon Islands. Only in the past 10,000 years or so did the bay fill with water, as the ice-age glaciers melted and global sea level rose accordingly. This interval is the geological blink of an eye; contemporary Indigenous Californians may well have seen it happen.

The shape of San Francisco Bay protects nearly the entirety of its shores from ocean waves, making it one of the best natural harbors in the world. This same protection means that its coastal habitats experience little

A long-billed curlew (*Numenius americanus*) wades along the shore, intermittently probing the soft sediment for small invertebrate prey.

A European green crab (*Carcinus maenas*; lower left) nestles among filaments of green algae in a shallow bay. First observed on the West Coast in San Francisco Bay in 1989, green crabs are considered to be among the world's most destructive invasive species. Nonnative Japanese mudsnails (*Batillaria attramentaria*; scattered through-out) are also invasive in habitats such as this.

serious wave energy and that sediment is more likely to accumulate than to be swept away, although wind-driven waves erode the leading edges of marshes, contributing further sediment back to the bay. The shallow depths along the estuary's edges create large temperature swings over the course of hours for intertidal creatures, and substantial freshwater input, particularly in the more northern parts of the bay, require species to tolerate a wide range of salinities. The result is a suite of hearty generalist species occupying salt marshes, mudflats, and other low-energy environments that are more similar to Humboldt Bay or Puget Sound than they are to the wave-swept ocean shores just a few miles to the west. There is a lot of mud and fine sand here, and therefore untold numbers of worms, small crustaceans, and other infaunal animals, plus legions of shorebirds—wintering stilts, godwits, willets, curlews, and others—that eat them.

Nonnative species have found these waters particularly welcoming, consistent with a worldwide trend in which shipping ports and other sheltered coastal environments accumulate a disproportionate share of "weedy" species from afar. There are more than a hundred species in San Francisco Bay that hail from elsewhere. These include the European green crab (*Carcinus maenas*), Asian date mussel (*Arcuatula senhousia*), the incredibly abundant Japanese mudsnail (*Batillaria attramentaria*), the smooth cordgrass (*Spartina alterniflora*), and many others that can dominate soft-sediment habitats, alone or in concert.

## Western San Mateo Peninsula

Almost three-quarters of California's shoreline consists of rocky cliffs and coastal bluffs. San Francisco and the Pacific-facing side of the San Mateo Peninsula offer instead a mainly sandy shore, much of it backed by high bluffs. The shoreline heads in an almost straight line for thirteen miles between the Golden Gate and the Montara headland that divides Pacifica from Half Moon Bay. Monterey cypress (*Hesperocyparis [Cupressus] macrocarpa*) reach out of the fog with skeletal branches, flanked in many places by stringy, fragrant eucalyptus.

Although it is not at all obvious, sandy habitats often have subdivisions, zones akin to the more-apparent zonation of the rocky intertidal. In the case of rocky intertidal zonation, a mix of species interactions and physical forces delimit the size and height of, say, the band of mussels running along shore. In the case of a sandy beach, it seems physical factors alone strongly influence what lives where. For example, lower-elevation habitats are saturated with water and host particular species of amphipods and polychaete worms, while relatively drier sand a few feet higher may harbor a completely different suite of small crustaceans, insects, and worms. In fact, sandy beaches even feature commuters, species that move up and down the beach with the tides—the mole, or sand, crab (*Emerita analoga*; see Species of Interest in chapter 8, Long Beach to San Diego) is one of them. Taken together, a square yard of beach can support hundreds of thousands of small animals.

As a general rule, beach slope is dependent upon beach grain size, with finer-grained beaches having lower slopes than coarse-grained beaches. Beaches of fine sand and shallow slope tend to support a greater diversity of species than their steeper, coarse-grained counterparts, for a few reasons. First, it seems that wave energy on the sand increases primary productivity via the growth of diatoms. More diatoms, in turn, support more diverse and larger food webs. Second, flatter beaches have much longer backwash periods—the time period, after a wave breaks, during which the water flows back into the sea. Longer backwash periods give suspension feeders a chance to eat in that thin layer of flowing water and also give waterborne individuals a chance to move around. A coarser, steeper beach will not support all of the small crustaceans and worms and others that require these conditions.

Moss Beach features Fitzgerald Marine Reserve, a habitat of rocky benches within one of the state's network of marine protected areas (MPAs). California has protected the site since 1969, long before establishing the larger network of MPAs in 2012. Fitzgerald Marine Reserve offers one of the more accessible habitats for visitors in the area, and as the price of waterfront homes has continued to skyrocket over decades, the state has fought to maintain public access to the shore, resulting in more than one US Supreme Court case.

# MARINE PROTECTED AREAS

California's coastline is at the heart of the state's identity: the ocean's beauty and productivity fuel the imagination and soothe the soul, all the while supporting a robust tourist and maritime economy. Various human pressures on marine systems have come and gone over the years—from the sea otter fur trade and whaling to intensive abalone harvesting, industrial-scale fishing, and oil spills—transforming marine ecosystems along the way.

The state legislature passed the Marine Life Protection Act in 1999 to protect, sustain, and rebuild marine life and marine ecosystems by establishing a network of marine protected areas (MPAs) spanning the entire length of the California coast. Following the formation of a public-private partnership, a lengthy consultation period, and considerable planning, sites were selected to meet the objectives of the legislative act. In all, more than 850 square miles of coast and ocean were protected at some level—including some no-take marine reserves—across 124 individual sites, making up just over 15 percent of state waters.

The benefits of MPAs include safeguarding habitat for the state's iconic marine species, providing educational and recreational opportunities, and marking scientific reference points against which to compare ecosystem changes elsewhere. More generally, the MPAs are intended to protect California's natural heritage, acting as a buffer against localized ecological change.

The point of creating a network of MPAs—rather than individualized, one-off designations akin to most city parks—is the emergent benefits of strategically located and linked sites; the idea is that the network is more than the sum of its parts. In the case of California's MPAs, the state Ocean Protection Council governs the network to ensure that the benefits envisioned by the Marine Life Protection Act are realized.

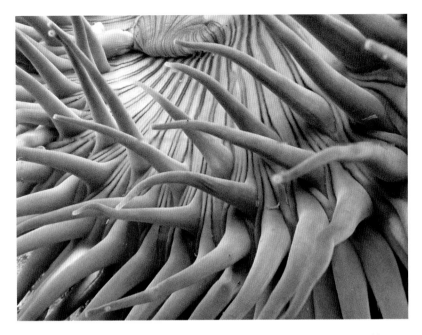

The starburst anemone (*Anthopleura sola*) occupies rocky habitats at Fitzgerald Marine Reserve. This species of anemone can be distinguished from similar species by its solitary habit and its striped oral disc.

High in the intertidal zone, brown and black turban snails (*Tegula brunnea* and *T. funebralis*, respectively) meander among tufts of seagrass. These two are the most common of several closely related turban snails along the shore, and they subdivide intertidal real estate where the two co-occur, minimizing direct competition, with black turban snails (see Species of Interest) occurring at somewhat higher elevations than their brown cousins. Larger individuals tend to be older, and large black turban snails can be up to thirty years old at colder-water sites, while in the warmer waters of Southern California they generally live less than a decade.

Molecular work on these and other turban snails reveals a key detail of evolution among closely related species that live in the same habitat. In these snails, the proteins by which sperm and eggs recognize one another evolve rapidly, such that the gametes of each species have a distinctive

For those willing to wade through the wrack, beach-cast seaweeds offer a glimpse of the diversity of species and life forms occurring nearby, all tossed into one elegant mess.

lock-and-key relationship. This way, turban snails minimize the chance of hybridizing with other species when spawning into the surrounding seawater, where sperm and eggs mix freely in the surf.

At the Fitzgerald Marine Reserve, sea urchins feed on a diverse suite of seaweeds that they catch with their tube feet and spines. The urchins then gradually move the food to their downward-facing mouths, gracefully coordinating their many appendages to do so. Countless hermit crabs (*Pagurus* spp.; see Species of Interest in chapter 8, Long Beach to San Diego), porcelain crabs (*Petrolisthes cinctipes*; see Species of Interest in

The lined chiton (*Tonicella lineata*), with its bright pink color and vivid markings, is perennially delightful. This chiton, which relies on crustose coralline algae for food, typically lives right on top of its food source.

A hermit crab (*Pagurus samuelis*) wearing a distressed turban shell makes its way across an ochre sea star (*Pisaster ochraceus*). Hermit crabs have only two pairs of walking legs on their uncalcified abdomen and use two other pairs of legs to hold on to their purloined shells.

chapter 3, Far Northern California), black-clawed crabs (*Lophopanopeus bellus*), tiny snails (*Margarites pupillus*), and other small invertebrates dwell amid the shell debris and small pebbles that underlie the site's larger, more stable rocks.

Porcelain crabs and hermit crabs belong to a group (Anomura) that also includes king crabs and the sand-burrowing mole crabs (also called sand crabs; see Species of Interest in chapter 8, Long Beach to San Diego). While these would all appear to have little in common, given their enormous differences in body size, habitats, and lifestyles, each has a reduced number of walking legs—three pairs, or in the case of hermit crabs, only two. True crabs (Brachyura) always have four pairs of walking legs. In total, however, both anomurans and brachyurans have ten paired appendages (including claws), and hence both are groups of decapods (meaning "ten feet").

At Pillar Point, just south of the Fitzgerald Marine Reserve, huge waves rolling in from the Pacific break at the big-wave surf spot known as Mavericks. Quirks of underwater topography help to focus wave energy and amplify the height of the breakers, creating occasional monster waves when conditions are just right. To the south along State Highway 1, the expansive sands of Half Moon Bay and San Gregorio taper to form small pocket beaches. Throughout the region, diving brown pelicans (*Pelicanus occidentalis*; see Species of Interest in chapter 8, Long Beach to San Diego) fold tightly as if airborne umbrellas, gravity taking hold as they convert from ungainly fliers into streamlined missiles entering the water to forage.

## Pigeon Point and Año Nuevo

On a map, discrete bits of shore poking out into the ocean nearly always signal rocky intertidal habitat. Such places are subject to intense wave action and local upwelling, thus having a mix of hard substrate, energy, and productivity that often result in a great diversity of intertidal life. The area around Pigeon Point Lighthouse offers this kind of high diversity at an accessible site, with a conglomeration of habitat types both to the north and south of the lighthouse itself. Seagrass, medium-sized cobbles, and boulders offer a range of microhabitats set amid rocks from the age of the dinosaurs.

Pigeon Point is named for the clipper ship *Carrier Pigeon*, which ran aground off its rocky shores in 1853 before the lighthouse was built.

Seabirds exploit the deep nearshore waters at Pigeon Point, making it a destination for bird-watchers, particularly in spring, when thousands of migrating gulls, terns, cormorants, shearwaters, loons, and other seabirds head northward along shore.

Just down the coast from Pigeon Point, Año Nuevo is a larger headland through which run at least five distinct branches of the San Gregorio–Hosgri Fault. Featuring interior wetlands and coastal scrublands, Año Nuevo has since the mid-twentieth century been most famous as a breeding site for northern elephant seals (*Mirounga angustirostris*). Northern elephant seals spend up to nine months each year foraging at sea, coming to land only to reproduce and molt. Large male elephant seals are the first to arrive at the rookery each year, wasting no time in establishing their reproductive territories. They use their inflatable elephantine nose (proboscis) to audibly challenge competing males, bellowing and sometimes subsequently engaging in vicious battles. These males move with surprising speed despite being enormous—up to 5,000 pounds and sixteen feet long—and legless. Females are smaller, but still impressively large at up to 1,800 pounds and twelve feet long. Yard-long pups weigh about 75 pounds at birth and quickly gain hundreds of pounds from the nutrition of their mother's milk alone. Exceptionally large pups—up to 600 pounds—are endearingly referred to as "super weaners."

The seals haul out by the thousands each winter to give birth and mate, in that order. Pups are born in winter, with only a single pup produced per mother per year. Females nurse pups for about a month, then mate again at the end of the nursing period. The egg acquired in this mating is fertilized but further development is paused for some months, a process known as delayed implantation—a neat biological trick, shared with skunks, kangaroos, and selected other mammals, that has the effect of synchronizing births across a rookery. Females leave their weaned pups

Sea foam fills a surge channel near Pigeon Point. Often associated with the breakdown of algal blooms, sea foam forms naturally when the organic remains of planktonic microbes, algae, and zooplankton are whipped up by intense wave action. The foam supports a transient community of living microbes.

and head to sea to forage for about two and a half months, then return to the beach to molt around the first of May. During the molting period, the fertilized egg implants to initiate the eight-month gestation period and begin the next reproductive cycle.

Biologists tend to use the northern elephant seal as the canonical example of a genetic bottleneck. After being hunted to a population size of only double digits in the late nineteenth century, the species has dramatically rebounded. The result is a very small gene pool. modern elephant seals are all fairly close relatives of one another, with little genetic diversity in the species as a whole. Despite low genetic diversity, the limited degree of migration among colonies in California has allowed the seals to develop behavioral differences among populations: for example, local dialects in the vocal displays of breeding males have come and gone in the scope of decades.

## Santa Cruz

The very name of the town of Santa Cruz conjures images of sun and mellow surf set against a backdrop of dun-colored sandstone terraces, hillsides giving way to dark-green canyons, and sunlit clearings. Bay laurels (*Umbellularia californica*), madrone (*Arbutus menziesii*), and nonnative eucalyptus (*Eucalyptus* spp.) insinuate themselves among the quiet groves of looming redwoods (*Sequoia sempervirens*) as the forest slopes toward the sea, where sand accumulates in the lee of the exposed coast and creates a respite from the Pacific's wrath much of the time.

Santa Cruz is the northern pole of Monterey Bay, facing south across the bay toward the city of Monterey, which is in many ways Santa Cruz's opposite. Sitting in the protected crook of the bay, occupying an upwelling shadow—an area of warmer water and lower productivity relative to surrounding areas of more active upwelling—Santa Cruz has more sun and less wind and fog than does Monterey. Summer high temperatures average about 9 degrees Fahrenheit warmer in Santa Cruz than in Monterey, which faces into the teeth of winds from the northwest and experiences routine coastal upwelling. Moreover, the rocky habitats at the two sites look and feel completely different, with those at Santa Cruz

This spongy, brain-like mass is an unusual green seaweed (*Codium setchellii*). Composed of a network of microscopic tubes, or siphons, the seaweed grows on rocky substrates in low sandy areas and is favored by a sea slug (*Placida* cf. *dendritica*) that feeds by slicing open the algal cells and ingesting their contents.

The sedimentary substrates—mudstones, siltstones, and sandstones—found along much of the California coast can be covered in cavities known as tafoni. Common in granular surfaces, they are likely created through abrasion, wind erosion, salt weathering, and other mechanisms.

formed of mudstone, siltstone, and sandstone while at Monterey, bright-white granite dominates.

The sandstone of Santa Cruz offers constant reminders of coastal dynamics. Natural Bridges State Park, for example, refers to the set of three connected stone arches that graced the beach in the late nineteenth and early twentieth centuries. The first of these collapsed into the sea early in the twentieth century, and the second followed in 1980, leaving only a single arch remaining. Such constant erosion and reshaping is the normal state of affairs along the coast—creating, for example, the sea stacks common to exposed rocky headlands along the West Coast (see "Sea Stacks" in chapter 1, The Tumultuous Earth). But sedimentary rocks, in particular, are no match for the waves, making the area around Santa Cruz an especially vivid illustration of coastal processes.

## SPECIES OF INTEREST
### Coralline Algae

Pink may not be a color we immediately associate with intertidal habitats, but on closer inspection, it's seemingly everywhere on rocky shores. What might at first appear to be bushy pink tufts or pale pink crusts on rocks or shells are in fact coralline algae. Found growing in the tidepools of California and everywhere else along the West Coast, coralline algae occupy both shallow and deep habitats all over the world.

Coralline algae form a group of red algae that is distinct from fleshy red seaweeds. Although their architecture varies by species, all coralline algae deposit calcareous minerals in their cell walls, making them hard and somewhat stony. These hard parts are left behind when the algae die, quickly turning chalky white as the pink pigments are lost.

Because of their stony exteriors, coralline algae tolerate a moderate amount of disturbance, including sand scour and wave action. They take two primary growth forms: one is flat and encrusting, adhering tightly to rock and other solid substrates and sometimes looking like pink paint splashed on rocks or shells. The other is upright and bushy, with jointed branches that can bend with wave action—these branched forms are called articulated corallines.

Branching forms of coralline algae gain flexibility via narrow uncalcified joints known as genicula, seen here as very fine whitish lines interspersed between rigid barrel-shaped sections.

Encrusting forms of coralline algae sometimes cover the shells of limpets and snails, perhaps affording them a bit of protection from their visual predators. For example, the shell of the whitecap limpet (*Acmaea mitra*) is bright white, but living individuals typically are covered by pink encrusting coralline algae—the same alga that makes up the limpet's primary food source. Covered in pink, these limpets blend in with their algal buffet and, perhaps relatedly, are among the few local limpet species that don't appear to mount a protective response against predators.

Coralline algae tend to be more resistant to grazing than many of the fleshy algae, but they can easily be overgrown by faster-growing seaweeds and invertebrates. Only a handful of specialized grazers favor coralline algae as food, and those that do tend to have hardened mouthparts that can handle the stony exterior—among these are a few species of chitons and limpets, including the aforementioned whitecap limpet. Other invertebrates make use of crustose corallines in a very different way: the larvae of some species such as abalone choose these algae as a place to settle and grow, cued by chemicals produced by the alga or its bacterial associates that indicate a favorable habitat.

## Dead Man's Fingers

The velvet-green fronds of dead man's fingers (*Codium fragile*) are, biologically speaking, somewhat peculiar. These green fingers are remarkably resistant to the pounding of waves, despite their soft and spongy nature. Like some other green algae, *Codium* is siphonous—that is, instead of being composed of many individual cells, it consists of a series of tubes, or siphons, woven densely together to give the seaweed its form. Different from the typical cell that you may recall from biology class, in which a single nucleus runs the show, the gelatinous cytoplasm that fills *Codium*'s tubes contains many, many nuclei (and a corresponding number

Dead man's fingers (*Codium fragile*) have a branching, velvet-like appearance.

of chloroplasts) that can move through the tubes as if they were subway tunnels. If tissue is damaged, the seaweed can mount a wound-healing response to prevent the loss of cytoplasm, a tactic that has functional similarities to blood clotting in mammals.

Both native and invasive forms of *Codium* inhabit temperate shores, and they can be difficult to distinguish. Invasive forms are highly problematic on the East Coast of the US and in Great Britain and were likely introduced to the West Coast with oyster aquaculture. In earlier times, *Codium* often was used as natural packing material for shipping live oysters due to its moist and spongy texture, but hardy bits of the seaweed survived transit, allowing the species to move around the globe. Many other invasive species in marine and estuarine environments have the same backstory.

The unusually keen observer will note two species of sea slugs that feed on *Codium*, both specialized seaweed-eaters from the order Sacoglossa: *Elysia hedgpethi* and *Placida* cf. *dendritica* (the latter is part of a global complex of similar-looking species that have not yet been distinguished and given names). Sometimes white egg spirals are more obvious than the slugs themselves, which are colored green and match the alga that is their food and habitat. These slugs feed by punching a tiny hole with a single tooth and slurping out the cytoplasm, turning green as their guts fill with the chloroplasts from *Codium*. If removed from its seaweed host, the fluffy *Placida* cf. *dendritica* digests the chloroplasts in its guts and loses its color. Remarkably, *Elysia hedgpethi* can remain green for weeks after feeding. Its highly branched gut takes up ingested chloroplasts and keeps them alive *within* the slug's cells. These ultimate vegetarians thus become a virtual fusion of plant and animal, surviving on the products of photosynthesis. How slugs maintain chloroplasts apart from the algal nuclei, which normally supply vital proteins for harvesting light, is currently a mystery under study.

## Pickleweed

Across mudflats in protected estuarine habitats throughout California grow herbaceous plants quite different from the eelgrass (*Zostera marina*;

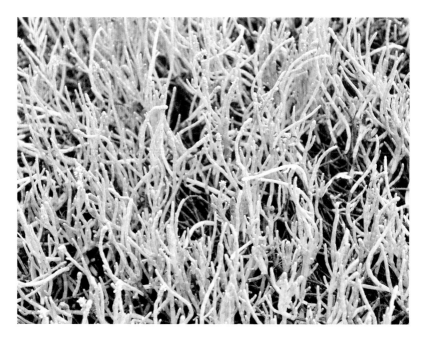

Pickleweed (*Salicornia* spp.) dominates many salt marshes along the California coast.

see Species of Interest in chapter 3, Far Northern California) that's common there. This herby greenery often is pickleweed (*Salicornia* spp.), a salt-tolerant flowering plant that grows in estuaries along both coasts of the continental US. Pickleweed stores salt in the plant's tips; when that gets to be too much, the tips turn red and fall off, shedding excess salt. Even though most animals do not feed on pickleweed, it's nevertheless an important plant ecologically: it stabilizes muddy sediments; numerous bird species use it for nesting; small mammals use it to seek cover. Humans use pickleweed too—in the summer, when its new growth yields tender green tips, people harvest them to use in salads, either raw or steamed. Pickleweed can host dodder (*Cuscuta californica*), a bright orange parasitic vine that looks like nothing so much as a tangle of spaghetti tossed across the mudflat. Dodder is almost entirely stem—hence the resemblance to noodles—and has tiny white flowers in summer, betraying its identity as a flowering plant.

## Brooding Sea Anemone

The brooding sea anemone (*Epiactis prolifera*) is far smaller than most other intertidal anemones, reaching only about two inches in basal diameter, but it is nevertheless remarkable. Small individuals are female, but individuals become hermaphroditic with age, developing male reproductive organs as well. Eggs are fertilized within the animal's gastrovascular cavity—essentially, in their gut—and then expelled. Tiny projections on the mother's exterior move the fertilized eggs to the base of the disc where they become attached in small pits. There they remain, feeding and growing, for several months, and thus adult females are usually found with a brood of baby anemones attached in a circle around their base, an adorable intertidal nursery. Young later crawl away to find a new attachment spot on rock, coralline algae, or seagrass. Brooding sea anemones are eaten by nudibranchs and leather stars and reportedly are not very tasty to humans, even when fried in butter.

The brooding sea anemone (*Epiactis prolifera*) sports minuscule juvenile anemones on its central column, which here is compressed. All individuals of this species begin life as females, developing over time into hermaphrodites with two different sets of reproductive organs.

## Black Turban Snail

The black turban snail (*Tegula funebralis*) is nearly ubiquitous in mid- and high-intertidal zones along California's exposed coasts. Its stout shell is black or dark purple in color and can be about an inch across at its widest point; older individuals are larger, and exceptionally large snails can be thirty years old or more. The snails aggregate conspicuously, reaching densities of over a hundred individuals per square foot.

Their shells offer stability to smaller animals in habitats that are otherwise space-limited, and accordingly, the shells of black turban snails often feature ride-along slipper snails (*Crepidula adunca*), the larvae of which settle on the larger snail, and small black limpets (*Lottia asmi*), individuals of which can switch among *Tegula* hosts.

Black turban snails feed on coralline algae, fleshy algae, and detritus; in turn they are prey for sea otters, sea stars including ochre stars,

Black turban snails (*Tegula funebralis*) aggregate alongside limpets (*Lottia* sp.) and barnacles (*Chthamalus dalli*) in favorable habitats. Specialized organs on their gills allow the snails to sense predatory sea stars from a distance, affording them a chance to escape.

enterprising rock crabs (*Cancer antennarius*), and even octopuses. When the snails sense danger, they can make a quick turn and more than double their typical crawling speed in an attempt to flee. Or, if positioned on a vertical face, they can simply release their foot, rolling downhill to escape.

Several other species in the genus co-occur in California (see Western San Mateo Peninsula, above), and archaeological evidence points to the importance of these snails to humans over the past 12,000 years—middens contain not only multitudes of turban shells but also special tools for cracking their shells and extracting the meat.

## Kelp Crabs

Kelp crabs (*Pugettia* spp.) are common in nearshore areas all along the West Coast. While often associated with kelp, they are not restricted to kelp habitats and can be found among other seaweed species and

Color-matching between northern kelp crabs (*Pugettia producta*) and the substrates they inhabit may help protect them from predation.

seagrasses. They tend to be herbivorous, favoring seaweeds as food, but will eat invertebrates when seaweeds are scarce, and for herbivores they can be quite aggressive, claws packing a fierce pinch. Their long, spindly, spider-like legs help them climb and hold onto kelp stipes and other vertical structures such as pilings.

Individual kelp crabs can be brown, olive green, orange, or deep red, matching their surroundings closely, and depending on species, can be smooth (northern kelp crab, *P. producta*) or covered in bumps (graceful kelp crab, *P. gracilis*, occurring north of Monterey) or spines (cryptic kelp crab, *P. richii*). Even so, all kelp crabs share a shield-shaped carapace that is distinctive to the group. Kelp crabs are vulnerable to parasitic barnacles that can commandeer the crab's body as a means for their own reproduction.

## Brittle Stars

A seashore visitor, on finding beneath an overturned rock a tangle of writhing arms covered in stiff bristles, might well wonder how such frenetic, delicate-looking things can live for long in such a habitat. And yet for millions of years, brittle stars have endured.

These relatives of sea stars resemble their stouter cousins, insofar as each generally has five arms radiating out from a central disc, on which is located its mouth and other important bits. But whereas sea stars are hearty enough to take a punch from oncoming waves, brittle stars would fall to pieces. And in part, this is a strategy: they lose arms easily, a mechanism for escaping from predators, and quickly regrow those arms later. Each arm is loaded with hydraulic tube feet, as are sea stars' arms, although brittle stars' tube feet lack suckers and aren't as conspicuous.

Brittle stars can be difficult to differentiate, and in many cases, genetic data has shown the scientific names of these species underestimate their diversity. It's quite likely there are many more species than the more than 2,000 that are currently described worldwide.

## Shiner Surfperch

Rocky intertidal habitats are full of fish, although it may not seem so at low tide. As the tide flows out, fish move out with it, or they remain

A brittle star (center, with red central disc) makes its way across shell and rock fragments, some adorned by pink coralline algae. Brittle stars can be found all along California's coast, from intertidal habitats to depths of thousands of feet; depending on the species and substrate, they can be remarkably difficult to distinguish from their surroundings.

submerged and hidden in pools to avoid desiccation. As the tide flows back in, intertidal fish return to feed, mainly on invertebrates and sometimes on algae. Estuaries, too, are full of fish. Shiner surfperch (*Cymatogaster aggregata*) are among the most common fish in bays and estuaries of the West Coast, inhabiting eelgrass beds (see Species of Interest in chapter 3, Far Northern California) and other sheltered habitats, including the calm waters around piers. Typically reaching a few inches in length, their silvery sides sport three vertical yellow bars, though the bars disappear in breeding males as their color turns dark and blotched. Shiner surfperch are carnivorous, feeding on small zooplankton, and different from most other fishes, they give birth to live young. Many larger animals, from halibut to seals to birds, make a meal of them.

## Sooty Shearwater

Sooty shearwaters (*Ardenna grisea*), present along the California coast in summer and fall, are the most numerous of the six shearwater species that visit this coast. A member of the petrel family, shearwaters have prominent tube-shaped nostrils thought to help them excrete salt—hence the common name "tubenose." Breeding on isolated islands in the South Pacific and south Atlantic, shearwaters are impressive migrants, heading to the northern hemisphere once breeding is completed. Birds observed in California may have begun their journey in New Zealand, flying more than 45,000 miles en route. Equally impressive are their diving skills: sooty shearwaters can reportedly dive to depths of more than 220 feet, using their wings to propel themselves as they pursue small squid and anchovies. In summer, large flocks of up to a million individuals can converge in upwelling areas where prey are abundant.

An incident in 1961 during which thousands of sooty shearwaters descended upon Santa Cruz at nighttime and behaved as if crazed—slamming into houses, severing television antennas, and regurgitating meals of fish—inspired the plot of Alfred Hitchcock's *The Birds*. The frenzy appears to have been caused by poisoning brought on by a toxic algal bloom.

Gulls have adapted to humans and their infrastructure: here, a western gull (*Larus occidentalis*) rests on a piling.

## Western Gull

Gulls are seemingly ubiquitous at coastal sites and as likely to be found eating out of trash cans as diving into schools of nearshore fish. As ecological generalists, gulls appear to have benefitted from human alteration of shorelines—that is, they are able to do well under a variety of conditions, eat a variety of foods, and withstand the host of challenges that come with human occupation of coastal areas. About a dozen species of gulls live in or migrate through coastal California. The western gull (*Larus occidentalis*), with a wingspan approaching five feet, is a year-round resident and is among the most common, nesting on offshore islands and coastal rocks. Western gulls forage both at sea, where they take fish and pelagic invertebrates, and in the intertidal, where they feed on a range of benthic invertebrates. The noticeable red spot on an adult western gull's beak triggers chicks to peck at the bill, in turn causing the adult to regurgitate a meal for the baby bird; investigating these instincts led to a Nobel Prize for researchers who pioneered studies of genetically programmed behavior in animals.

**6**

Relicts from a glacial era, cypress trees line the shore of Whalers Cove at Point Lobos.

# MONTEREY, BIG SUR, AND THE CENTRAL COAST

S tate Highway 1 hugs the perfect crescent of Monterey Bay for twenty-five miles from Santa Cruz to Monterey and Pacific Grove. The community of Moss Landing, at the mouth of Elkhorn Slough, sits dead center between the more-developed poles of the bay. Along the route southward, the sedimentary rock of the Santa Cruz coast gives way to granite on the Monterey Peninsula, after which the wide-open feel of Monterey Bay disappears as the mountains pinch the highway against the sea in Big Sur.

Visitors feel the surf, salt wind, and fog, but they miss the giant submarine canyon that descends from Moss Landing, bisecting the bay beneath the waves. The canyon walls are a mile high in some spots. In total, the canyon runs almost a hundred miles offshore, ending up more than two miles below the ocean's surface, forming the largest canyon on the West Coast. Standing on the beach, it's hard to imagine that there's an entire Grand Canyon gouged into the seafloor just out of sight.

Mere trickles do not create such canyons. This kind of deep erosion requires a large volume of water flowing over a long stretch of time; the fan of sediment at the canyon's tail suggests something more along the lines of the Mississippi or the Amazon. The story of the canyon's formation is complicated and not completely understood, but the sheer size of the canyon—its length and depth—suggests powerful forces at work across geological timescales.

Elkhorn Slough, in the crook of Monterey Bay's wide arc, is a large estuary that is home to sea otters, shorebirds, and an associated soft-sediment ecosystem. A hulking power plant creates a jarring backdrop to

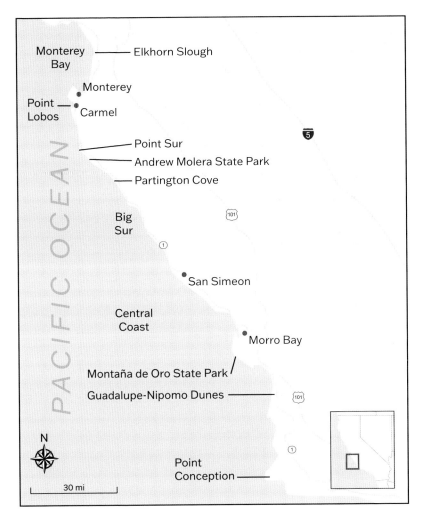

Monterey Bay, Big Sur, and the central California coast.

this tranquil scene, sitting astride the freshwater outlet and dominating the skyline. Shoreline power plants such as this one use ocean water as coolant, discharging heated water back to the sea; the ocean itself provides the logic for their locations.

Humpback and gray whales transit close to shore where deep water abuts coastal terrain, the former chasing schools of sardines or anchovies and the latter feeding on small crustaceans. The presence of deep water so close to shore supports cold-water communities throughout the area and helps fuel a productive food web, as decades of commercial fishing attest. Anomalously warm events such as El Niño can allow warmer-water species to invade or expand into cooler, more northerly areas—examples include subtropical urchins (individuals of *Centrostephanus coronatus*, *Lytechinus pictus*, and *Arbacia stellata*), the six-foot-long predatory Humboldt squid (*Dosidicus gigas*), and others. The resultant mingling of warm- and cold-water faunas is part of the reason more species of animals live here than most other places on the West Coast.

Rocky intertidal communities here stand inshore of elegant stands of giant kelp that are impossible to miss. Kelps grow in temperate nearshore environments around the world; their rapid growth and large size require the steady supply of nutrients that coastal upwelling and turbulent mixing readily supply. So kelps—and giant kelp (*Macrocystis pyrifera*) in particular—are generally restricted to sites with abundant nutrients and sunlight and a hard, rocky bottom offering secure attachment at reasonably shallow depths. Suitable sites abound in Monterey and along California's central coast, favoring the formation of kelp beds that shape the nearshore ecosystem.

Tall, tangled, and enormously productive, giant kelp creates biological structure similar to that of terrestrial forests. Anchored at the bottom in depths of up to ninety feet, the fronds grow toward the surface where a profusion of blades creates a thick canopy that intercepts sunlight and shades the habitat below. Once the blades reach the water's surface, the fronds can continue to grow, extending laterally to reach impressive lengths. Small floats (pneumatocysts) at the base of each blade provide buoyancy that keeps the entire structure upright in the water column. These same small floats are the reason that detached fronds are so likely to wash up on shore: the buoyant fronds are carried by currents and waves.

Kelp forests change nearly everything about a nearshore ecosystem. Apart from reducing light and altering its spectrum beneath the canopy, kelps slow currents and moderate surge, taking the edge off a sometimes-violent sea. Their rapid growth consumes nitrogen from the

Giant kelp (*Macrocystis pyrifera*) is the largest seaweed on the planet, creating undersea forests that harbor other seaweeds plus many species of invertebrates, fish, and marine mammals. Photo by Allison Vitsky Sallmon.

water column and releases organic carbon in return. The three-dimensional structure created by kelps attracts a wide variety of species, leading to communities rich in invertebrates, fish, and mammals. Invertebrate larvae accumulate in the lee of the kelp forest, setting the stage for repeated generations of growth, competition, and predation among a distinctive assortment of species. Kelp associates include ephemeral life stages—which last mere days in some species—to those that, like rockfish, can live for a century or more.

## PLACES TO EXPLORE
### Monterey and Carmel

Monterey sits atop granite, the whole peninsula forming a white headland that intrudes into a sapphire sea. Fragments of the pale rock, ground by waves, create immaculate white-sand beaches. In tidepools, pinks and greens and reds stand out against the granite background, and startlingly clear water seems to magnify the small dramas playing out within their confines. The peninsula points northwest, directly into weather coming

Fog creeps in from the sea, filling low-lying valleys along the Big Sur coast.

from the open ocean. The result is year-round wind and more fog than rain, in a setting that is cool and damp even by coastal standards.

The Monterey Peninsula divides the sandy expanse of Monterey Bay from the rocky habitat of Big Sur, with most points along the peninsula exposed to significant wave action. Accessible rocky-intertidal sites ring the peninsula and adorn points to the south along State Highway 1. These include Point Pinos, the northernmost point of the peninsula, facing into the bay and featuring the Great Tidepool made famous by John Steinbeck and Ed Ricketts.

Carmel-by-the-Sea, tucked into the peninsula's south-facing crook, is only somewhat more sheltered than sites facing the open ocean. Just south of Carmel lies Point Lobos State Natural Reserve, a gem in a system of state parks already replete with riches, and Garrapata State Park's Soberanes Point. These sites and many others feature kelp forests, marine mammals, seabirds, and an array of intertidal habitats along their cragged margins.

The city of Monterey's breakwaters protect a still-active fishing fleet that reached the height of its fame and profitability in the 1930s and '40s. The rise and fall of the region's sardine fishery is a story of the linkage between social and ecological prosperity, and indeed the sardine boom and bust followed Monterey's earlier adventures in unsustainable extractive industries, which had serially focused on sea otters, whales, and abalone. The midcentury collapse of sardines (*Sardinops sagax*) followed a period of intense exploitation, and around the same time decadal-scale oceanographic patterns appear to have shifted away from a sardine-friendly warmer phase. The fishery turned its sights to anchovies (*Engraulis mordax*), which suffered the same fate as sardines, and soon both the great schools of fish and the fishing and canning jobs that had relied entirely upon them were gone.

A more sustainable fishery still operates, particularly in spring as market squid (*Doryteuthis opalescens*) arrive in the bay to spawn. Commercial fishing boats target them at night, shining bright lights to attract the squid into their nets by the thousand and creating a picturesque scene on the darkened bay. Market squid is one of the state's most valuable

(above) A purple shore crab (*Hemigrapsus nudus*; left) and black turban snails (*Tegula funebralis*; right) seek shade amid cobbles at low tide. The small white coils covering the cobbles are the calcified tubes of polychaete worms in the genus *Spirorbis*.

(left) Purple sea urchins (*Strongylocentrotus purpuratus*), where abundant, can quickly remove fleshy seaweeds, leaving only calcified algae and bare rock.

fisheries, although unlike the sardines of Cannery Row's past, they are shipped to Asia instead of being processed locally, while some of Monterey's former canneries now are occupied by hotels, restaurants, and the Monterey Bay Aquarium.

On sunny days the local granite seems to intensify the sun's effect, warming high-intertidal pools beyond expectation and leaving only the hardiest species to survive in the warm waters and fluctuating oxygen concentrations. Hermit crabs (*Pagurus* spp.; see Species of Interest in chapter 8, Long Beach to San Diego) scramble among tiny periwinkles (*Littorina* spp.) in crevices only occasionally refreshed by waves. Outside the pools, shore crabs and turban snails occupy shaded spots among cobbles. Coastal scrub, poison oak (*Toxicodendron diversilobum*), and invasive ice plant (*Carpobrotus edulis*) dot the shore as granite gives way to the sea. Gulls ride updrafts powered by the consistent winds, while red-tailed hawks (*Buteo jamaicensis*) circle overhead.

Purple sea urchins (*Strongylocentrotus purpuratus*) are abundant here and all along the California coast. They can quickly multiply in the absence of predators, devouring kelps and other fleshy seaweeds, leaving behind calcified algae in wonderful shades of pink, meanwhile depriving competitors of food. At small spatial scales—say, the scale of a tidepool—areas dominated by urchins often host scant fleshy algae and few large-bodied invertebrates. At larger scales, intense urchin grazing can lead to the development of extensive urchin barrens that are denuded of kelp and other seaweeds and accordingly depleted of other invertebrates, fish, and mammals. By consuming marauding urchins and other grazers, sea otters that reoccupied Monterey Bay transformed the urchin-dominated habitats of the 1960s into kelp forests in the 1970s, helping to restore a productive system and fueling a subsequent tourism boom. Ecologists point to this and similar stark transitions as evidence of phase shifts in response to intense disturbance.

## Big Sur

The drive south from Monterey feels like an expedition from an earlier era, a departure from everyday life. State Highway 1 passes over the

The iconic Bixby Bridge spans a chasm along the precipitous Big Sur coast. The first major section of State Highway 1 to open was along the Big Sur coast in the 1930s; today the highway totals more than 650 miles, running for most of its length within sight of the ocean.

granite mass of the Monterey Peninsula, down across the floodplain of the Carmel River, and past Point Lobos. The terpene perfume of blue gum (*Eucalyptus* spp.) and the arthritic forms of Monterey cypress (*Hesperocyparis [Cupressus] macrocarpa*) unmistakably mark the more developed parts of the central California coast. Then after a few twists, the road takes on the rhythm of the Big Sur coast, undulating through canyons as the road hugs the cliffs above the breakers.

Seventy-five miles offshore of the Big Sur coast, the Davidson Seamount is an underwater volcano nearly 7,500 feet in height, although its peak is still 4,000 feet below the waves. The submarine mountain stands out from its flatter surroundings to such an extent that it creates localized upwelling of nutrients from the deep to the surface—akin to a terrestrial mountain creating its own weather system—fueling a productive food web at the surface. More than two dozen cold-water coral species flourish here in the dark, far from the sunlight that their better-known, tropical reef-building relatives require. But like tropical corals, deep-sea corals are

# BLUE GUM

The scent of the blue gum (*Eucalyptus globulus*) frequently penetrates the populated areas of coastal California, subliminally mixing with the native bay laurel (*Umbellularia californica*) to create a fragrant punctuation mark for the visitor's sense of place. Despite the blue gum's origins half a world away in Australia, it has been a fixture of California ecology for more than 150 years.

In the wake of the California gold rush and following statehood, new California residents planted eucalyptus beginning in the 1850s. Whether it was planted for shade or wind block; for medicine, timber, or firewood; or to stand in for the eastern hardwoods (of which the new state had none), the ensuing decades saw plantations of the trees seeded from nurseries

Native to Australia, blue gum (*Eucalyptus globulus*) is common in coastal California.

throughout California. The University of California even once offered free eucalyptus seed to those interested in cultivating the plant. Of the hundreds of species of *Eucalyptus* in Australia, just a few rose to prominence in California—the blue gum being the most common.

Among its many supposed uses, perhaps the most intriguing was as a living antiseptic: in the nineteenth century, the tree was thought to disinfect the surrounding ground and air, thus preventing malaria. And remarkably, the tree does indeed fight malaria . . . but it does so by drying the soil and thereby hindering the development of mosquito larvae.

Customers found the new trees fast-growing and aesthetically pleasing, although it soon became clear that their wood left much to be desired. Much to the disappointment of the Central Pacific Railroad company—which had invested in substantial experiments with the trees—the wood was not suitable for railroad ties. In fact, eucalyptus turned out to be unsuitable for nearly all timber and construction purposes, due to a propensity of the wood of California's young trees to warp and crack after being harvested. Oil, gas, and electricity replaced the need for fuel wood in the early part of the twentieth century, and California's ardor for planting the Australian trees cooled.

The landscapes of coastal California still reflect the nineteenth- and early-twentieth-century enthusiasm for eucalyptus, although in more recent decades their dangers have become more clear. Hard winters, it seems, cause the trees to drop large limbs and even more debris, accumulating fuel for aggressive fires the following year. Add to this tinder the oily nature of the wood and leaves, and eucalyptus seems a poor match for a region that struggles with long-term water shortages and catastrophic fires.

ecosystem engineers, generating durable three-dimensional structures that host many other animal species that make up the vibrant communities of the deep.

The Santa Lucia Mountains slope at impressively sharp angles toward the Pacific as the native coast redwoods and bay laurels take refuge in shaded creekside canyons. The land is dry in most years and warm enough to support the occasional palm tree along with century plants (*Agave americana*) that pepper the hillsides—images that evoke lower latitudes than the map would suggest for Big Sur. The distinctive scent of California sagebrush (*Artemisia californica*) welcomes visitors.

Topography has largely prevented human development here, with the notable exception of the highway itself. Before the highway's opening in the 1930s, access to the Big Sur coast was extremely limited, and even now, the road regularly washes out in wet years, stranding residents and eliminating north-south travel and commerce. The Big Sur coast accordingly features stretches of rocky habitat that are difficult to access both as a cause and a consequence of topography and limited human development. Some of the most accessible parts of the Big Sur coast are in fact the least rocky: Andrew Molera State Park and Pfeiffer Beach feature sandy beaches, thanks in part to the generally modest outflow of the Big Sur River at Molera Point. Almost everywhere else, the region's steep, rocky terrain creates tidepools and boulder habitats at the shore.

The tidepool flora and fauna here largely mirror that of Monterey, owing to similar ecological conditions consisting of cold water, high wave-energy, and durable rocky substrate. No rivers of any size cut through the coastal range here, and like Monterey, there is little freshwater influence on the intertidal communities.

At Partington Cove, for example, granite boulders bathe in cold, clear water, the cove itself a niche shaded by steep hillsides. The wave action here is serious and sustained, and even during the relatively calm summer months this high-energy environment can catch unwary visitors by surprise. Below the waves, visible in pools and beneath overhanging rocks, a wild mosaic covers the substrate: colonies of red-orange sponges and cream-colored bryozoans compete for space with tunicates, pink

The intertidal community at Big Sur's Partington Cove is typical of high-energy environments where wave-tolerant species dominate the shore. The intense wave energy here makes it hard to believe that the cove once served as a landing point for ships carrying timber.

A mosaic of bright colors and contrasting forms fill a tidepool at Partington Cove.

coralline algae, and larger seaweeds in hues of red and brown. Snails and urchins graze at the margins, mussels discreetly filtering particles from the water, as anemones sit patiently awaiting a meal.

This abundance of intertidal life reflects the combined forces of oceanography and ecology. Ocean conditions that promote the growth of phytoplankton at the bottom of the food web, combined with those that retain or transport larvae toward shore, favor larval settlement and the development of rich ecological communities. Consider this: to sustain their populations over multiple generations, the millions and millions of invertebrate larvae that are cast into the water column need to survive their time at sea and either remain close to shore or use ocean currents to return to shore where they can settle and grow.

This is no mean feat—a host of biological and environmental factors have to align for success. One helpful factor is the existence of chemical cues that guide larvae to precise spots for settlement. Unsurprisingly, the presence of adults of the same species offers one reliable indicator of favorable settlement sites—in fact, the adults often are the source of those guiding chemical cues and can help explain why, for example, larval bryozoans settle near adult bryozoans (see Species of Interest in chapter 7, Santa Barbara to Los Angeles), and larvae of colonial worms settle near similar adults. The same applies to many sponges, tunicates, barnacles, and other sessile species. Coupled with reproductive strategies that, in many species, involve asexual reproduction by budding or other forms of cloning or, for sexually reproducing species, the proximity of mates at high densities, these processes help create and maintain the vibrant tapestries found all along this shore.

Alternatively, important settlement cues can be produced by unrelated species. For example, the larvae of abalone, chitons, and other grazers use chemical cues from coralline algae or their associated microbial films as signs of suitable habitat. The coralline algae themselves present an ecological enigma: these calcium carbonate-based species occur throughout polar and tropical environments and locations in between, are highly abundant (though often go unnoticed), grow slowly, are often overgrown by other species, and tend to do best where grazing

Crustose coralline algae play important roles in intertidal systems, resisting grazing and desiccation while promoting larval settlement.

is most intense. Indeed, there may be a deep evolutionary association between the crustose corallines and their invertebrate grazers (see Species of Interest in chapter 5, San Francisco to Santa Cruz). The evolution of ever-more-efficient invertebrate mouthparts to enable the excavation of calcium carbonate, and the corresponding evolution of morphological and reproductive traits of crustose corallines, may have fostered a relationship whereby the grazers prevent the corallines from overgrowth by competing species. Modern-day coralline crusts often have both grazers and competitors in close proximity, suggesting the complicated relationships at play.

Black abalone (*Haliotis cracherodii*) are among the suite of invertebrate species associated with coralline crusts. Historically abundant along much of the California coast, in places the species reached densities as high as a hundred individuals per square yard. As the only abalone

Barnacles encrust the shell of a black abalone (*Haliotis cracherodii*) in an intertidal habitat; this individual is about six inches across.

species in California that lives principally in the intertidal, black abalone have been used by humans for more than 10,000 years, valued both for their meat and their iridescent large shells. Decades ago, the more southerly populations of this species succumbed to a temperature-associated disease known as withering syndrome that caused their muscular foot to atrophy, rendering individuals unable to cling to the substrate and exposing them to predation and dislodgement by waves. The disease, combined with historical overexploitation, caused the species to become rare, and it remains endangered despite recovery efforts. In Big Sur, however, these giant snails can still be found among low-intertidal rocks, tucked in deep crevices, feeding on drift kelp and other seaweeds (also see Species of Interest in chapter 4, Mendocino, Sonoma, and Marin).

Likewise, Big Sur was the last redoubt of the southern (or California) sea otter (*Enhydra lutris nereis*), which survived here in small numbers

A small population of the southern sea otter (*Enhydra lutris nereis*) avoided extinction in the last century in Big Sur and since then has grown in numbers and expanded its range.

even as it was hunted to extinction elsewhere. (Southern sea otters are distinct from their cousins to the north, the northern sea otter, *Enhydra lutris kenyoni*, which inhabit the waters of Washington, British Columbia, and Alaska.) Today's southern sea otters are descended from the remnant population in Big Sur, discovered near Bixby Bridge in the late 1930s. The population has grown slowly over the past century to span the region from San Mateo County to Santa Barbara, with a total population size of several thousand. As sea otters repopulated Monterey Bay in the 1960s and early 1970s, they swiftly altered the nearshore ecosystem, consuming sea urchins and other invertebrate grazers and facilitating a system dominated by giant kelp.

## The Central Coast

Heading south from Big Sur, the central coast seems to open up at Piedras Blancas, creating broad vistas that are a departure from the hemmed-in feel of the Big Sur coast. The historic Piedras Blancas Light Station is prominent here, but perhaps more notable are the thousands of northern elephant seals (*Mirounga angustirostris*) that fill the beach at certain times of year. One of fifteen breeding sites in California and Mexico, the colony at Piedras Blancas was first populated in the 1990s as the species expanded its breeding territory, continuing its recovery from near-extinction in the nineteenth century.

Continuing south from Piedras Blancas, the shoreline consists of a series of shallow, sandy crescents, each representing the landward end of a northwest-pointing valley running out to sea. Repeatedly folded and faulted, this landscape continues to Morro Bay, where Morro Rock stands embedded in sand and water, dominating coastal sight lines for miles. At approximately 580 feet tall, the rock would tower over every state capitol building in the US.

Morro Rock dominates the view from the harbor in Morro Bay, framed by a shoreline garden of lion's tail agave (*Agave attenuata*; left foreground and right middle), a plant species native to the arid plateaus of western Mexico, and pride of Madeira (*Echium candicans*; right foreground), native to its namesake Atlantic island.

Morro Rock is, astonishingly, a volcanic plug—it is the remnant *inside* of a volcano, a neck of solidified volcanic rock that has stood in place for more than 20 million years, even as the external mountain has eroded away. And it is not alone, being part of a chain of nine volcanic mountains—the Nine Sisters—that stretch inland to San Luis Obispo. Morro Rock is a state historical landmark, as well as a reserve for peregrine falcons (*Falco peregrinus*).

Within the protected waters of Morro Bay itself—the drowned remnant of an ice-age river valley—sea otters, harbor seals, and sea lions make a home beside the vessels of the active fishing fleet. More than 200 species of birds reportedly use the mudflats and salt marshes of Morro Bay in their migrations along the Pacific Flyway, probing the sediments for invertebrates or feeding and resting among the emergent vegetation. In shallow habitats, eelgrass (*Zostera marina*; see Species of Interest in chapter 3, Far Northern California) appears to be recovering following sharp declines over the past decades, and at slightly higher elevations a suite of salt-marsh plants connects the estuary with upland habitats. Invasive species have

A sandy arc anchored by Morro Rock separates the calm waters of Morro Bay from the open ocean, creating estuarine habitat that supports eelgrass, invertebrates, and fish.

The striations of sedimentary rock formations, shown here in the upper intertidal at Montaña de Oro State Park, create a corrugated landscape that provides varied microhabitats for invertebrates and seaweeds.

found a home here, too, covering a large fraction of the hard substrate in the bay, most of which consists of man-made structures.

Although Morro Rock itself offers some stable habitat for intertidal life, the best rocky habitat lies a few miles south, in Montaña de Oro State Park. The park sits upon a prominent headland that separates Morro Bay from Pismo Beach—as such, it is the most accessible rocky intertidal habitat for many miles, with the next closest being south of Point Conception and thus decidedly in Southern California.

Montaña de Oro's rock ledges poke out into the sea, tilted reminders of a dynamic earth: as with other sedimentary rocks, the layers here were originally horizontal, sand and mud accumulating and slowly forming into stone as mass and pressure built up. Tectonic movement over the eons since has twisted and folded them into their present-day positions, the long striations and overhangs creating space for intertidal life of all kinds.

Surfgrass (*Phyllospadix* spp.; see Species of Interest in chapter 8, Long Beach to San Diego) attaches to these hard surfaces using short rhizomes and fine root hairs; kelps including *Laminaria setchellii* use holdfasts, entirely different structures, to accomplish the same feat in the face of breaking waves. Together, the two blanket the low-intertidal shelves of Montaña de Oro, painting the seaward margin in tones of green and gold. This mat of vegetation offers protection to other species when the tide is out, concealing small prey from visual predators such as birds, and shading others from the sun's heat and drying power: here, the tidepools and crevices are wholly covered in vegetation even during the lowest tides.

Isopod crustaceans of the genus *Idotea* live among the nearshore surfgrasses and kelps here and elsewhere along the central coast. These animals are well adapted to life on wave-swept shores: in addition to being flattened from top to bottom, adults have hooked claws on their walking legs that they use to hang on to vegetation. Various closely related species of *Idotea* live and move between microhabitats over the course of their individual development, with adults frequenting the surfgrass or kelp in higher-energy areas while young occupy the relative shelter

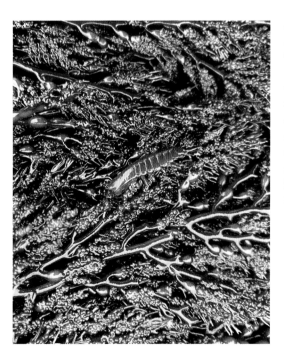

An isopod of the genus *Idotea* (center) clings to branches of the brown seaweed called chain-bladder kelp (*Stephanocystis osmundacea*), though this common name is misleading because the seaweed is not a kelp at all—instead, it's more closely related to rockweed.

of red algae and other vegetation closer to shore. The small crustaceans remain camouflaged as they move, using specialized structures called chromatophores to concentrate or disperse pigments to match the color of their background. Color matching provides protection from fish and other visual predators. Intriguingly, adults swim upside down through the water when displaced and brood their young in pouches.

Spaghetti worms (family Terebellidae) build long tubes of coarse sand pressed against vertical rock faces, their red or orange tentacles sometimes visible when the tubes are submerged. Shiny black patches of the crustose alga called tar spot, or Petrocelis, cover high- and mid-intertidal rocks adjacent to the fleshy stage of the same species, commonly called Turkish washcloth (*Mastocarpus papillatus*), that is more easily recognized as a red seaweed (see Species of Interest). Sharing the upper-intertidal habitat with *Mastocarpus* is the red seaweed referred to as turfweed or sea moss (*Endocladia muricata*; see Species of Interest), though it is not a moss at all.

Intertidal seaweeds on exposed rocks give way to larger forms below the water's surface.

The calcareous tubes of worm snails (family Vermetidae) snake among anemones on mid-intertidal benches, creating a reef-like crust on top of the rock. These animals are indeed snails, despite looking superficially like tube worms. In some species of worm snails, a round operculum (a tiny lid) seals the tube's opening, just as the operculum does in more standard-shaped snail shells. Like many other snails, these odd snails have a round foot and sensory tentacles on their heads, but because they're cemented in place, they have evolved a style of feeding in which they repeatedly cast mucous nets to ensnare particulate matter, later digesting both food and net.

South of Montaña de Oro lies the wide arc of Pismo Beach and the Guadalupe-Nipomo Dunes. These coastal dunes extend eighteen miles along the coast, one of the largest dune formations along the West Coast. Other surviving dune ecosystems include the Oregon Dunes (near Florence, Oregon) and Fort Ord Dunes (in Monterey Bay); much of western San Francisco—including Golden Gate Park—consisted of similar dunes well into the twentieth century.

Such dunes form when sand blows inland from the beach. Prevailing winds from the west and an ample supply of dry sand have built the dunes over millennia, helped along by changes in sea level. Many of these waves of sand were formed long before the last ice age, and some have risen to more than 500 feet tall.

Open, shifting sands create a landscape that seems alive. The persistent wind tends to cover tracks in the sand, the transient evidence of human presence—both bonfires and motorized vehicles are legal on the beach here—as well as that of foxes, weasels, rodents, and any number of other species.

## SPECIES OF INTEREST

### Turfweed

The red seaweed variously referred to as turfweed or sea moss (*Endocladia muricata*) can be found all along the California coast; indeed, the species ranges from northern Alaska to northern Mexico and can be quite abundant in places. Low-growing, bushy, and covered in short spines, this

Turfweed (*Endocladia muricata*; upper right and lower left) is common in upper intertidal areas all along this coast. It is especially tolerant of desiccation at low tide. Turfweed often can be found growing intermixed with the red seaweed known as Turkish washcloth (*Mastocarpus papillatus*; lower center).

seaweed is common in high-intertidal areas where it is subject to prolonged emersion, in some settings more often exposed to air than water. Turfweed resembles a kitchen scouring pad and dries quickly at low tide, becoming photosynthetically inactive but more resistant to heat when desiccated. With its short, bushy architecture, turfweed offers excellent places for invertebrate larvae to settle, and its presence can influence the community that develops around it—indeed, nearly a hundred species are known to associate with turfweed on California's central coast.

## Turkish Washcloth and Tar Spot Alga

Occurring from Alaska to Mexico, the red seaweed known as Turkish washcloth (*Mastocarpus papillatus*) is so named for the papillae, or small bumps, that cover its surface. Typically less than six inches tall, blades vary in width and range in color from nearly black to red to almost yellow.

Turkish washcloth (*Mastocarpus papillatus*; upper right) is a fleshy red seaweed that is in fact a different life stage—but the same species—as the blackish crust known as Petrocelis, or tar spot alga (upper left). Grazing by limpets (center) of various species can clear rocky substrates of *Mastocarpus* and other fleshy seaweeds while the crustose phase is more resistant to grazing.

That is to say, there is a great deal of variation among individuals and populations of this species, leading some to suggest that what we commonly refer to as a single species may instead be a complex of closely related species that are difficult to tell apart except at the molecular level.

And that's not all: the fleshy, bladed form of this species—known as the gametophyte phase—alternates with a crustose sporophyte phase that looks entirely different. Formerly known as *Petrocelis franciscanus*, and more commonly referred to as the tar spot alga, the crust was for many years thought to be an entirely different species from *Mastocarpus*. We now know that the two phases alternate, from blades to crusts and back again to blades, and the Latin name *Mastocarpus papillatus* is used for both phases.

## Black Pine

Typically forming dense mats on low rocky shores, black pine (*Neorhodomela larix*) is a red seaweed that occurs from the Bering Sea to Baja California, though it is rare toward the southern end of its range. The stiff, whorled branches of this species are loosely evocative of pine branches, albeit in miniature. Dark red in color, the seaweed typically reaches about four inches in length, with axes emerging from a small crustose holdfast that can persist for many years, even after the axes themselves have been torn away by waves. Black pine does well in sand-inundated habitats, tolerating sand scour and burial, and does just as well where sand is absent. Along with mussels, black pine can be a dominant space-holder on rocky shores, its dense mats harboring a range of small invertebrate and seaweed species, protecting them from thermal stress on warm days when the tide is out.

The red seaweed called black pine (*Neorhodomela larix*) creates dense mats in rocky areas with or without sand.

## Sea Lettuce

Sea lettuce (*Ulva* spp.) is common throughout California, easily recognized by its ruffled bright-green blades that can be long and broad in northern regions and somewhat shorter in southern regions. These blades are only two cells thick, their translucence an indicator of their fragile nature. Sea lettuce often is abundant in bays and estuaries, where a combination of quiet waters, sluggish circulation, copious sunshine, and nutrient pollution can lead to rapid growth and the accumulation of quantities so large they are referred to as green tides. Generally noxious but not locally harmful to humans in California, a green tide caused an unusual event in Europe in 2009 in which a horse and rider strode into a mass of rotting sea lettuce several feet thick, releasing sulfur dioxide gas. The horse collapsed and died, and the unconscious rider was dragged to safety.

It can be difficult to distinguish between different species of sea lettuce in the field. Some are cryptogenic (of uncertain origin), and nonnative species originating from distant regions may be among the sea lettuce found on California shores.

Sea lettuce (*Ulva* spp.) has an unmistakable bright-green color and is common in intertidal areas throughout California.

## Pink Volcano Barnacle

First described by Darwin, the pink volcano barnacle (*Tetraclita rubescens*) grows in low- and mid-intertidal areas where the surf is strong, where individuals can live up to fifteen years and reach two inches across. This species tends to be solitary—that is, not aggregating like acorn barnacles—but still can reach densities greater than 2,000 per square yard. Each barnacle is hermaphroditic and can fertilize another individual at a distance of up to four inches. Once fertilized, the eggs develop internally before being released into the plankton. For many years, this species was thought to reach its northern range limit around San Francisco, but in past decades the species has pushed its way north to about Cape Mendocino. Recent evidence suggests that recruitment at northern sites may be associated with pulses of warm water.

The pink volcano barnacle (*Tetraclita rubescens*; here decorated by a periwinkle, *Littorina* sp.) stands out against the granite substrate of the Monterey Peninsula. The calcareous shell of the barnacle may offer relatively cool substrate for heat-stressed periwinkles at low tide.

While most gooseneck barnacles (*Pollicipes polymerus*) in intertidal habitats are cloaked in shades of black, white, and gray, those living under overhangs or otherwise shaded from direct sunlight display the vibrant red color of hemoglobin in their blood. In sun-exposed individuals, the red color is obscured by a protective black pigment.

## Gooseneck Barnacle

Gooseneck barnacles, or simply goose barnacles (*Pollicipes polymerus*), differ from their more recognizable volcano-shaped cousins by the absence of the typical outer shell. Gooseneck barnacles instead attach to the substrate via a flexible stalk, or peduncle, that bears calcified plates at the top. Feeding appendages slip out from between these plates when the barnacle is immersed. Like other barnacles, gooseneck barnacles feed with their feet—highly modified though they are—by plucking small particles out of the plankton. But unlike more standard barnacles, they don't do the work of waving their feeding appendages around; instead, they rely on water motion to carry plankton to them, combing particles from the backwash of waves, as water flows back out to sea. This arrangement restricts gooseneck barnacles to wave-swept shores replete with a steady supply of planktonic food. And the feeding appendages can serve another handy purpose: the barnacles can use these feathery sieves to capture sperm when mates are not close by.

Gooseneck barnacles are gregarious, typically growing in clumps. Larvae tend to settle on the stalks of adults, which may improve the larvae's chances of survival and growth. Often growing alongside mussels and competing with them for space, gooseneck barnacles are preyed upon by sea stars and birds.

And how did these odd crustaceans get their common name? Supposedly, gooseneck barnacles bear a vague resemblance to the head and neck of a goose, or at least enough of a resemblance that it led to centuries of European mythology surrounding them. The story, it seems, went like this: not understanding the migratory patterns of geese in northern Europe, people were at a loss to explain how they hadn't ever seen baby geese, yet the birds continued to show up each year, fully grown. The European gooseneck barnacle was thought to be the fruit of a kind of barnacle tree that, when mature, would (somehow) turn into a grown bird. And cleverly, some Catholic clergy saw this as a way to allow eating meat on days when doing so was otherwise forbidden: because the goose hadn't been born in the usual way, it didn't count as meat.

California mussels (*Mytilus californianus*) and gooseneck barnacles (*Pollicipes polymerus*) often share space in mid-intertidal habitats.

## California Mussel

The California mussel (*Mytilus californianus*) lives on wave-swept rocky intertidal shores along the California coast—and, indeed, much of the West Coast from Alaska to Mexico. From the perspective of other organisms that live attached to bare rock, California mussels are a competitive dominant that forms dense aggregations, or beds, as larvae settle out of the plankton onto existing adults; juveniles can move around a fair bit, but adults are usually fairly well stuck in place within a bed. Mussels secrete a liquid protein molded by a groove on their foot into tough strings called byssal threads, gluing their shells to the rock and to each other. The crush of shells anchored by the strong byssus lets mussels outcompete most organisms for space. However, beds are a complex three-dimensional habitat: the interstices between neighboring mussel shells harbor a constellation of small invertebrates and algae, from tens

Spatial patterns in the intertidal can tell stories. Here, California mussels (*Mytilus californianus*) occupy fissures in fractured sedimentary rock, suggesting small-scale differences in settlement or survival.

to hundreds of species at any location, making mussel beds high in biological diversity, despite their overall appearance of uniformity. Thus, along the California coast mussels are recognized as a foundation species: one that is at once food, habitat, and ecosystem stabilizer, turning (in this case) bare rock into refuge for myriad other species.

California mussels carpet the rocks in some places but are spread more thinly in other areas. Their abundance is influenced by local food supply, predation, and competition and is further affected by factors such as water motion and substrate availability, creating mosaics that vary from location to location and from year to year.

Remove a patch of mussels and it may be slow in returning, depending on season and the other species present. Just noting whether mussels are present at a site can tip off an observer to other species that are likely present, including predators like the ochre sea star (see Species of Interest in chapter 4, Mendocino, Sonoma, and Marin), frequent cohabitants like the gooseneck barnacle (see above), or the many small invertebrates that dwell within the bed.

California mussels can experience sharply varying body temperatures over the course of a tidal cycle, heating rapidly at low tide on a sunny day and cooling just as quickly as the tide comes in. Rapid heating can cause heat stress, which one might expect to put intertidal mussels at risk in a warming world. However, research has shown that California mussels can acclimate to high temperatures after just one short exposure to heat stress and that the benefits can last up to three weeks, thereby offering helpful protection from fiercely hot conditions in the intertidal.

## Keyhole Limpets

Keyhole limpets belong to a family of gastropods (snails) that, despite being similar in size and shape to many "true" limpets, have a distinct evolutionary lineage. Shield- or cone-shaped shells are common in the fossil record and have evolved independently at least fifty-four times among gastropods over the course of evolutionary history, a good example of convergent evolution—that is, the evolution of structures that are similar despite having different evolutionary origins. Today, organisms

The volcano keyhole limpet (*Fissurella volcano*; upper photo) is common in California south of San Francisco; the rough keyhole limpet (*Diodora aspera*; lower photo) occurs from Alaska to Mexico and very often lives with a commensal scale worm (*Arctonoe vittata*) in its mantle cavity.

with superficially limpet-like shells occupy highly diverse habitats from freshwater streams to the very deep sea.

Keyhole limpets have a characteristic hole at the apex of their hat-shaped shells. The hole is the exit point for water and waste products from the animal's mantle cavity. The rough keyhole limpet (*Diodora aspera*) displays a couple of adaptations to life in rocky intertidal settings where sea star predators are common. Several sea star species and even a sea urchin species can trigger an escape response in this limpet, causing the animal to extend its soft mantle tissues up and over its shell, and down and around its foot, while at the same time pushing its siphon through the keyhole aperture. This defensive response seems to prevent the sea star from gripping the limpet with its tube feet, thereby deterring the predator. This escape behavior is aided by a commensal scale worm (*Arctonoe vittata*), a polychaete that lives in the gill groove of the limpet. The scale worm can reach lengths of nearly four inches, which is large relative to the size of the limpet. As the limpet crawls around searching for food, the scale worm preys on polychaete tube worms and other sessile species but does not prey on its host—instead, it defends its host from sea star predators by biting their tube feet until they retreat.

## Bat Star

The bat star (*Patiria miniata*) has a webbed shape that sets it apart from California's other sea stars. It is most often orange in color, although it can range from yellow to green to blue to mottled brown, and adults can grow to be several inches from the tip of one arm to the tip of another. Each of those tips ends in an eyespot that can detect light (but cannot resolve images), a valuable sensory addition to the chemosensors that dot their tube feet, allowing the star to taste its meals with its means of locomotion. Bat stars are generalist feeders, although they seem to prefer to eat tiny animals over seaweeds, and like other stars they evert their stomachs to feed, partially digesting their food outside their bodies before ingesting it.

Apart from the stubby shape of their arms, bat stars are also distinguished by their texture from other local sea stars. Bat stars lack the fuzzy

Stubby arms and a webbed shape distinguish bat stars (*Patiria miniata*) from California's other intertidal sea stars.

gills and tiny pincers (pedicellariae) that line the upward-facing surfaces of many sea stars, and thus appear scaly. On its downward-facing side, a single star can harbor up to twenty individuals of a commensal worm species (*Ophiodromus pugettensis*) in grooves that radiate away from its central mouth along the surface of each arm.

Bat stars in California have no close relatives in the region—their nearest relatives are species in South America and Asia—and have an unusual disjunct distribution along the West Coast, being common in California and British Columbia, but not in between.

## Tunicates and Sponges

Low down in the intertidal zone, under overhangs and tucked away in crevices, patches of bright color create living collages. Such colorful splashes are probably either sponges or tunicates, two radically different kinds of animals that have evolved similar lifestyles.

A purple encrusting sponge (*Haliclona* sp.) has telltale raised bumps (osculae) that distinguish sponges from colonial tunicates which are often found in the same habitats.

Sponges are familiar from the tropical examples that find their way into bathtubs, but local species tend to have low growth profiles more akin to a crust on low-intertidal rocks. Those crusts are slightly spongy to the touch and sport an irregular set of raised bumps (osculae), each bump having a single opening through which water exits the sponge as food is filtered out. Along West Coast shores, different species of sponges can be nearly any color of the rainbow, from red to pink to purple to yellow and white. Although they may not strike you as animals at all, they are indeed sessile animals in need of food, and in this they are incredibly efficient, filtering up to 99 percent of plankton (and all bacteria—notably, the water exiting a sponge is nearly sterile) in their target size range from the seawater passing through microscopic channels within their bodies. Despite having the most primitive body plans in the animal kingdom, they nevertheless sport bits of calcium carbonate or even glass in their tissues, firming up the body wall and deterring would-be predators.

Tunicates are at the opposite end of the animal tree of life, and despite all appearances, they are some of our closest relatives in the tidepools. Tunicates belong to the group of animals called chordates, which includes everything with a dorsal nerve cord, from fish to humans. Adult tunicates look nothing like vertebrates, but the giveaway is earlier in their development: tunicates have a larval stage that looks quite like a tadpole, but adults have lost many of the features that make the larvae recognizable as our relatives.

Different species of tunicate can look quite different from each other, but along West Coast shores, those that live in colonies are among the most conspicuous. Colonial tunicates frequently live alongside sponges, both taxa preferring low-intertidal habitats protected from the sun. Colonial tunicates feel a bit slippery to the touch, almost rubbery, with a translucent outer layer (the "tunic") made of cellulose, a material more often associated with plants than animals. Solitary tunicates, those that don't form colonies, are known as sea squirts, and although they look quite different from colonial species, they can be found in similar habitats.

In other regions of the world, larger forms of both tunicates and sponges are conspicuous. Impressive specimens of both groups can be found in tropical waters—for example, the giant barrel sponges of Caribbean reefs. One genus of tropical tunicates called *Pyrosoma* can form huge tube-shaped colonies that swim through the water column emitting a bluish light. These are large enough to show up on radar, and indeed, there is some evidence these tunicates were perceived as enemy torpedoes during the Gulf of Tonkin incident that led the US into the Vietnam War—a rare case of a marine invertebrate playing a role in international hostilities.

## Great Blue Heron

The great blue heron (*Ardea herodias*) was originally named by Linnaeus in the eighteenth century and the name has not changed since. It's been suggested that the species name *herodias* comes from medieval mythology, referring to a female spirit doomed to forever wander the skies, allowed repose only in treetops, and only at night—seemingly apt for a

Equally at home in freshwater and marine environments, great blue herons (*Ardea herodias*) typically forage alone and gather in colonies when nesting.

bird of graceful flight that nests in treetops, but perhaps less fitting for a bird most often observed standing stock-still in shallow water waiting to skewer hapless prey.

Great blue herons are common year-round along the California coast where small fish are abundant. And they are unmistakable: at up to four and a half feet in height, they are the tallest birds in the intertidal. Offshore, they can sometimes be seen standing atop floating mats of kelp. In California's coastal habitats, great blue herons eat an array of small fish species, including sculpins, top smelts, perch, flounders, and bass, and they can take invertebrates, too, including crabs, all of which they swallow whole (and sometimes choke on). Their sharp vision allows them to hunt day and night, using lightning-quick movements to lance their prey with their blade-like beak. Specialized feathers on their chest serve as a sort of bib, helping to keep their other feathers free of the fish slime that inevitably comes with their piscivorous diet.

## California Sea Lion

California sea lions (*Zalophus californianus*) are common along California's coast, intimidatingly large and graceful in the water, and often loud when on land. The sea lions inhabiting California waters belong to one of five distinct populations of the species, differing from their relatives to the north and south based in part on where they breed. The California Channel Islands are the primary breeding ground for the state's population, although some breeding may occur in Northern California. The sea lions use both rocky and sandy beaches as haul-outs and breeding

The California sea lion (*Zalophus californianus*) is easily distinguishable from other pinnipeds by the shape of its head and small external ears, among other features. Although typically found in marine waters, these sea lions are capable of living in freshwater for limited periods of time. One errant individual was observed nearly a hundred miles upstream from San Francisco Bay in Merced County, apparently resting on a country lane. Photo by Claire Fackler.

sites, and nonreproductive individuals sometimes haul out on docks and buoys and boats where the audible bark of the males contributes to the distinctive coastal soundscape. They are gregarious breeders, with multiple animals sharing a single raucous rookery in which breeding males aggressively defend territories that can contain more than ten females. Mothers care for pups until they wean.

California sea lions generally feed offshore in coastal areas and consume a range of prey species—squid, anchovies, mackerel, rockfish, and sardines—that are common in areas of coastal upwelling. Their prominent whiskers, or vibrissae, function somewhat like those of a cat and are a highly sensitive means of detecting movement in the water, thereby helping to detect prey. Being relatively large-bodied, the sea lions' only real predators are mammal-eating killer whales and large sharks, and—having been protected from human exploitation by the Marine Mammal Protection Act of 1972—their numbers have increased greatly in recent decades (see "Seals, Sea Lions, and People" in chapter 8, Long Beach to San Diego).

7

California's Channel Islands dominate the horizon from Santa Barbara.

# SANTA BARBARA TO LOS ANGELES

At Point Conception, California makes a sharp turn, both literally and figuratively. North of this point, temperature and other variables change relatively smoothly according to latitude, following the north-south-trending coastline. South of this point the shoreline makes an abrupt ninety-degree turn to the east before trending southeast, carving out the landward margin of the Southern California Bight. Offshore, California's eight Channel Islands form a loosely knit archipelago of varied geologic origins (five of which are designated a national park). South of Point Conception lie Santa Barbara, Ventura, and Los Angeles Counties. The coastal zone here enjoys warmer weather and calmer seas than places north of Point Conception.

This is Southern California, geographically and ecologically. Species that can't tolerate the colder waters to the north tend to disappear, while warmer-water species become relatively common. Tellingly, a local guide in Ventura said about a trip to the shore, "We're south of Point Conception! So I skip the boots and just go with flip-flops or bare feet."

Geologically, coastal Southern California is a dynamic mosaic dominated by the Transverse Ranges in the north and the Peninsular Ranges in the south. The land here is among the most rapidly deforming in North America, if not the world, and frequent earthquakes are just one indication of this constant physical change. But over most of ecological time—that is, for the species in place at the moment—we can treat Point Conception as a relatively stable boundary between northern and southern suites of

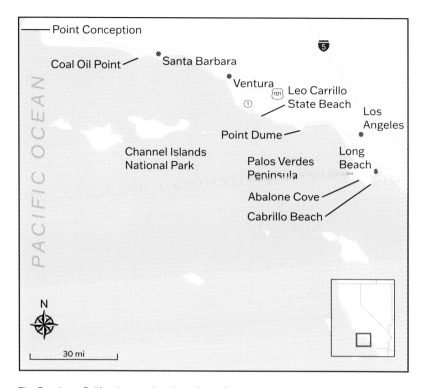

The Southern California coastline, from Point Conception to the Palos Verdes Peninsula.

populations or species. For species that span Point Conception, populations north and south of this break point are often genetically distinct, and other species are found only north or south of Point Conception.

Sea-surface currents explain much of the oceanographic transition from Northern to Southern California. The California Current flows relentlessly southward along the West Coast from southern British Columbia to Mexico, mostly hugging the shore. At Point Conception, the California Current continues its southbound trajectory even as the land turns sharply eastward, forcing the colder waters of the California Current offshore, to the west of the Channel Islands. The current splits near the US-Mexico border with one arm curling northward to form the Southern California Countercurrent, which, as the name suggests, flows from south to north. This countercurrent, along with the seasonally associated

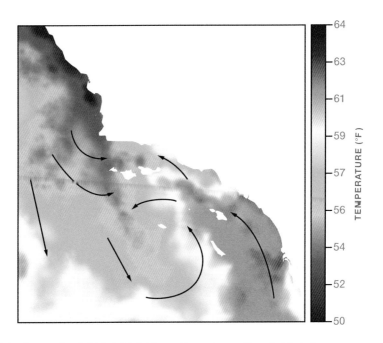

Point Conception (middle left) divides colder-water northern habitats from warmer-water habitats to the south. As the cold California Current moves southward, the Southern California Countercurrent brings warm water northward from Mexico, at the same time trapping waterborne larvae within the Southern California Bight.

Southern California Eddy, bathes the Southern California Bight in waters that are much warmer than those to the north and west.

The Southern California Bight is therefore distinct from coastal waters to the north: its dominant current is warmer and runs in the opposite direction, it is on average shallower, and it is calmer, with smaller wave heights than those of coastal waters to the north. The prevailing winds tend to be mild and onshore, out of the west.

The influence of wind-driven upwelling on primary production is more limited in Southern California compared with areas to the north; in summer, there is only minimal local upwelling here. Water temperature is fairly stable year-round, with average maximum and minimum temperatures hovering around 57–66 degrees Fahrenheit. (El Niño, however, can increase the temperature by up to 10 degrees Fahrenheit, a huge departure.) And perhaps equally important for local species, the circulation in the Southern California Bight can trap a given parcel of water for several months, so that larvae and juveniles are likely to be retained within the bight rather than being transported away from shore.

Southern California receives little rainfall and is a landscape heavily modified by twentieth-century human infrastructure. Accordingly, rivers deliver only minimal freshwater to the coastal zone, and natural sediment and nutrient transport to the coast is sharply curtailed. In fact, discharges from municipal wastewater treatment are three to four times greater than the volume of freshwater flow from rivers into the Southern California Bight—a striking comparison that reflects the equally mind-boggling wholesale reengineering of freshwater flows throughout the American Southwest.

In sum, nearly everything about coastal conditions in Southern California is different from Northern California: the wind, the weather, the currents, the rocks... all of the things that set the stage for ecological dramas to play out. And so it's a wonder that not all of the species change; indeed, a good many are consistent between northern and southern habitats.

## THE RESHAPED SOUTHERN CALIFORNIA COAST

Some of the Southern California coast—parts of northern Malibu (near Point Dume) and Camp Pendleton (see chapter 8's map) between Orange and San Diego Counties—looks much as it has for millennia, but the vast majority has been extensively reshaped by humans. Many waterways and shorelines have been armored, channeled, straightened, dredged, nourished, and fortified. Consequently, it takes a rich imagination to picture today's land-sea interface as it was even a hundred years ago.

Mission Bay in San Diego is the largest human-made marine park in the US. In the 1850s, the US Army Corps of Engineers began modifying the original marshland, called False Bay by Spanish explorers, to protect San Diego's Old Town from flooding. Between the 1940s and 1960s, efforts to develop a tourist attraction wholly reshaped the bay into an artifice of islands and shoreline, which required dredging 25 million cubic yards of sand and silt. The bay is widely used for boating, waterskiing, swimming, and other water sports, while the vestigial wetlands are restricted to a few protected fragments.

The fingerprints of wholesale human reengineering are nearly everywhere in Southern California, from Oxnard, Port Hueneme, and Point Mugu (just south of Ventura) to Los Angeles's Venice Beach and Marina Del Rey, to the massive ports at San Pedro (Cabrillo Beach is nearby) and Long Beach, to points farther south such as Newport Beach, Dana Point, and Oceanside. These are merely the most extreme examples of shoreline modification; more subtle alterations abound, too, from seawalls and breakwaters to large-scale beach nourishment, with tons of sand imported to maintain the region's iconic beaches.

Armoring helps keep shorelines in place, at least temporarily. Such artificial structures reduce coastal erosion locally—but may increase erosion elsewhere—and also replace existing nearshore habitats that would otherwise harbor a more diverse complement of species.

## Santa Barbara and Ventura

The young chaparral-clad Santa Ynez Mountains rise abruptly from the relatively narrow Santa Barbara coastal plain, influencing everything from local weather to patterns of human settlement. Flights of uplifted marine terraces mark former shorelines, with younger, higher terraces toward the west and older, lower terraces toward the east. Sand, not rock, dominates this stretch of coast, originating from rivers and streams as distant as the Santa Maria River and generally moving toward the south and east within littoral cells. Weather conditions are mild and Mediterranean, characterized by cool, dry summers, daytime sea breezes, and a marine layer that clings to the coast on summer mornings. In the lee of the northern Channel Islands, Santa Barbara experiences a combination of a relatively warm current and calm waters. Over ecological time, one effect of this relative serenity is exceptionally fine layering in the Santa Barbara Basin's submarine sediments, allowing geologists to reconstruct ancient climatic and oceanographic changes with nearly annual resolution over tens of thousands of years.

# OIL PRODUCTION IN CALIFORNIA WATERS

The Santa Barbara Basin is rich with oil and gas reserves trapped in folded, faulted, and fractured sedimentary rocks. Oil and other hydrocarbons ooze naturally from fissures in the seafloor and have done so for at least 500,000 years, releasing tens of tons of oil per day—more than enough to be noted by Captain James Cook's navigator, George Vancouver, in 1792. Onshore seeps are also present throughout Southern California, with the La Brea tar pits in Los Angeles being a visible example (*brea* is Spanish for "tar").

Natural oil slicks are accordingly common in the Santa Bar-

Sedimentary rocks slightly north of Coal Oil Point in Santa Barbara offer a visible indication of the unseen seep field that lies just offshore. The Coal Oil Point seep field is among the largest in the world. Located at depths of about 60 to 250 feet, these seeps have been active for 500,000 years or more. Oil and gas released from the seeps affect air and water quality in the vicinity, and weathered petroleum released from the seeps regularly washes ashore on local beaches in the form of tar balls.

bara Channel, and tar balls have been found on the beaches for millennia; the indigenous Chumash people used the tar-like substance to bind canoes and to seal vases and pitchers for holding water. Modern place-names, too—for example, Coal Oil Point on the campus of the University of California, Santa Barbara (UCSB)—are contemporary indications of the oil-rich geology here.

The obvious presence of oil here led to the development of offshore drilling in the late nineteenth century, when oil was brought to shore via the construction of piers extending into the ocean. In the 1950s, artificial islands in nearshore shallow waters extended industry's reach somewhat farther away from shore, and by the 1960s hulking rigs on metal stilts, still highly visible, were built some miles out in the channel. More than two dozen would eventually dot the coastline between Point Conception and Huntington Beach (south of Long Beach).

In 1969, a blowout on Union Oil's Platform A off the coast of Santa Barbara spilled 80,000–100,000 barrels of crude oil into the water, slicking the ocean's surface and tarring wildlife. At that time, it was the largest oil spill in US history, and its disastrous effects were widely televised, bringing images of environmental catastrophe for the first time into the living rooms of Americans across the country. The spill, credited with birthing the modern environmental movement, is responsible for launching the first environmental studies program in the country, at UCSB.

California has not issued any new oil leases since that 1969 spill, and the rigs are in various stages of decommissioning. But ecologically, the oil platforms have become artificial habitats supporting rich marine communities, the hard structures mimicking rocky reefs and giving organisms solid substrate on which to attach. The metal pilings thus sustain a diversity of fishes and other marine life, and the naturally escaped oil fuels a microbial food web in which the oil is consumed by specialized microbes that convert it into products such as hydrogen, which in turn are consumed by other microbes, and so on.

Offshore oil platforms signal the existence of rich seabed petroleum reserves.

Only a small fraction of the coastline here consists of rocky intertidal habitats, and those that do exist tend to be relatively soft multilayered sedimentary outcroppings and reefs with small crevices in which marine life finds purchase. Elsewhere, boulders seasonally peek out from the sand, anchoring anemones and other invertebrates that endure burial for some period of time. As everywhere in the marine environment, even the smallest bit of stable structure is a magnet for marine life, and even partially buried boulders awash in sand may harbor a suite of resident hermit crabs, olive shells, and other small motile invertebrates. Seaweeds seasonally cover some of the harder rocky substrates, including boulders, but tend to be less abundant on the softer sandstone formations where their attachment can be tenuous at best.

Sandy beaches dominate this stretch of coast. The food webs on these beaches are fed from outside sources that consist chiefly of seaweeds and seagrasses that have been tossed ashore. These food subsidies can be quite large, especially in the vicinity of offshore kelp beds, and they support tens of species of small invertebrates that collectively can reach abundances approaching 100,000 individuals per square yard of shoreline. Beach hoppers (several species of amphipods in the genus *Megalorchestia*) are especially common in these wrack communities, where they feed primarily on beach-cast kelps and show preferences for some kelp species over others.

The prevalence of intertidal sandy habitats in the Santa Barbara region tends to obscure the rich ecological communities that exist just offshore. Subtidal rocky reefs support beds of giant kelp (*Macrocystis pyrifera*), the largest seaweed on the planet and one that can grow in mass by about 3.5 percent per day in summer, a remarkable rate that would see a 150-pound person gaining over 5 pounds per day. Despite the rapid rate of growth and high level of biological productivity of giant kelp, its foremost ecological benefits appear to lie in the three-dimensional structure it creates. The shade from its dense canopy tends to exclude many understory seaweeds, favoring sessile invertebrates and their roving predators and ultimately increasing diversity and biomass within the kelp forest. Evidence of some of these subtidal species can be found cast ashore after

Giant kelp (*Macrocystis pyrifera*) modifies the nearshore environment, creating a three-dimensional structure that is used by a slew of species for shelter or food.

storms, when careful beachcombing can offer a tiny glimpse of this rich subtidal community.

As Santa Barbara County bleeds into Ventura County, the mountains fall away to the east and the road opens up on the wide floodplain of Ventura's Santa Clara River. Sand continues to dominate intertidal habitats here, challenging surfgrass, seaweeds, and invertebrates to colonize stable surfaces at unpredictable intervals. Such a mosaic of habitats (in space) and disturbances (in time) plainly influences the mix of species present. For example, both the sandcastle worm (*Phragmatopoma californica*) and the aggregating anemone (*Anthopleura elegantissima*) conspicuously occupy space at mid-intertidal sites where there is purchase to be had, and both species tolerate some sand. The worm typically outcompetes the anemone for space, but sandcastle worms can't readily survive being buried; the aggregating anemone, in contrast, can elongate its extensible body to feed above the level of the sand, outlasting its competitor in more dynamic habitats buried by ever-shifting sand.

This is merely one example of sand's influence on what lives where. More broadly, those opportunistic species that quickly colonize intermittently sand-scrubbed habitats tend to be short lived and produce many offspring—a live-fast-die-young demographic strategy. Examples include bladed and filamentous green seaweeds (such as *Ulva* spp., *Cladophora* spp., and *Chaetomorpha* spp.) and small invertebrates that remain glued in place as adults (barnacles such as *Tetraclita rubescens* and *Chthamalus dalli* and tube worms like *Phragmatopoma californica*). Meanwhile, larger, longer-lived motile species such as turban snails (*Tegula* spp.), abalone (*Haliotis* spp.; see Species of Interest in chapter 4, Mendocino, Sonoma, and Marin), and large owl limpets (*Lottia gigantea*) escape sand inundation by taking refuge at slightly higher elevations. Surfgrass (*Phyllospadix scouleri*; see Species of Interest in chapter 8, Long Beach to San Diego) has blades sufficiently long to escape inundation and often flourishes in sandy habitats.

The aggregating anemone moderates the upper intertidal's desiccating conditions, playing the role of facilitator. Clonal mats of anemones can reach densities of hundreds of individuals per square foot; these soft mats retain water and substantially cool their immediate surroundings, such that a host of other species that are more sensitive to light and heat can survive in their presence. The erect pink coralline alga *Corallina vancouveriensis* is a prominent example, drying and bleaching in the absence of aggregating anemones, particularly during Southern California's hot, dry Santa Ana winds.

Between Ventura and Malibu, the coast is thoroughly human engineered. Oxnard, just south of Ventura, encompasses a large agricultural and industrial plain that touches the Pacific at Oxnard Shores, Port Hueneme, and Point Mugu, themselves angular testaments to industrial activity. These are previews of the massive rearrangements of the coastal zone more common to points farther south, where human population densities are far higher.

## The Channel Islands

Relatively few visitors ever set foot on the Channel Islands or in the national park that encompasses five of them, yet walk any mainland coastal bluff on a clear day and island silhouettes loom on the horizon, seemingly just out of reach, commanding attention. The four northern islands—San Miguel, Santa Rosa, Santa Cruz, and Anacapa—are, geologically speaking, an extension of the Santa Monica Mountains of the mainland. These peaks arose from shear between the Pacific and North American tectonic plates, as coastal Southern California rotated into its current position. The islands comprised a single landmass (Santarosae) as recently as the last ice age, when sea level was as much as 360 feet below present, although the island remained disconnected from the mainland even then.

The four southern Channel Islands—San Clemente, San Nicholas, Santa Barbara, and Santa Catalina—are geologically and geographically distinct. These islands are more dispersed than their northern counterparts and belong generally to the coastal mountain range that runs north

California's Channel Islands tend to have steep cliffs interspersed with sandy coves.

to south through Southern California and Baja California. Only Santa Catalina has permanent residents to speak of, mostly concentrated in the resort town of Avalon.

Unlike much of mainland Southern California, most of the islands' shores are rocky, although the steep topography of the northern islands, and their isolation, results in few opportunities for tidepool exploration. However, the islands' position between the colder, more nutrient-rich California Current (to the north and west) and the warmer protected waters of the Southern California Bight (to the south and east) creates favorable conditions for a host of species. Giant kelp (*Macrocystis pyrifera*) supports a wide diversity of fish and large invertebrate species such as the spiny lobster (*Panulirus interruptus*) and the two-spot octopus, whose common name actually refers to two nearly indistinguishable species (*Octopus bimaculatus* and *O. bimaculoides*). Isolated stands of elk kelp (*Pelagophycus porra*) create a sparser canopy that only occasionally reaches the surface. Garibaldi (*Hypsypops rubicundus*), the state marine fish, are prominent here—this bright-orange damselfish (see Species of Interest) is not shy and can easily be spotted on a ferry ride from Los Angeles to Avalon Harbor.

The islands support a terrestrial fauna and flora that is less diverse than that of the coastal mainland, having evolved and persisted in isolation from its mainland counterparts. Examples include a gopher snake that behaves like a rattlesnake, an endemic oak, and a subspecies of the rare Torrey pine, as well as the spotted skunk and several bird species. The island fox (*Urocyon littoralis*) is perhaps the most notable endemic; with distinct subspecies on each of six channel islands, the fox evokes Charles Darwin's evolutionary insights that arose from the great naturalist's visits to the Galapagos Islands. During the most recent ice age, the Channel Islands even hosted pygmy mammoths (*Mammuthus exilis*), human-scale descendants of much-larger Columbian mammoths (*Mammuthus columbi*) that had crossed the Santa Barbara Channel by swimming from the mainland.

Notably, California's Channel Islands provide important clues to the early history of Native Americans in coastal California. Evidence suggests that Native Americans occupied the Channel Islands for about 13,000 years prior to the early nineteenth century. The archeological record here is among the best in California, being well preserved relative to mainland sites. Early evidence of marine voyaging, shellfish consumption (in the form of shell middens), and fishing all have been reported. Over time, cultural and environmental changes occurred, in some places allowing the development of dense human settlements, the construction of permanent houses, and the establishment of rich cultural traditions. The abundance of nearshore marine life, including shellfish (especially abalone), fish, and marine mammals, provided important subsistence resources. The long archaeological record of the Channel Islands helps bring to life an understanding of California's earliest coastal residents, not just here but at sites all along the California coast, offering a longer-term perspective on human occupation in the state.

## Leo Carrillo State Beach

The iconic shoreline of Los Angeles is dominated by wide, human-enhanced beaches of *Baywatch* fame, extending from Malibu to Redondo Beach. The City of Angels sits on a broad, sandy arc of coastline almost precisely the same distance across as Monterey Bay. This crescent of coast, Santa Monica Bay, is lined with beach communities and lies between two rocky headlands: Point Dume (Malibu) to the north and Palos Verdes to the south. Each features a rich intertidal flora and fauna despite the environmental degradation that is almost inescapable this close to a sprawling megalopolis like Los Angeles County, home to one-quarter of the residents of California.

Located along State Highway 1, Leo Carrillo State Beach offers easy access to a beach featuring a rocky point, famed sea caves, and a broad expanse of cobble habitat. An extensive field of boulders and small cobbles is exposed at low tide, with sandy shallow pools draining the rocks. Cobbles are adorned with strands of green seaweed and shaggy tufts of red turf algae that are a tangled mess of several different species.

Clumps of large California mussels (*Mytilus californianus*; see Species of Interest in chapter 6, Monterey, Big Sur, and the Central Coast) and

Leo Carrillo State Beach, pinched between the Santa Monica Mountains and the Pacific, includes both rocky and sandy habitats in northernmost Los Angeles County.

empty shells of the wavy turban snail (*Megastraea undosa*; see Species of Interest) lie partly buried in the sand along with beach-cast seaweeds. Many small hermit crabs inhabit shells of the purple olive snail (*Olivella biplicata*); olive snails burrow in sandy substrates using their large foot, which seems to overflow their bullet-shaped polished shell. Olive snails hide by day and are hunted by the far-larger moon snail (*Neverita lewisii*), which uses its radula to drill a hole in the olive snail's shell, providing a meal for the moon snail and, in the bargain, a steady supply of available housing for the hermit crab population. The sides of rocks are densely colonized by calcified snail tubes (see Palos Verdes Peninsula, below) and hinged shells of oysters; sheets of bryozoans (see Species of Interest) coat rock and algae alike, looking a bit like white or gray cornflakes plastered on surfaces. Mounds of the sandcastle worm (*Phragmatopoma californica*, a tube worm) stabilize the space between some rocks; in other places, the sides of a mound are exposed and eroded by wave action where rocks have shifted away, providing a view of the internal architecture of the worm-built reef.

The rocky point's sheer vertical face showcases zonation, a pattern that reveals essential ecological processes. An abrupt boundary demarcates the lower edge of the mussel bed: large California mussels and gooseneck barnacles (*Pollicipes polymerus*; see Species of Interest in chapter 6, Monterey, Big Sur, and the Central Coast) grow above the line; below persist tiny barnacles, anemones, and the sandcastle worm but no mussels. This sharp break in the mussel bed reflects a tension between physical and biological stress. Physical stress increases higher up on the rock, as heat and desiccation intensify with tidal height; growing too far from the water, a mussel can bake in its shell at low tide. Less immersion time also means less time to feed during high tide. Lower down, however, predation risk increases. Consumers like the ochre sea star (*Pisaster ochraceus*; see Species of Interest in chapter 4, Mendocino, Sonoma, and Marin) and sometimes the giant sea star (*Pisaster giganteus*; see Species of Interest in chapter 8, Long Beach to San Diego) lurk near the base of rocky outcrops during low tides, moving up to forage at the lower edge of the mussel bed on the rising tide.

More sea stars are tucked away in nooks along this rocky point than in most other places along the Los Angeles shoreline, particularly since a wasting disease decimated many populations in Southern California in 2013. At Leo Carrillo, large sea stars abound in hues of magenta, pale orange, and purple—a stable array of color morphs that remains something of an ecological mystery—clamped tightly to the rocks and even partly buried in sand as they wait for the tide to return. Large anemones (*Anthopleura* spp.) are interspersed on the rocks in shades of pale yellow, deep blue, and green, holding their ground against the crush of mussel shells.

Purple sea urchins occupy the low rock formations here, nestled into pits carved into the sides of rock walls. Using their pyramid-like five-sided tooth known as Aristotle's Lantern, urchins can easily chew through tubes of the sandcastle worm and then patiently grind down the very rock surface beneath. In fact, purple urchins actually eat rock, ingesting the rock as they chew beneath their bodies, excavating the perfectly sized pits they

**(left)** Ochre sea stars (*Pisaster ochraceus*), purple sea urchins (*Strongylocentrotus purpuratus*), and anemones share space in a tidepool at Leo Carrillo State Beach. **(right)** Sea caves at Leo Carrillo, as elsewhere, offer shade and cooler temperatures, sometimes mimicking conditions more often found lower in the intertidal zone.

then occupy. Urchins may contribute to the bioerosion of rocky shores through this slow-motion drilling operation, to a degree previously unappreciated. From the safety of their homes bored into rock, they present a wall of purple spines to any would-be predator that tries to dislodge them from their pits. Other urchins of the same species live more exposed lives, free to move about in the search for kelp, but at greater risk of predation—risk and reward, one of many trade-offs that can decide the fate of an individual when no single strategy consistently has the highest payoff.

Sea caves are a main attraction at Leo Carrillo. Pirates and hidden treasures are lacking, their places usurped by a diversity of marine species clinging to walls and ceilings: snails and chitons hang amid algae, barnacles cling, and even sea anemones droop here, surprisingly far from the water. These animals and algae live much higher on the shore than they would outside of the protection of cool, shaded caves.

## Palos Verdes Peninsula

The Palos Verdes Peninsula is a significant chunk of rock in a Southern California landscape that, in the popular imagination at least, is otherwise synonymous with sandy beaches. Despite—or perhaps in addition to—its sandy appeal, the landscape around the peninsula bears clear evidence of geologic activity: folding, faulting, sliding, and uplift. Indeed, thirteen distinct marine terraces have been identified here, formed as land that was then an island was lifted above sea level by tectonic forces. Palos Verdes, which offers the most substantial rocky intertidal habitat south of Point Conception, is a wonderland of rocky benches, pools, and boulders that California has designated as a pair of marine protected areas. Consequently, the state prohibits the taking of nearly every species here.

Abalone Cove, facing south from the larger peninsula, is one of several broad inlets accessible from a roadside parking lot and associated trails. Here, kelp grows along the rocks in the persistent wave surge, while farther out on the point are deeper pools, sometimes carpeted with purple and red sea urchins. In these pools, one can occasionally find soft corals like the golden gorgonian (*Muricea californica*) growing intertidally among cowries and urchins—an exceptional find in Southern California and a testament to the unusual vitality of Abalone Cove. This is one of the most likely sites in all of Southern California to find a two-spot octopus (*Octopus* spp.), usually hiding under a rock but sometimes out prowling in a tidepool in broad daylight. On occasion an octopus has even shot a tentacle out of the water here, to grab the finger of an explorer infiltrating the cephalopod's personal space a little too closely.

The pools here are excellent habitat for the black sea hare (*Aplysia vaccaria*), the world's largest slug; these plushy basketball-sized black mounds weigh up to thirty pounds and can rival the weight of a small child. The California sea hare (*A. californica*) is a close relative and also lives here. This sea slug is only somewhat smaller—sized more like a football than a basketball—and is a blotchy dark purple color; it can produce a robust mucus layer to avoid drying out if stranded by the low tide.

Both species of sea hares would appear to be the perfect lunch for a legion of marine predators, yet nothing seems to eat them. When disturbed, sea hares squirt concentrated purple ink and slime that gum up the antennae of lobsters, letting the slugs escape. Sea hares also store chemical defenses from their respective diets: the black sea hare eats brown algae, while the California sea hare prefers red algae. Each retains bad-tasting algal compounds in their skin and ink, helping to ward off any would-be consumer. Licking a sea hare will illustrate the effects of their foul flavor on a hungry mouth.

Sea hares can form hermaphroditic mating aggregations of more than a dozen individuals. Their egg strands often festoon the rocks, looking

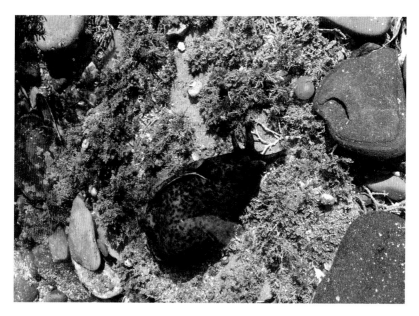

A dark-colored California sea hare (*Aplysia californica*; center) grazes in a tidepool among pale pink coralline algae, releasing defensive ink (darker pink color at left).

like pink or yellow glass noodles and containing hundreds of thousands of tiny embryos. The Nobel Prize in medicine was awarded in 2000 for studies using *Aplysia* to understand how nerve cells record experience as memory; thus, these memorable tidepool creatures are helping scientists understand how we remember things like an amazing outing to the tidepools.

Other fairly large molluscs prowl here as well, including the wavy turban snail (*Megastraea undosa*), an appealingly robust, long-lived herbivore that grows to five inches in diameter and whose shaggy brown outer surface hides a pearlescent inner shell (see Species of Interest). The tapered shell of the Kellet's whelk (*Kelletia kelletii*) can be nearly seven inches long. It is a scavenger and a predator, sensing dead or dying animals from some distance away, deploying its preposterously long feeding organ— a proboscis with a rasping radula—to bore into its meal. Like *Megastraea*, Kellet's whelk is a warm-water species ranging throughout Southern California and Baja California, but its range is expanding northward as the climate warms. The smooth brown kelp snail (*Norrisia norrisii*) is smaller (about two inches) and common here as well, given its close association with the large kelps that attach to the Palos Verdes Peninsula's rocky substrate.

The sandcastle worm (*Phragmatopoma californica*) builds large aggregations of tubes that appear as solid as the surrounding rocks, their individual tubes being hard to distinguish. These polychaete worms are easily overlooked but can transform the intertidal through their collective reef-building activities. Each worm is only half an inch long and cements sand grains together to make a tube around its body using a special underwater glue—a solid foam that becomes powerfully adhesive when extruded into the surrounding water. After growing for several weeks in the plankton, microscopic larvae return to shore and attach to preexisting worm tubes—another example of gregarious settlement—causing reefs to expand and fill space between rocks like foam insulation in a house. Worm reefs are no castles of sand, however; these formidable structures withstand the surge of water, crash of waves—and even being stood upon by careless visitors—buffering some of the local physical stress. Other small invertebrates take up residence in empty sand tubes, and because colonies can persist for years, diverse communities may form.

A second ecosystem engineer, easily confused with *Phragmatopoma* at a glance, is actually a snail that looks nothing like a snail: *Thylacodes squamigerus* (family Vermetidae; snails of this family are often referred to as a group, simply as "vermetid snails"). This snail is adapted to a sessile life, attached to rock by a modified shell. Their shells resemble calcified worm tubes and form tangled reefs rising from the base of rocks or creating a raised surface on rock walls. Vermetid tubes can carpet rocks, with over 650 tubes per square yard reported for *T. squamigerus* and an extraordinary 50,000 tubes per square yard reported for its northern relative *Petaloconchus montereyensis*. Thus, immobile animals can gradually transform their environment and provide shelter for myriad other species through the simple processes of gregarious settlement and tube-building. The snails extend a mucus net to catch suspended particles out of the water for food; imagine the millions of mucus webs covering a short stretch of rocky coast at high tide, a vast slime trap hoovering organic particles out of the sea to feed hidden snail reefs.

On the south side of Palos Verdes's Portuguese Point lie spectacular sea caves through which breaking waves send water surging. Broad rock platforms rise above the sea here, stretching out from the base of the cliffs and serving as resting spots for seals, surprisingly well camouflaged until they raise a lazy head to give a look, perhaps curious, perhaps annoyed to have their rest disturbed. In deeper tidepools, male garibaldi tend to their algal gardens, seemingly content to forego the nearby ocean for life in a figurative goldfish bowl.

What explains the great diversity at Palos Verdes, not far from the largest port on the West Coast and a serious footprint of industrial destruction? Most likely, it's a mix of several factors. First, the rock itself is a set of substantial boulders on a hard sedimentary reef providing lots of nooks and crannies for species to accumulate and hide in and eat one another; second, biological structures from sandcastle worms, vermetid snails, and kelp add to this structural diversity. Third, as the largest rocky habitat for many miles in either direction, the peninsula is probably a

Portuguese Point on the Palos Verdes Peninsula is part of a dynamic landscape that features folding, faulting, sliding, and uplift. The surrounding land has been sliding for about 250,000 years.

The calcareous tubes of vermetid snails form coils that can create massive reefs on Southern California's intertidal rock surfaces.

magnet drawing larvae of all kinds of rocky-intertidal species out of the plankton. And there is a bit of upwelling and primary production associated with this headland that, combined with ample sun and warmth, make for good growing conditions. In any event, it's a treat to find such a site so near the heart of LA.

Farther south along the Palos Verdes Peninsula, White's Point is easily accessible, and low tide reveals extensive rock platforms angling out into the receding sea. On the tops of platforms, mossy chitons (*Mopalia muscosa*) seem unafraid of exposure. Like all chitons, *Mopalia* has eight shell plates embedded in a muscular thick girdle, but whereas other large chitons tend to hide under rocks by day, *Mopalia* boldly stays in the open.

Ida's miter (*Atrimitra [Mitra] idae*), an unusual snail found here, exemplifies the bizarre twists and turns evolution can take in intertidal species. This snail's shell is jet black, pointed like a teardrop, and its body is bright white, from crawling foot to long extended siphon; the contrast makes *Atrimitra* the Oreo cookie of snails. Along rock ledges and in mussel beds, Ida's miter hunts one food only: peanut worms called sipunculans, animals so strange they were until recently given their own phylum but are now recognized as just highly unusual worms. Sipunculans rest with their bodies rolled up like socks in a drawer; they unfurl to feed, becoming long and thin until their mouth finally opens at the end of a sleeve-like extension, before the whole body rolls back in on itself. A curious thing to prize as your only meal ticket, but Ida's miter swallows peanut worms whole—maybe a good reason to stay rolled up as if in a drawer or nestled deep in a mussel bed.

## Cabrillo Beach

In San Pedro, at the Port of Los Angeles, the Cabrillo Marine Aquarium is an excellent child-friendly place to learn more about local ecosystems with a focus on community outreach and education. Wide sandy white beaches (Cabrillo Beach) stretch to the east and south. Just to the north, a small fenced-in wetland—the Salinas de San Pedro salt marsh—acts as nominal mitigation for all the wetlands lost in the construction of the LA Harbor. Here, blue herons stalk small fish trapped by receding water, and rays dig pits in the shallow stream that drains the mudflat, hunting for invertebrates; lined shore crabs scurry under the oyster-covered rocks that line the sides of this protected habitat.

A raised walkway curves along the base of the bluff to a series of inter-tidal platforms, ending at a remnant concrete wall extending perpen-dicular to shore into the sea. A field of cobble and small boulders gives way to tilted rock platforms cut through with channels moving north around the peninsula. These platforms lie beneath the locally famous Sunken City ruins remaining almost a century after a landslide dam-aged cliff-top homes. Above, the site has become somewhat legendary for a mix of street art, references in popular culture, and the allure of its inaccessibility—the ruins are fenced off due to persistent safety concerns given the still-unstable cliffs. Below, the tidepools are safe and accessible, though the surviving seawalls and rocks are everywhere draped with surfgrass and feather boa kelp (*Egregia menziesii*; see Species of Interest), so slippery underfoot.

The vertical sides of the seawalls are striped with bands of tufty, calci-fied red algae above snarled growths of vermetid snails in chalky white tubes; gaps in the wall are filled in by mounds of sandcastle worm tubes. This is a good site to look for some impressive intertidal hunters. Two-spot octopuses (*Octopus* spp.) dart slyly from one shadowy overhang to

Rock platforms ring the base of the San Pedro bluffs below Sunken City, near Los Angeles Harbor.

A northern kelp crab (*Pugettia producta*) tries to decide between waving its claws in an aggressive display or ducking below the surfgrass for protection.

another. Juvenile lobster are abundant beneath ledges, yellow-framed eyes peeking out amid a flurry of antennae. Winter king tides reveal dense aggregations of the northern kelp crab (*Pugettia producta*); these large red crabs are often barely concealed in a few inches of water under a thin layer of surfgrass—though they're not especially aggressive, their flexible long claws are not trivial. These crabs seasonally migrate in and out of offshore kelp beds and form mating aggregations to spawn (see Species of Interest in chapter 5, San Francisco to Santa Cruz).

Molluscan consumers are abundant here as well. Cone snails are one of the most species-rich groups of molluscs, with over 500 species occurring mostly in tropical waters; much sought after by shell collectors, cone snails are aggressive predators of other snails, worms, or fish, using a modified harpoon-like radula to inject paralytic neurotoxins into their prey. California has but one species, boasting a modest brown shell but with the classic cone shape; however, the "cookies-and-cream" speckled foot and exceptionally long siphon on a crawling California cone snail make it quite distinctive from other local snails. Cone snails regularly prowl the sandy pools here in search of prey, a very on-the-go habit for a snail.

Cowries are another highly diverse group of molluscs comprising hundreds of species—many of which have been used around the world

(above) A chestnut cowrie (*Neobernaya spadicea*) nestles amid branching coralline algae (top and bottom); note the cowrie's maroon spotted mantle tissue extending upward, polishing and partly covering the white and brown shell.

(right) The giant keyhole limpet (*Megathura crenulata*) is one of the largest keyhole limpets in the world. Copper compounds cause its blood to appear blue when oxygenated.

as jewelry and currency for centuries. There exists but one local species in Southern California, the chestnut cowrie (*Neobernaya [Cypraea] spadicea*), which is seasonally very common in channels and under ledges. Whereas cone shells are collected for their distinctive shape and speckled patterns that differentiate each species, cowries are prized for the polished sheen imparted to the egg-shaped shells by the live snail's mantle. This thin organ is often hidden inside the protective hard shell, which the mantle also produces by crystallizing calcium carbonate from seawater. In cowries, the mantle can also extend to cover the shell on either side like wing flaps, polishing the shell and making it hard for predators like sea stars to grab hold. The mantle of the chestnut cowrie is a lovely pink or purple with polka dots, often seen creeping up the sides of a resting snail like a reverse bed skirt. Cowries scrape encrusting invertebrates like sponges and sea squirts (ascidians) from the rock, occupying a similar niche as the giant keyhole limpet (*Megathura crenulata*), also common here (see Species of Interest in chapter 6, Monterey, Big Sur, and the Central Coast).

The pools and channels here are reliable places to find a range of sea slugs. In shallow, sandy areas between boulders at the southern end, look for both local sea hares: *Aplysia californica* with its red and purple colors, and the giant black *A. vaccaria*. Sea hares and nudibranchs are two different types of sea slugs, like cats and dogs are two kinds of pets (or two different kinds of mammals); "sea slugs" informally refers to the larger group of animals that traded the heavy protective shell of their snail ancestors for alternative lifestyles, often depending on a foul taste and warning colors for defense. In the surge channels, every crack and crevice is lined with colorful patches of invertebrates: sponges, ascidians, bryozoans, and hydroids, each species the food for a different nudibranch. The red nudibranchs *Aldisa sanguinea* and *Rostanga pulchra* are highly camouflaged when resting on the sponges they rely on for food, even mimicking the sponge's pores, but dot the intertidal with bright splashes of color when crawling about.

Other sponge eaters such as the San Diego dorid (*Dialula sandiegensis*), cream-colored with dark rings, glide along like pale ghosts. The spotted dorid (*Triopha maculata*) may be orange, red, or yellow, with

Two sea slugs below Sunken City are distinct yet similarly festive in their appearance: McDonald's dorid (*Limacia mcdonaldi*; top) and the Spanish shawl (*Flabellinopsis iodinea*; bottom).

conspicuous mouth tentacles used to feed on upright bryozoans. Individuals of McDonald's dorid (*Limacia mcdonaldi*) are even more striking, with orange tips on white tentacles radiating in all directions as they pluck the microscopic zooids from encrusting bryozoan colonies. Sea slugs are extremely fussy eaters: each species of slug usually eats one type of food, and often just one species of prey. While that can make finding food difficult, specialization allows over 300 species of sea slugs to coexist along the West Coast without much competition. Most nudibranchs are tiny compared to their giant sea hare cousins, so keen eyes are essential for visitors; peer along the edges of channels, or even on the surface of the water in a still tidepool at dawn or dusk, when sea slugs crawl upside down on the water's surface tension.

Notably absent here are the thick mussel beds and sea stars that are common elsewhere along the coast. But the deeper platforms resemble Swiss cheese, having been carved and pitted by purple sea urchins, tucked safely into holes they've eaten into the softer rock. Here the red sea urchins are less prone to hide, either too large to fit handily in the rock cracks or better protected by their longer spines from predators.

## SPECIES OF INTEREST

### Feather Boa Kelp

The feather boa kelp (*Egregia menziesii*) is unmistakable—it's the only intertidal seaweed that can be worn (however briefly) as fashionable

Feather boa kelp (*Egregia menziesii*) is one of the largest of the intertidal kelps, creating dense mats in wave-swept low areas.

neckwear. Its scientific name is apt too: *Egregia* comes from the Latin for "illustrious" or "extraordinary," and *menziesii* honors Archibald Menzies, a Scottish naturalist who accompanied the late nineteenth-century Vancouver expedition. The kelp's strap-like fronds arise from a substantial holdfast and are covered with diminutive blades and small floats. Fronds can reach lengths of several yards and at low tide splay across sand or rock in a somewhat messy fashion.

Beyond its striking appearance, this seaweed has remarkable mechanical properties. Growing in wave-swept environments, its tissues increase in strength with age and tend to be strongest at the base of the frond, close to the holdfast, and stronger in winter than in summer. And while the species is distributed all along the California coast, the shape of the seaweed and even the shape of its small blades can vary with water motion and latitude. All else being equal, the shape of *Egregia* hints at overall conditions at a site: individuals exposed to greater wave action have longer, narrower blades, while those in more protected habitats have shorter, wider blades.

## Sulfur Sponge

Spectacular examples of the sulfur sponge (*Aplysina fistularis*) grow as bulbous yellow masses beneath overhangs and along the edges of Southern California's rocky channels. Sponges feed by drawing in water, beating tiny hairs to generate currents within their body, filtering bacteria from the water for food, then pumping the water out again (see Species of Interest in chapter 6, Monterey, Big Sur, and the Central Coast). The excurrent pores (osculae) are visible on the sponge as openings on the volcano-like fingers that poke up from the animal's body. Spending long periods out of the water at low tide can cause this sulfurous yellow species to turn brown, signaling a change in metabolites.

Most sponges make fine needles (spicules) of silicate glass or calcium carbonate for internal support, but the sulfur sponge belongs to a family that uses only protein fibers as their skeleton. This sponge is soft whereas other species can be quite hard, despite our common association of sponges being squishy.

A large sulfur sponge (*Aplysina fistularis*, right) grows in a shaded spot eneath a rocky overhang. This yellow sponge has volcano-like osculae through which water exits the animal. Nearby, a smaller encrusting red sponge (left) takes advantage of the same shady spot.

The sulfur sponge releases mildly toxic compounds into the water exiting its pores to keep its surface clear of fouling organisms, which would clog the pores (like leaves filling a house's rain gutters) and starve the fouled sponge. The clean surface of the sulfur sponge is consequently free from algae, barnacles, and other common fouling organisms. Most sponges and ascidians produce chemicals that render the animal distasteful to fish and crabs and ward off spores and larvae that would otherwise colonize their surface.

## Wavy Turban Snail

The wavy turban snail (*Megastraea undosa*), common from the mid-California coast through Baja California, is the largest among marine gastropods in the intertidal. It gets its name from the wavy whorls that spin up its sturdy conical shell. It cruises tidepools and subtidal environments searching for kelps and coralline algae to feed on, avoiding predators like lobsters and sea stars by climbing into the kelp canopy where it can. Like many other animals with shells, the wavy turban snail provides a hard surface that other species, like barnacles, can secure themselves to.

A wavy turban snail (*Megastraea undosa*) creeps along in a tidepool in Southern California, its shell encrusted with gray bryozoan colonies.

When disturbed, most snails snugly shut themselves inside their shells using a kind of trapdoor (operculum), but the wavy turban snail displays a distinct curiosity, typically hanging its face out of its shell to have a look around when picked up.

### Feather Boa Limpet

In most intertidal spots, some searching can reveal the specialized feather boa limpet (*Discurria insessa*), which spends its life living on—you guessed it—the feather boa kelp (see above). This limpet has a beautiful highly peaked brown shell that affords camouflage on its host seaweed. Oval depressions along the seaweed's strap-like central stipe (rachis) are a clue that limpets are present. These empty home scars indicate spots where a limpet formerly resided, scraping away the algal tissue. The scars

The feather boa limpet (*Discurria insessa*) lives on the central stipe (rachis) of feather boa kelp (*Egregia menziesii*), the snail's glossy brown shell offering it camouflage. Empty home scars (elliptical depressions, center) previously occupied by limpets weaken the rachis and can result in breakage.

can wear right through the blade, causing it to be torn away, thereby illustrating one of the dangers of eating one's own home. This natural pruning can also prevent the frond from growing too long and being torn away by winter storms.

## Surfgrass Limpet

Like the feather boa limpet, the surfgrass limpet (*Tectura paleacea*) is adapted to live solely on blades of surfgrass (*Phyllospadix* spp.; see Species of Interest in chapter 8, Long Beach to San Diego). Unlike the round shells of most limpets, the surfgrass limpet's shell is roughly the size and shape of a penny sawed in half and stood on its flat edge: exactly wide enough to permit the limpet to crawl along the narrow blades of surfgrass, and tall enough to fit the body of the animal within its laterally compressed dimensions. The limpet grazes on surfgrass and incorporates a compound from the surfgrass into its shell, which may act as a chemical camouflage. Predatory sea stars generally ignore this species and instead attack other snail species, which escape by dropping off the surfgrass or using their mouthparts to fight back. This limpet is especially common at Shaw's Cove (see chapter 8's map) compared to most Southern California localities.

## Bryozoans

A patch of pale white on a large kelp blade, or a translucent glob with a hint of internal structure on rocks low in the intertidal, may catch the eye of the curious visitor. Or perhaps it's a feathery, almost algal-looking clump poised under rocky overhangs. In each case, the object of curiosity is likely a bryozoan, one of the tiny animals whose colonies take a wide variety of forms and that can be quite common along the shores of Southern California. These are interesting creatures in tiny packages, and because they are small they are generally recognized by the shapes of their colonies rather than by the individuals themselves.

Bryozoans have diversified into many species-specific growth forms and shapes, despite sharing the same underlying body plan. All are composed of microscopic individual units (zooids) produced as clones to form a colony. Zooids differentiate to hold down different jobs (feeding, defense, reproduction) within the colony but work together for their

Several colonies of encrusting white bryozoans (*Membranipora membranacea*; center, left, and bottom) grace a well-worn frond of feather boa kelp (*Egregia menziesii*).

mutual survival. Some species (such as *Membranipora membranacea*) encrust the flat blades of red and brown seaweeds, growing like white lace.

Other species (for example, *Bugula* and related genera that only experts can differentiate) grow in finely branching, erect brown clumps. Along the south face of rock channels where water surges at high tide, these arborescent (tree-like) bryozoans grow alongside tiny sponges that look like miniature white vases. These simple sponges are anchored to the rock by a stalked base, their skeletons made entirely of calcium carbonate (no glassy spicules like most sponges; see Species of Interest in Chapter 6, Monterey, Big Sur, and the Central Coast).

## Garibaldi

South of Monterey, the garibaldi (*Hypsypops rubicundus*) often enlivens rocky shores, its striking bright orange coloration standing out against the water's greens and blues. This is California's official state marine fish; for its distinctive color, it is (mis)named after the Italian general and nationalist Giuseppe Garibaldi, whose followers wore red (not orange) shirts.

Garibaldi (*Hypsypops rubicundus*) were formerly known as Catalina goldfish—and indeed, the individual pictured holds territory in the shallow waters of its former namesake, Santa Catalina Island.

Garibaldi are typically associated with the kelp forests of Southern California but can often be seen from piers or docks, and occasionally even in deep tidepools. They are the largest of all damselfish, a group of mostly tropical fishes that is perhaps better known from coral reefs than from the coast of California. Like many other damselfish, garibaldi are territorial, with males vigorously guarding their territory all year long, routinely driving off other fish and even humans who swim too close. The males are gardeners, actively cultivating patches of small red algae to create nests on which females deposit eggs. Once the eggs are deposited, the males fertilize them, then clean and guard them until they hatch, without help from the female. Juvenile garibaldi sport iridescent blue spots that are lost as the fish ages.

## Grunion

The grunion runs of Southern California are part routine phenomenon, part mirage. For a handful of nights in spring and summer, during the highest tides, the wide sandy beaches south of Point Conception are over-taken by thousands of slender iridescent fish breeding madly in the sand, only to disappear entirely a few hours later. These are grunion (*Leuresthes tenuis*), one of only a few fish species worldwide that emerge from the water to spawn. Females ride the shore break as high as possible onto the beach, digging tail first into the wet sand to lay eggs; males entwine them-selves around the females to fertilize the eggs and are back in the water within minutes. The eggs then hatch during the subsequent high tide two weeks later, washing as larvae into the sea. Individual grunion can spawn many times during a lifetime, and even during successive tides.

8

Sandstone bluffs back a beach of cobble and sand in northern San Diego County.

LONG BEACH
TO SAN DIEGO

The warm, sandy beaches of Orange County stretch south and east from Long Beach, marked by pervasive human development and only occasionally interrupted by accessible rocky intertidal habitat. Southern California's arid climate is evident in the few natural spaces that remain between suburbanized population centers. Streams deliver only small amounts of freshwater to the coastal zone here except during rare torrential rains, during which channelized rivers deliver large volumes of water to the shore over short spans of time. Absent such storms, persistent aridity is the norm, accompanied by relatively warm air and water temperatures, and these are key environmental differences that distinguish tidepool life in Northern versus Southern California.

Orange County ends and San Diego County begins at San Onofre, site of a coastal nuclear power plant, now decommissioned, and of the adjacent Cristianitos Fault, now dormant. The fault marks a horizontal break between a prominent younger band of sandstone (5 million years old) and the older underlying Monterey shale (15 million years old), neatly illustrating the land's relative motion north and south of the fault: the missing sandstone to the south was uplifted by tectonic activity and shaved off by the waves of a formerly higher sea.

The land of San Diego's sandstone mesas and canyons begins in earnest south of the sprawling US Marine Corps Base Camp Pendleton. Eroded canyons mainly run from east to west to the ocean, complicated by north-south faults, creating a distinctive coastal landscape. A series

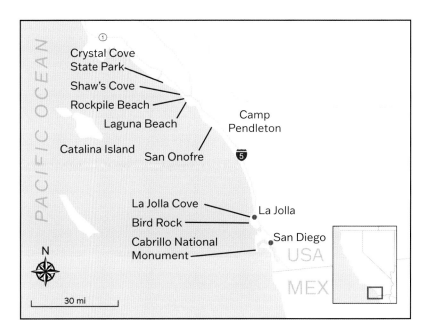

The Southern California coastline, from Long Beach to San Diego.

of shallow, brackish lagoons occupies the downstream end of creeks and rivers, their condition influenced by sedimentation and runoff, intermittent flooding, invasive species, and human interventions. Throughout the region, fragile coastal bluffs rapidly erode into the sea, a process as ancient as the continent itself.

The mesas here are wave-cut terraces and, as elsewhere in California, are the products of competing forces: as tectonic plates collided, the land rose, only to be shaved flat by breaking waves over the millennia. The central mesa on which much of San Diego's human infrastructure is built is about a million years old—quite young in terms of geological time, but respectably mature relative to many of Southern California's seaside landforms.

## PLACES TO EXPLORE

### Laguna Beach

The rocky intertidal of Laguna Beach hides its secrets well, beneath a heavy carpet of surfgrass (*Phyllospadix torreyi*) that covers tidepools like green spaghetti. Organisms that would typically hide under rocks or ledges to evade sun and predators can be more active by day or grow in places that otherwise would be inhospitable. Just as hair protects a person's scalp from sunburn, surfgrass protects sensitive species from sun and heat. Beneath the mat of surfgrass, a rainbow of encrusting sponges graces the tops and sides of rocks, places these colorful and vulnerable animals might not otherwise survive. Various animals climb onto the surfgrass and seaweed that cover tidepools in order to move about as the daylight fades, when juvenile kelpfish (*Gibbonsia elegans*) or snails like

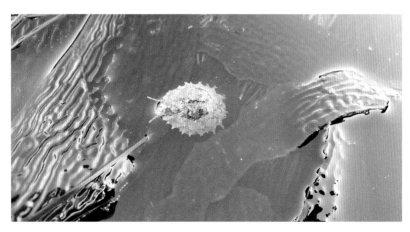

A juvenile spotted kelpfish (*Gibbonsia elegans*) crawls across surfgrass (top), while a trivia snail (*Pusula [Trivia] solandri*; bottom) meanders among kelp blades at low tide.

the spectacular trivia (*Pusula [Trivia] solandri*) cruise atop the tangled blades, half out of water but momentarily free from the snarl.

Surfgrass is a true angiosperm (flowering plant), not a seaweed (see "Algae and Seaweeds" in chapter 2, Living Between the Tides), and is a critical foundation species along the Southern California coast. It provides nursery habitat to animals like the spiny lobster at vulnerable stages in its life, while at the same time stabilizing sediment, modifying water flow, and acting as substrate for small seaweeds and invertebrates. Surfgrass is an important primary producer, fixing carbon through photosynthesis and helping to fuel nearshore food webs (see Species of Interest).

Most of the shoreline of Laguna Beach is protected in a series of marine reserves, which prohibit recreational and commercial removal of any marine resource. The intertidal life is especially rich as a result of this protection from the typical pressures coastal organisms face living near dense human populations.

Easy beach access at Shaw's Cove, south of Crystal Cove State Park, provides entry to extensive rocky intertidal areas. As elsewhere in Orange County, the coast here consists of sedimentary formations of different ages; much of the rock in the exposed seaside cliffs is visibly organized in folded layers that are eroding into the Pacific. The topmost of these layers

Shaw's Cove in Laguna Beach consists of extensive rocky shelves along the base of bluffs north of the beach.

is only about 120,000 years old, while the bottommost is about 25 million years old; the cliffs therefore show a cross section through a long period of time compared to the age of most of the California coastline.

Marine life exists even in the shallowest of pools here, far from the edge of the shore, and platforms of rock extend from the base of the bluffs. The edges of these platforms are lined with surfgrass (*Phyllospadix* spp.; see Species of Interest) and festooned with long strands of the feather boa kelp (*Egregia menziesii*; see Species of Interest in chapter 7, Santa Barbara to Los Angeles).

Shallow pools on rocky platforms reveal a reliable ecological association. The green alga sometimes referred to as sea emerald (*Chaetomorpha* sp.) grows in long strands, each a string of cells large enough to see with the naked eye; a sea lettuce (*Ulva intestinalis*; see Species of Interest in chapter 6, Monterey, Big Sur, and the Central Coast) also grows here in flat green tangles, but unlike *Chaetomorpha*, its cells are too small to be visible without a microscope. A black sea slug with white patches surrounding forlorn-looking eyes (*Aplysiopsis enteromorphae*) lives here and eats only *Chaetomorpha* and not *Ulva* (whose genus used to be *Enteromorpha*, which was the basis for the slug's species name—unfortunately, scientific names cannot be changed merely because they were ill considered when bestowed). Remarkably, the microscopic swimming larvae of *Aplysiopsis* spend a month in the plankton, then must get splashed into these pools at high tide, sniff out *Chaetomorpha*, and metamorphose into baby slugs without being washed out by ensuing waves; they can complete their life cycle and colonize pools in the crash of a wave this high on the shore.

Colonies of the sandcastle worm (*Phragmatopoma californica*) cover the sides of surge channels where intensified flow facilitates feeding. When submerged at high tide, the worms open to reveal purple tentacles encircling their mouths. They use these tentacles to capture food and select sand grains with which to reinforce and repair their tubes.

Deeper into the channels, a dense cover of anemones and mussels gives way to red seaweeds and invertebrates situated among clusters of the southern sea palm (*Eisenia arborea*; see Species of Interest). The kelp snail (*Norrisia norrisii*) often occurs alone or in clusters around the base

Reefs of the sandcastle worm (*Phragmatopoma californica*) dominate space beneath rock ledges at Shaw's Cove, Laguna Beach. Each cell pictured is about a quarter inch across and houses an individual worm.

of this large seaweed; the snail's smooth brown shell contrasts sharply with the deep orange-red of its foot, making this one of the most strikingly colorful animals in California's rocky intertidal realm.

Encrusting invertebrates line the rock walls of sandy channels, surviving the abrasive scour of waterborne sand. Patches of smooth-surfaced vivid red and orange sponges mingle with purple ascidians that resemble irregularly shaped blobs of clay, oddly molded and textured. In lower areas, anemones open to reveal their vibrant greens, yellows, and blues, in places extending up out of the sand on hidden pedal discs attached to buried rock below.

At points, the rocky platform rises higher to form a shelf dominated by expanses of mussels and turf algae. Here, abundant purple sea urchins (*Strongylocentrotus purpuratus*) nestle in depressions on the flat top of the ledge. Rarer, larger red urchins (*Mesocentrotus franciscanus*) are found in deeper, more protected channels, along with a few ochre stars (*Pisaster ochraceus*; see both in Species of Interest in chapter 4, Mendocino, Sonoma, and Marin) within foraging reach of their mussel prey. Kelp blades flail in the surging currents that flow through the deep channels dissecting this rocky point, a picturesque spot from which to observe marine life up close and from a lofty vantage point.

Rockpile Beach extends north from Bird Rock and Heisler Park as a sandy beach dotted with boulders; the northern nook of the cove is exposed at low tide to reveal extensive rocky ledges dissected by channels, overhangs, and deeper pools. An old oil pipeline offers a somewhat treacherous path through fields of surfgrass that render the route slick to navigate. Beneath the surfgrass, rocks are carpeted with dense cushions of fleshy red seaweeds and tufts of coralline algae, while tiny brittle stars climb on fern-like clumps of the red seaweed called sea comb (*Plocamium pacificum*) in the shade of the surfgrass canopy. Small stands of the southern sea palm line the sides of rocky ledges. Standing out against the maroon turf, strands of green algae (*Chaetomorpha spiralis*) decorate shallow pools like strings of unlit fairy lights, twisting into corkscrew helices.

Beneath ledges, sculpins flash bits of iridescent blue as they dart from hiding spots. Giant keyhole limpets (*Megathura crenulata*; see Species

Rockpile Beach in Laguna Beach boasts rocky shelves and intertidal pools covered by mats of surfgrass (*Phyllospadix torreyi*).

Schooling fish circle around an octopus slithering across a tidepool at Rockpile Beach.

of Interest in chapter 6, Monterey, Big Sur, and the Central Coast) often prowl out of water, protected from desiccation by their fleshy mantle. Sometimes an oily jet black, sometimes a striped beige reminiscent of 1970s decor, the mantle of these large snails may only partially cover the shell but pokes up through the circular "keyhole" center. Slow moving, these predators hunt for sessile invertebrates like sponges and ascidians to scrape from the rocks. Their stalked eyes and snouts are often on display, giving them ample personality.

A short distance to the north, rocky reefs emerge at low tide where overhanging rocks and deeper channels protect a different suite of animals from heat and sun. Rockpile Beach is the rare place in Southern California where an abalone might be spotted clinging to the underside of a ledge, yet some of the most common tidepool inhabitants are strikingly uncommon—for instance, anemones and purple sea urchins are rare. The sides of small caves are lined with colorful encrusting invertebrates that filter food from the water at high tide. White and purple colonial ascidians grow in patches the shape and texture of liver. Orange sponge covers a tangled medusa's wig of vermetid snail tubes at the base of many rocks, a colorful reef that seems to grow from the stone itself.

Colorful sponges in strange shapes grow under rock ledges at Rockpile Beach. The pale blue species (*Dysidea amblia*; upper left) produces noxious chemicals to ward off encroaching ascidians, tube worms, and bryozoans that carpet the rock.

Extraordinary examples of intertidal sponges are visible beneath overhangs during low king tides. Large white sponges the size of basketballs hang down from the roof of rock ledges and drip eerily into pools, their contoured surfaces seemingly brain-like. Shaded spots allow sponges to persist without competition from faster-growing seaweeds (which require sunlight), but few sponges can survive long periods out of water, so large individuals are found only on the lowest of tides (see Species of Interest in chapter 6, Monterey, Big Sur, and the Central Coast). Sky-blue mounds of the sponge *Dysidea* grow alongside deep red and orange encrusting sponges in crevices, hidden murals of life painting the rock. On large sponges, if you hold your hand over the visible holes (osculae) you'll feel a jet of water like air from a fan, such is the force of the sponge's feeding currents.

Distinctive strawberry-pink patches of an encrusting bryozoan (*Integripelta bilabiata*) hug rock surfaces in crevices or small pits (see Species of Interest in chapter 7, Santa Barbara to Los Angeles). Where there is pink encrusting bryozoan, there is often its predator: the nudibranch known as Hopkins rose (*Okenia [Hopkinsia] rosacea*). This ornate sea slug stands out against the darker strawberry color of its bryozoan food source as a splash of neon pink, boasting a crown of waving anemone-like projections on its back. Feathery branched gills on the slug's posterior end and two rhinophores (antennae) on the head are also often visible, along with pink ribbons of egg masses on nearby rocks. *Okenia* steals the bright pink pigment of its food, becoming one of the most glamorous (if elusive) species in the California intertidal.

## La Jolla Peninsula

La Jolla itself is a sandstone terrace cut into Soledad Mountain, uplifted by a curve in the local Rose Canyon Fault. Waves carve out caves, creating a diversity of habitats for marine life with small-scale gradients in sunlight, temperature, desiccation, and wave exposure. Here as elsewhere, caves often host more-diverse suites of species than exposed sites just steps away.

Fingers of sandstone carpeted in turf algae and surfgrass extend offshore near Children's Pool (see "Seals, Sea Lions, and People") in La Jolla.

Immediately offshore, the La Jolla submarine canyon is one of several that cross the continental shelf in the vicinity of San Diego. The canyon is relatively young—only about 1.2 million years old—and is still active, interrupting the alongshore flow of sand by trapping and transporting sand into its depths, in the process yielding the most prominent rocky habitat south of the Palos Verdes Peninsula some eighty-five miles to the north. Add to this a surface countercurrent that flows northward from Mexico, supplying warm water to nearshore habitats: San Diego's surface seawater can reach 70 degrees Fahrenheit, far warmer than elsewhere in California. The combination of warm water and solid, rocky habitat creates tidepool conditions that may more closely resemble conditions in parts of Baja California than those elsewhere on the West Coast.

The La Jolla Peninsula is an island of rock in a sea of Southern California sand. For intertidal species that require solid substrate for attachment, such habitats are like literal islands where adults of many species are confined to the habitat at hand, unable to colonize suitable space elsewhere by walking, crawling, or otherwise traversing solid ground. And so, somewhat like adult coconut palms on a remote tropical island, the dispersal strategy of these place-bound species often is to cast their propagules—in this case, spores, gametes, or larvae, rather than coconuts—into the sea and hope for the best. In Southern California, larval dispersal likely connects places like Malibu (Point Dume) and Palos Verdes to the Channel Islands and La Jolla, microscopic larvae serving as intrepid voyagers in search of distant territories, linking intertidal populations via gene flow.

La Jolla Cove, within the Matlahuayl Marine Protected Area, offers a chance to explore sea caves and nearshore rocky habitats. Garibaldi (*Hypsypops rubicundus*; see Species of Interest in chapter 7, Santa Barbara to Los Angeles) are common in La Jolla Cove, but the real attraction here may be the seals and sea lions lolling about onshore. Just to the south, a seawall partially encircles Children's Pool, a once-popular swimming hole now largely occupied by these pinnipeds; more often than not, the beach here is covered by snoozing harbor seals seemingly indifferent to the throng of visitors snapping photographs from above.

## SEALS, SEA LIONS, AND PEOPLE

It is called Children's Pool, and indeed its patron—philanthropist Ellen Browning Scripps, who together with her brother Edward Willis Scripps also was a founding sponsor of the nearby Scripps Institution of Oceanography—intended it to be a swimming area protected from the vigorous waves and currents common to the rocky La Jolla Peninsula. A seawall dating from 1932 curls around a quiet sandy nook, creating an inviting space for families . . . or, as it has turned out instead, for harbor seals (*Phoca vitulina*).

Since 1972, the US Marine Mammal Protection Act has prohibited hunting marine mammals—or really even closely interacting with them—without a special permit. The law has been a great success for marine mammal conservation, and most marine mammal populations on the West Coast have increased substantially as a result. But more marine mammals has meant more potential for conflict with beachgoers, as Children's Pool illustrates nicely.

Sometime in the early 1990s, a group of harbor seals began

Harbor seals (*Phoca vitulina*), appearing languid and uncontroversial, warm themselves on dry sand near the water's edge at La Jolla's Children's Pool.

using the beach as a haul-out, and as seal numbers increased, the area could accommodate fewer human visitors without putting the two species in direct conflict. By the end of the decade, the city closed the area to swimming because of poor water quality—there was too much seal poop in the water. As local (human) beach-access and marine-mammal advocates each grew more strident in their attempts to define the beach as a place for people or a place for seals, tempers flared, lawsuits were filed, statutes and ordinances were passed, rope barriers were erected and then taken down, and so on. Much-larger California sea lions (*Zalophus californianus*; see Species of Interest in chapter 6, Monterey, Big Sur, and the Central Coast) joined the haul-out at Children's Pool at some stage, spilling over from nearby coves. Despite the best (and worst) efforts of many people, the competition for waterfront access and land use continues here, as elsewhere along the coast. Ultimately, a group of hundreds of marine mammals is going to have its own logic, and as mammal populations continue to rebound after centuries of exploitation, conflicts like this are bound to continue.

As for the marine mammals themselves, seals and sea lions are distinct groups that are often confused in the popular imagination. Technically, they are distinguished by the presence or absence of external ears—sea lions have them, seals don't—but, more practically, if it looks like a sausage wallowing around awkwardly on land, it's a seal; if it's more coordinated, using its front flippers to move about, it's a sea lion. The harbor seal, the West Coast's most common marine mammal, lives in coastal regions throughout the northern hemisphere. Individual seals often are seen hauled out of the cold water on beaches or small islands, draped across boulders or sprawling on rocky benches; they can grow to six feet in length and weigh up to 370 pounds. In contrast, the more-intimidating California sea lions can be nearly eight feet long and weigh more than 700 pounds—and unlike seals, they have a loud bark that can be heard for miles around.

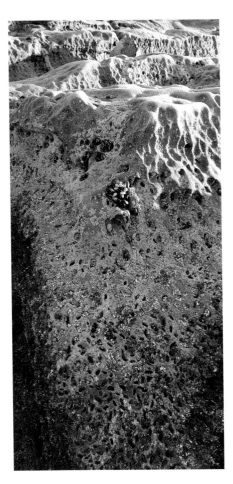

Soft sedimentary rocks have been sculpted by wind and waves and further carved by grazing molluscs.

To the south of Children's Pool, rocky shelves poke out along the shore below grassy bluffs. At South Casa Cove the sandstone is carved into intertidal platforms subsequently eroded into uneven ridges and troughs. The upper reaches are kept fastidiously clean by owl limpets (*Lottia gigantea*; see Species of Interest) except for a dusting of tiny barnacles (*Chthamalus dalli*) that can endure longer periods out of water than other barnacle species found lower down on the rocks. Below this, beds of mussels spill across rocky ridges interspersed with aggregating anemones (*Anthopleura elegantissima*) and red algal turf, the resilient denizens of the upper intertidal. Lower still, the soft rock appears pitted where chitons have scraped deep grooves, forming home scars in which they nestle. Shallow pools are dominated by finely branched calcified red algae, with solitary anemones extending tentacles in striking green and blue hues. Shore crabs dart for cover in this zone, and at dawn sea slugs take advantage of surface tension to crawl across the water's surface when the pools are still and dark.

In the lowest zone, long surge channels run parallel to shore, cutting through broad, flat platforms of rock; the sides of the channels are festooned with surfgrass and brown and red seaweeds, while fast-moving tidal surge supplies food to invertebrates that line the walls. Spiny lobsters frequent deeper, darker edges along these channels. A variety of sponges and ascidians attract a range of sea slugs and snail predators. Notably, the channels contain a hot-pink bryozoan (*Integripelta bilabiata*) and its nudibranch consumer, Hopkins rose (*Okenia rosacea*). With its tentacle-like cerata waving in the tidal slosh, the nudibranch stands

A Hopkins rose sea slug (*Okenia rosacea*) brightens a surge channel at South Casa Cove, La Jolla.

Sandstone is carved into channels and spires at Bird Rock in La Jolla.

out against a sandy channel bottom or among tangles of seaweed. For thirty years, individuals of Hopkins rose, which live only about one year, consistently have been found here, illustrating a central mystery of marine ecology: how does a short-lived species persist for long periods at one site while remaining patchy or ephemeral elsewhere? Ecologists keep very busy studying the local persistence of otherwise rare species to test their understanding of why things are found where they are, to unravel the factors at play.

At the southern edge of La Jolla, where Bird Rock Avenue ends at the sea, a prominent formation known as Bird Rock becomes a resting place for seabirds at high tide and a playground for children and spry adults at low tide. To the north, a narrow channel between twisted spires of rock leads to a sheltered cove. The rocky zone extends south, forming smaller rocky channels and platforms, cobble and boulder fields.

The shallow pools here are dominated by a diverse suite of red seaweeds. This is one of the relatively few sites along the Southern California mainland where the preferred algal foods of the California sea hare (*Aplysia californica*) occur: bright red pepper dulse (*Laurencia pacifica*) and sea comb (*Plocamium pacificum*) decorate pools favored by sea hares. The pigments from these seaweeds are metabolized and then released as purple ink when the animal is disturbed.

Several species of coralline algae cover the rocks in a shallow pool.

Rocks submerged in pools are partly or entirely covered by calcified red algae, which tend to be more pink than red. Some have knobs or bumps protruding from their surface, while others take on fine, feathery shapes. Being calcified, these algae can be difficult to distinguish from the rocks they coat except for their romantic color palette.

The many overhangs, caves, and flat rocks provide the opportunity to peer into dark corners and explore the intertidal life that prefers to remain hidden by day. Small two-spot octopuses (*Octopus* spp.) are abundant here, usually found lurking under rocks. Their common name comes from the two iridescent blue spots on either side of the head that could be mistaken for eyes, possibly tricking predators and, in combination with their color-changing abilities, deterring predation. The spiny lobster (*Panulirus interruptus*) is here, often aggregating in groups that hide in the many caves and crevices, sometimes given away by their exceptionally long antennae and the stark contrast of their dark eyes set against a field of yellow. The giant sea star (*Pisaster giganteus*; see Species of Interest) is also here, with its striking coloration of white spines rising up from patches grading from azure to cerulean blue, each re-creating the five-pointed symmetry of the animal itself and the colors of sky meeting sea. All three predators might well be hunting for the red abalone (*Haliotis rufescens*) that hides, clamped beneath rocks; all intertidal predators once feasted on these formerly abundant snails that are now a rare prize (see Species of Interest in chapter 4, Mendocino, Sonoma, and Marin).

From the moment a visitor steps into the intertidal at Bird Rock, tiny dots of bright orange are immediately apparent, as if someone had stuck bubblegum on rocks both in and out of the water. Closer inspection of a submerged blob reveals a striped edge and a crown of tentacles; these are the local color morph of the brooding sea anemone (*Epiactis prolifera*; see Species of Interest in chapter 5, San Francisco to Santa Cruz). In Los Angeles, this anemone usually occurs in shades of maroon and purple beneath rocks, but here orange individuals dominate and occupy even

A clique of spiny lobsters (*Panulirus interruptus*) nestles under a rocky overhang, given away in dark spaces by their bright yellow eyes.

A shallow tidepool at Bird Rock is crowded with red seaweeds, seagrass, and sponges.

high-intertidal pools and rocks; contrast this with lighter morphs that occur farther north in California.

The marine realm is rife with specialized associations that can reveal something about ecological relationships. For example, where the sulfur sponge occurs (see Species of Interest in chapter 7, Santa Barbara to Los Angeles), a splash of vivid neon yellow is often tucked along its edges: this is the yellow umbrella sea slug (*Tylodina fungina*), as fun to find as its name is to pronounce. Whereas most sea slugs are shell-less, some retain vestigial (even internal) shells that offer little protection from predators but serve as a reminder of their evolutionary origin from marine snails. The yellow umbrella slug feeds solely on the sulfur sponge and stores the sponge's defensive chemicals, relying for defense on camouflage and bad taste rather than a heavy shell; its remnant shell is like a thin brown "hat" that covers the slug, gradually reduced like many unused body parts (e.g., an ostrich's wings or the human appendix). This sea slug's vibrant yellow

The yellow umbrella sea slug (*Tylodina fungina*) bears a thin round shell, which is raised here, revealing a neon-yellow body camouflaged on its food source, a sponge.

The San Diego dorid (*Dialula sandiegensis*; center) sniffs for a favorite sponge using its sensory tentacles (rhinophores), shown here as grayish feelers at the slug's anterior end (middle right). No other sea slug has the telltale markings of this species—brownish ringed circles scattered across the pale dorsal surface.

egg ribbons are often tucked nearby, a lesson in the role of camouflage in the sea. Even toxic organisms often evolve to avoid detection as a first line of defense, with bad taste as a backup; best never to be seen at all, but better to be regurgitated than swallowed for good.

Encrusting invertebrates and algae line the channels at Bird Rock. Odd shapes and contrasting colors are splattered in seemingly haphazard ways that might be reminiscent of a painter's palette. The buffet of sponges and other invertebrates invites browsing by the giant keyhole limpet (*Megathura crenulata*; see Species of Interest in chapter 6, Monterey, Big Sur, and the Central Coast) and by the eponymous nudibranch, the San Diego dorid (*Dialula sandiegensis*).

South of the La Jolla Peninsula, sand reasserts its dominance in the intertidal landscape, in many areas enveloping bowling-ball-sized cobbles seemingly weathered out of the eroding cliffs. Human development has brought with it a layer of concrete that often reaches nearly to the water, broken here and there by public-access stairways to the surf. Cliffsides of prickly pear cactus (*Opuntia* spp.), coastal cholla (*Cylindropuntia prolifera*), and palms point out the juxtaposition between arid shore and the watery realm beyond.

Where there is hard substrate to be found, the combination of sunlight and nutrient-rich waters can yield a lot of primary production (algal growth), one indicator of which is the mounds of seaweed wrack that can be found washed up on San Diego's beaches after storms. These tangled masses of decaying seaweed and seagrass are the transient home of many species of beach hoppers and other small crustaceans, as well as kelp flies, beetles, and other insects. Shorebirds (plovers, sanderlings, godwits, and others), in turn, pick off these animals in large numbers, the wrack serving to connect marine and terrestrial species across several levels of the food chain.

## Cabrillo National Monument

The last chunk of intertidal rock north of the Mexican border is Cabrillo National Monument, straddling the narrow Point Loma peninsula that separates the Pacific from San Diego Bay. The west side of the peninsula is formed of sandstone, the older layers of which reportedly contain dinosaur fossils from the Late Cretaceous period.

Point Loma serves as the nautical entrance to San Diego Bay, now thoroughly engineered to accommodate all sorts of human activity. Military jets, helicopters, and ships come and go from the naval installations on the bay, and maritime traffic and infrastructure are dense throughout the bay, the concrete-laden built environment a jarring change from the more natural areas on the west-facing shores of Point Loma.

Cabrillo's sun-blasted sedimentary rock hosts diverse seaweeds and many limpets, chitons, and other small molluscs along its weathered ridges, with the most prominent invertebrate being the owl limpet

Tidepools at Point Loma's Cabrillo National Monument consist of boulders and sedimentary benches beneath a bluff-backed beach, much of which was deposited more than 70 million years ago, carried seaward from the foothills and mountains to the east. Despite their inhospitable appearance, these baked rocks and pools host several interesting and highly tolerant species.

(*Lottia gigantea*; see Species of Interest), ensconced in weathered hollows along the vertical surfaces. Surfgrass drapes across pools otherwise populated by red seaweeds; the lack of larger-bodied animals such as sea urchins and sea stars is likely due to large numbers of human visitors over the years.

Finally, hard by the international border in southern San Diego is the Tijuana River National Estuarine Research Reserve (NERR), a coastal wetland visited by over 340 species of birds and encompassing the tail end of a river that lies mainly in Mexico. The broader NERR system rings the US coastline, with more than two dozen saltwater sites dedicated to protecting and studying the roles of estuaries in the larger coastal ecosystems.

## Southern Sea Palm

The southern sea palm (*Eisenia arborea*) occupies the lower edges of surge channels and rocky benches in Southern California. A relative of the feather boa kelp (*Egregia menziesii*; see Species of Interest in chapter 7, Santa Barbara to Los Angeles) and giant kelp (*Macrocystis pyrifera*), the southern sea palm has a stout holdfast and single round woody stipe that flattens near the top where it branches in two. Each branch produces many blades that often are furrowed and nearly always have toothed edges. Individuals are perennial and can live for many years.

Southern sea palms (*Eisenia arborea*; foreground) crowd the mouth of a surge channel.

This kelp is notable for its spotty distribution along the coast. Occurring in British Columbia, but absent from Washington and Oregon, the species reappears in California around Monterey, then disappears again until south of Point Conception. Not only are the north-south populations disconnected but in Southern California shallow and deep populations of this kelp appear disconnected, some inhabiting low intertidal areas and others appearing only at depths of more than twenty feet where they can form dense canopies.

Southern sea palms growing in low intertidal areas are exposed to wave action that can be violent at times. They tolerate these conditions by being flexible enough to sway in the face of water motion, and this swaying is essential to their survival.

## Surfgrass

Surfgrass (*Phyllospadix* spp.) is a marine flowering plant related to eelgrass (*Zostera marina*; see Species of Interest in chapter 3, Far Northern California). Unlike eelgrass, which sends roots and runners through muddy, soft-sediment habitats, surfgrass uses compact roots to anchor itself directly to rocky substrate in the surf zone. Surfgrass can form large, dense beds that modify water flow, create protective habitat for invertebrates and seaweeds, and produce oxygen via photosynthesis—indeed,

A tangled mat of surfgrass leaves (*Phyllospadix* sp.) covers an encrusted boulder in a San Diego tidepool.

oxygen can sometimes be seen bubbling out of surfgrass beds on warm, sunny days.

Two species of surfgrass are common in Southern California. One species—*P. scouleri*—can be distinguished by its relatively broad, flat blades that can grow to be more than three feet long; diminutive flowers form near the base of the plant. In contrast, *P. torreyi* produces narrow, wiry, cylindrical leaves that can reach ten feet in length, with flowers growing on elongated stalks. Both species are perennial, persisting year over year.

## Jellyfish

At the risk of stating the obvious, jellyfish are neither fish nor jelly. They are instead animals that are nearly as different from a fish as it is possible to be, members of a group called cnidarians. The group consists of generally squishy animals that tend to be radially symmetrical and armed with tiny harpoon-like stinging cells. Anemones and corals are in the same group. One could think of jellies as carnivorous upside-down anemones, stinging tentacles trailing out below the animal's main body.

In fact, most jellyfish species alternate body forms with each generation: the familiar bell-shaped jelly (the medusa) gives rise to a stationary small form (the polyp) attached to the seafloor. Then, in an elegant series of steps, the polyp cuts off small buds (a process called strobilation) that eventually turn into independent tiny medusae.

The familiar medusa phase of most jellies is planktonic. They are active swimmers, by virtue of the muscular bell that contracts rhythmically to propel them upward, countering a tendency to sink. Many have primitive eyespots that can at minimum tell light from dark, and some may even process images, which is quite a trick in the absence of a central nervous system. And jellyfish have, as a group, been around at least 750 million years, a testament to the durability of their seemingly simple body plan and life-history strategy.

Along the California coast, jellies are commonly seen at the water's surface or stranded on beaches in summer, when they are most numerous. The most prevalent species in these waters include one with a harsh sting: the purple-striped sea nettle (*Chrysaora colorata*). And yes, the

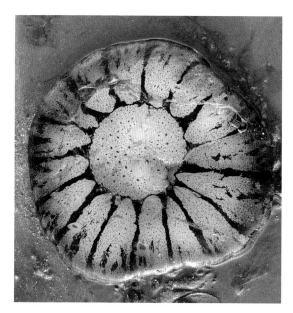

A stranded purple-striped sea nettle (*Chrysaora colorata*) is a common sight on California beaches. The bell of these jellies can reach two feet in diameter, though this specimen is half that size. Even stranded jellies can sting unsuspecting beach goers. Photo by Cricket Raspet.

tentacles can sting you even if you find the animal washed up dead on the beach. Graceful moon jellies (*Aurelia* spp.) are a complex of very difficult-to-distinguish species that can be common in less-exposed waters. Only distantly related to the sea nettle, these are recognizable by four horseshoe-shaped gonads visible through the translucent bell.

Finally, and also only distantly related to the true jellies, the by-the-wind sailor (*Velella velella*) illustrates connections between sea, sand, and air. This cerulean-blue and transparent species lives at the very interface between ocean and air, with gas-filled pockets in its body that help keep it there. Out of the water sticks a sail—a fin of tissue that catches the wind and propels the animal along, giving rise to its common name. It lives in oceans worldwide, a single cosmopolitan species. Perhaps most oddly, each individual is in fact a colony of many smaller individuals called hydroids. Given that they catch the wind but have no means of steering, by-the-wind sailors are driven onto beaches by the thousands under certain wind conditions. After a few days, beachgoers find their gelatinous discs crisped in the sun, stranded voyagers from the open seas delivering ocean-derived nutrients to the shore.

## Owl Limpet

Limpets are flattened snails whose shells lack the torsion (twisting) associated with coiled snail shells, but whose soft bodies do not: like other snails, a limpet is twisted so that its anus is not far from its mouth. The owl limpet (*Lottia gigantea*) is by far the largest of the West Coast's many limpet species, with a shell up to four inches long and accordingly large enough to serve as substrate on which barnacles, other limpets, and chitons attach and grow. Its common name derives from a supposedly owl-shaped pattern on the inner surface of its shell.

Owl limpets reflect a remarkable series of evolutionary and behavioral adaptations. Like many molluscs, they scrape microalgae from rocks using the "teeth" of a specialized organ called a radula. Impressively, the owl limpet's radular teeth are self-sharpening, their leading edges infused with iron. The limpets are strongly territorial, excavating indentations in the rock, called home scars, to which they return when exposed at low

An owl limpet (*Lottia gigantea*) adorned with barnacles occupies a home scar on a San Diego shore. Owl limpets are protandrous hermaphrodites (they start out as males and transition to females as they grow). Large individuals are therefore female and can measure more than three inches across—as this one does.

tide. Home scars both reduce water loss at low tide—allowing the animal to better seal itself off from the air—and offer an additional measure of security against wave forces that could otherwise pull the limpet from the rock, much as wind rushing over an airplane's wing generates lift.

Like other limpets, owl limpets have a single large foot that remains in contact with the rock and that they use to move about. However, they attach not by suction, but by a layer of mucus between foot and rock face. The resulting mucus trail traps algal spores, which grow and become food for the limpet. From their home scars, owl limpets then tend species-specific gardens of algae, defending their gardens against both animal intruders and weeds. This territoriality limits the limpets' population densities, because there are only so many available territories in each intertidal area. As the tide drops, the animals appear to navigate back to their home scars by recognizing their own individualized trails and also by using external cues.

Owl limpets stake out territories in wave-swept areas, often on vertical rock faces—particularly where the predatory black oystercatcher (*Haematopus bachmani*; see Species of Interest in chapter 4, Mendocino, Sonoma, and Marin) is present, vertical faces are safer—and can spend their twenty-year life spans in one spot. Over the course of this life span, individuals mature first into males, then become reproductive females as they grow larger and older. Consequently, the larger individuals are the only females in the population, and so are disproportionately important to the persistence of the species. Among the owl limpet's other predators are humans, who are particularly fond of eating the larger female individuals.

### Bean Clam

In some years, beachgoers in Southern California may find the sand at the water's edge dominated by millions of inch-long multicolored bean clams (*Donax gouldii*). In other years, the same beachgoers may find no such thing, the clams' populations having gone from boom to bust—from 20,000 clams per square yard to fewer than one clam in the same area, one year to the next. The boom years appear to be brought on by a beach

Bean clams (*Donax gouldii*) appear to outnumber sand grains in some years in Southern California (as here, in La Jolla).

winning the larval lottery—that is, many larvae arriving from elsewhere all at once—in combination with tides and sea-surface currents that transport those larvae at a time favorable for their growth. The bust years, by contrast, seem to be disease-driven, with most clams dying over the course of days or weeks.

These triangular-shaped clams make a living at the sand's surface, an unusual lifestyle that puts them squarely in the sights of avian predators, and one that also demands far more metabolic expenditure than the average clam's: after each wave, bean clams use their muscular foot to reorient themselves and dig back into the topmost layer of sand, however temporarily.

Many bean clams are substrate for bushy greenish-brown filaments that may at first glance resemble algae. These are instead colonies of a tiny hydrozoan (*Eucheilota bakeri*), a relative of jellyfish and corals. This particular species has both a hydroid phase in its life cycle—the colonial hydroid is the thing anchored to the bean clam—and a free-living, swimming medusa stage, akin to a tiny jellyfish. One wonders what becomes of the populations of these tiny animals when the bean-clam population crashes.

## Sand Crab

In ankle-deep water on sandy beaches, pebble-sized sand crabs (*Emerita analoga*, also known as mole crabs) may bounce off your feet with the incoming waves. As the water recedes, the mini football shaped crustaceans quickly bury themselves, back end first, to leave their stalked eyes and feathery antennae poking out of the sand to catch particulate food passing by. They create a conspicuous V shape in the sand as the wave recedes, giving away their exact location. Larger individuals can be more than an inch long, and many of the females can be seen carrying bright orange eggs on their underside. Found on nearly all sandy beaches along the California coast (indeed, all the way from Alaska through Baja California, and also in South America), these common residents are an important food source for larger fishes and shorebirds, including willets, godwits, curlews, and plovers.

Two sand crabs (*Emerita analoga*; also called mole crabs), left exposed, dig for cover as the water recedes. The crabs move backward as they burrow (here, burrowing toward the center of the photo), often leaving the antennae on their heads exposed.

A hermit crab (*Pagurus samuelis*) is at home in the shell of a black turban snail (*Tegula funebralis*).

## Hermit Crabs

A hermit crab is a crustacean masquerading as a mollusc. Lacking a calcified abdomen, these soft-bodied crabs can squeeze themselves into abandoned shells of their choosing: as opportunistic shell dwellers, hermit crabs find discarded snail shells (or sometimes clam or other shells) to carry on their backs as mobile homes, protecting their soft bodies from predation. And when they outgrow the shell that they have, they drop it and find another, bigger shell to inhabit. Watch hermit crabs long enough and you might witness them battling over a newly available shell that is just the right size. Abundant in most tidepools, hermit crabs can sometimes be identified by their quick movements: they move faster than most snails.

Some species of hermit crab have preferences for the shells of particular snail species: for instance, *Pagurus samuelis* tends to prefer the shells of the turban snails (*Tegula* spp.). Other species of hermit crab in this region favor the shells of dog whelks (*Nucella* spp.), dire whelks (*Lira-buccinum* spp.), and periwinkle snails (*Littorina* spp.). Hermit crabs make their living by feeding on seaweeds, microalgae, and detritus (dead organic matter). These small crabs are full of character, some shy, some bold.

## Giant Sea Star

While the ochre sea star (see Species of Interest in chapter 4, Mendocino, Sonoma, and Marin) stands out because of its bright orange or purple coloration, the giant sea star (*Pisaster giganteus*) distinguishes itself with bright blue or white dots on a brown background. The dots are actually blunt spines that span the dorsal (upper) side of the animal's entire body, giving rise to its other common name: the giant spined star. It is similar in size and shape to the ochre star but is generally found at lower elevations than its congener and is mainly subtidal north of Point Conception. Like

A giant sea star (*Pisaster giganteus*) clings to the underside of a rock in Cabrillo National Monument. Pictured here in close-up, the animal can grow to be more than a foot and a half in size from tip to tip.

other stars, it moves around using its tube feet to secure itself to rocks and other hard surfaces, searching for its next meal, which may include barnacles, bivalves, or various sea snails. Few animals eat the giant sea star, but otters and birds consume them occasionally.

## Brown Pelican

The unmistakable form of the brown pelican (*Pelecanus occidentalis*) graces the West Coast and many other western hemisphere coastlines as it dives for fish and glides over the waves on a wingspan that can top seven feet. Pelicans dive steeply into the water to feed, stunning small fish with their bodily impact before scooping them into their expandable throat pouches. This species experienced especially steep losses resulting from widespread application of the industrial pesticide DDT and was federally protected under the Endangered Species Act until 2009. Its recovery, a direct result of the 1972 ban on DDT, is a clear success story for environmental science and policy.

A brown pelican (*Pelecanus occidentalis*) perches on a rock above the sea near San Diego. The species nests in isolated colonies, but nonbreeding individuals can be found all along the California coast.

A snowy egret (*Egretta thula*) stalks prey among dense mats of seagrass.

## Snowy Egret

Snowy egrets (*Egretta thula*) frequent coastal estuaries and inland wetlands in San Diego County. Common in fall and winter, and with a growing number of nesting colonies in the San Diego area, these birds eat fish, crustaceans, and an assortment of other small animals, stalking their prey in shallow water. They tend to breed in mixed colonies—in San Diego, they may share breeding sites with herons and other egret species—choosing eucalyptus, pines, or even fig trees as sites for heronries. Formerly depleted due to hunting for their plumage, snowy egret and great egret populations both have benefited from the protections offered by the Migratory Bird Treaty Act.

# CODA

Over 800 miles of coastline separates the windblown dunes at the state's northern extreme from the warm tidepools of San Diego. This is equivalent to the distance, on the Atlantic coast, from New York to Florida, but the Pacific's narrow continental shelf and recent geological history conspire to generate a far greater diversity of habitats and conditions—and therefore opportunities for ecological specialization—between the tides in California than exists along the opposite coast.

California's tidepool life routinely captivates visitors drawn to the shore for aesthetic enjoyment, the pull of seemingly alien shapes and colors often inspiring hours of exploration. But for many, the possibility of uncovering explanations—the mechanisms responsible for patterns we observe—holds an even deeper appeal. A wholly different suite of species lives in the intertidal zone than exists only a few feet higher or lower in elevation. Hundreds of unique life forms compete for space and resources, predators and prey alike trapped in the very narrow band between high and low tides. Closely observing intertidal life helps us to appreciate the diverse palette of life histories that often go unnoticed during a visit to the shore and to begin to understand what lives where, and why.

# ACKNOWLEDGMENTS

With deep gratitude, we thank the many people who have helped bring this book to life. Many colleagues, students, and associates have shared their knowledge with us over the years and have profoundly shaped these pages; we hope they see a reflection of themselves in this work. We are especially grateful to our editor, Mike Baccam, and the entire team at University of Washington Press for their expert guidance, and to copyeditor Kris Fulsaas for her keen eye for detail. We thank graphic designer Zoe Vartanian for creating figures and thank the handful of colleagues who generously loaned key photographs. Comments from two anonymous reviewers were particularly helpful. Funding from the National Science Foundation made some work on this book possible.

# FURTHER READING

Abbot, Isabella A., and George J. Hollenberg. 1992. *Marine Algae of California*. Stanford, CA: Stanford University Press.

Alt, David D., and Donald W. Hyndman. 1975. *Roadside Geology of Northern California*. Missoula, MT: Mountain Press.

Behrens, David W., Karin Fletcher, Alicia Hermosillo, and Gregory C. Jensen. 2022. *Nudibranchs and Sea Slugs of the Eastern Pacific*. Bremerton, WA: MolaMarine Publications.

California Coastal Commission. 2014. *California Coastal Access Guide*. 7th ed. Berkeley: University of California Press.

Carlton, J. T. 2007. *The Light and Smith Manual: Intertidal Invertebrates from Central California to Oregon*. Rev. ed. Berkeley: University of California Press.

Carson, Rachel L. 1951. *The Sea Around Us*. Oxford, UK: Oxford University Press.

Dale, Nancy. 1986. *Flowering Plants: The Santa Monica Mountains, Coastal and Chaparral Regions of Southern California*. Santa Barbara, CA: Capra Press.

Gaines, Steven D., and Mark W. Denny. 2007. *Encyclopedia of Tidepools and Rocky Shores*. Berkeley: University of California Press.

Garrison, Tom S. 2012. *Oceanography: An Invitation to Marine Science*. Belmont, CA: Cengage Learning.

Griggs, Gary B. 2010. *Introduction to California's Beaches and Coast*. Berkeley: University of California Press.

Iselin, Josie. 2019. *The Curious World of Seaweed*. Berkeley, CA: Heyday.

Kaufmann, Obi. 2022. *The Coasts of California*. Berkeley, CA: Heyday.

Kozloff, Eugene N. 2000. *Seashore Life of the Northern Pacific Coast: An Illustrated Guide to Northern California, Oregon, Washington, and British Columbia*. Seattle: University of Washington Press.

Love, M. S., and J. K. Passarelli, eds. 2020. *Miller and Lea's Guide to the Coastal Marine Fishes of California*. 2nd ed. Publication 3556. Davis: University of California Agricultural and Natural Resources.

Morris, Robert Harding, Donald Putnam Abbott, and Eugene Clinton Haderlie. 1980. *Intertidal Invertebrates of California*. Stanford, CA: Stanford University Press.

Palumbi, Stephen R., and Carolyn Sotka. 2012. *The Death and Life of Monterey Bay*. Washington, DC: Island Press.

Ricketts, Edward F., Jack Calvin, Joel W. Hedgpeth, and David W. Phillips. 1985. *Between Pacific Tides*. Stanford, CA: Stanford University Press.

Webb, Sophie, Joe Mortenson, and Sarah G. Allen. 2011. *Field Guide to Marine Mammals of the Pacific Coast*. Berkeley: University of California Press.

Wertheim, Anne. 2002. *The Intertidal Wilderness: A Photographic Journey through Pacific Coast Tidepools*. Berkeley: University of California Press.

# INDEX

Page references in *italics* indicate photos or other illustrations.

chestnut cowrie, *239*, 240

Children's Pool, 261, 262, 263–64, *263*

chitons, 35, 185, 231, 236, 266, 272; black katy, 128, *128*; environmental adaptations, 50, 94; feeding behavior and preferences, 62–63, 88, 101, *152*; gumboot chiton, 99, *100*, 101; lined chiton, *152*; mossy chiton, *114*, 236; predators, 128, 139

cholla, coastal, 272

*Chondracanthus exasperatus*, 112, *112*

*Chrysaora colorata*, 276–77, *277*

*Chthamalus dalli*, 110, *164*, 224, 265

*Chthamalus fissus*, 106

*Citharichthys sordidus*, 83

*Cladophora*, 224

clams, 35, 56, 108, 122; bean clam, 279–81, *280*

clapper rail, 121

climate and weather: California's Mediterranean climate, 142, 219; El Niño and the Pacific Decadal Oscillation, 10, 32–33, 216–17; intertidal microclimates, 44; marine fog and its influence, 27, 31, 35, 81, 82, 109, 142, *176*, 177; marine influence on the West Coast, 30–31, 35; past glacial cycles, 20, 21, 22; storm impacts, 50–51. *See also* temperatures; *specific locations*

climate change: marine pathogens and, 70; range shifts and, 106, 134, 233

*Clupea pallasii*, 83, 121

cnidarians, 134. *See also* jellyfish; sea anemones

$CO_2$, 45, 48, 51

Coal Oil Point, 220, *220*; map, *215*

coastal access rights, 14–16, 148

coastal ecosystem influences, 36–70; energy types and levels, 46, 48–50; exposure and disturbance, 49–51, 66, 93–94; geological context, 20–22, 23–27; interspecies dynamics

overview, 55–56, 58–69; land-sea linkages, 64–65, 272; nutrients, oxygen, and carbon dioxide, 51–53; salinity variations, 45–46, 91, 94, 110, 143, 147; sunlight and photosynthesis, 45, 51, 52–53; temperature variation and microclimates, 43–44; tidal cycles and their impacts, 39–41, 43; winds and their impacts, 53–55. *See also* climate and weather; coastal geology and geomorphology; interspecies associations and dynamics; ocean conditions and processes; *specific regions, life forms, and habitat types*

coastal geology and geomorphology, 5; biological diversity and, 27, 35, 85–86; biological productivity and, 272; fossil remains, 89, *89*, 108; larval dispersal/settlement and, 87, 234, 236, 262; marine terraces, 108, 109–10, 253; Pacific vs. Atlantic coast, 24, *26*, 27, 35, 287; past glacial cycles and, 20, 21, 22; sea caves, *230*, 231, 261, 262; sea stacks, 25, *25*; shoreline modification in Southern California, 217–18, 224; submarine canyons, 172, 262; tectonic processes and coastal characteristics, 23–27, *26*, 27, 108, 118–19, 142; time scales, 23; vulcanism and volcanic rock, 24, *26*, 82, 189–90. *See also* beach characteristics; rocky habitats; sandy habitats; tectonic processes; *specific regions, locations, and rock types*

coastal land-use management, 15–16

coastal upwelling, 27, 29–30, *29*, 31, 53; ecosystem impacts, 30, 35, 106–8, 109, 123, 180; in Southern California, 216, 236

coast redwood, 79, 80–81, *80*, 82, 89, 156, 183

human impacts, 22, 149; estuarine habitat losses, 91; fisheries declines, 131, 149, 177, 187; logging and the timber industry, 76, 81, 109; marine pathogens and, 69–70; oil drilling and spills, 220–21; San Francisco Bay, 145; in Southern California, 217–18, 220–21, 224, 227, 252–53, 272; water quality impacts, 51–52, 198, 220–21. *See also* climate change; commercial fishing; conservation and stewardship; invasive species

Humboldt Bay, 76, 78, 83, 90, 103, 109; map, 77

Humboldt Bay National Wildlife Refuge, 90

Humboldt Lagoons, 76, 82–84, 83; map, 77

Humboldt squid, 174

humpback whale, 173–74

hydrogen sulfide, 48, 66

hydrozoans, *Eucheilota bakeri*, 280–81

*Hypsypops rubicundus*, 226, 248–49, 248, 262

ice ages. *See* glacial cycles

ice plant, 84, 122, 179

Ida's miter, 236

*Idotea*, 192–93, *192*

Indigenous cultures and resource use. *See* Native cultures and resource use

insects, 64, 148, 272

*Integripelta bilabiata*, 260, 266

interspecies associations and dynamics, 55–56, 58; competition overview, 58–59; experimental methods for explaining, 8–10; facilitation overview, 66–67; parasitism and pathogens, 67, 69–70; predation overview, 60–64. *See also* competition; facilitation; predation; spatial distribution patterns; *specific life forms*

intertidal zone: fishes in, 63, 64; intertidal zonation, 68–69, *68*, 147–48, 229; moisture variations in, 43, 53; tidal and temperature variation in, 39, 43–44. *See also* coastal ecosystem influences; habitat types and variations

invasive species, 84, 122, *146*, 147, 161, 179

iridescent horn-of-plenty, 94–95, *95*

island fox, 22, 226

isopods, 103, 192–93, *192*

Japanese mudsnail, 122, *146*, 147

jellyfish, 276–77, *277*

Jenner, *116*, 117

Jug Handle State Natural Reserve, 110

*Katharina tunicata*, 128, *128*

*Kelletia kelletii*, 233

Kellet's whelk, 233

kelp crabs, *151*, 165–66, *165*, 238, *238*

kelpfish, spotted, 254–55, *254*

kelp forests, 10, 98, 174–76, *175*, 179

kelps, 35, 60, 174, 192; bull kelp, 10, 97–98, *97*, 110; chain-bladder kelp, *192*; dense-clumped kelp, 124–25, *124*; elk kelp, 226; feather boa kelp, 50, *113*, 237, 242–43, *242*, 245–46, *246*, 247, 256; giant kelp, 57, 72, 97, 174–76, *175*, 188, 222–23, *223*, 226; *Laminaria setchellii*, 72, 192; pompom kelp, *85*; sea cabbage, *87*; urchin predation, 10, 135, 179. *See also* sea palms

kelp snail, smooth brown, 233, 256–57

keyhole limpets, 203–5, *204*, *239*, 240, 271

killer whale (orca), 211

kinetic energy, 46, 48–49. *See also* waves and wave energy

La Brea tar pits, 219

mossy chiton, *114*, 236

MPAs (marine protected areas), 10, 148–49, 262

mud and muddy habitats, 48–49, 66, 120, 147. *See also* estuaries and estuarine habitats; *specific locations*

mudstones, *157, 158*

*Muricea californica*, 231

murre, common, 115

mussels, 6; Asian date mussel, 122; environmental adaptations, 50, 55; feeding behavior, 61, 185; spatial patterns and interspecies dynamics, 51, 66, 68. *See also* California mussel

mutualisms. *See* facilitation

*Mytilus californianus. See* California mussel; mussels

names and naming practices, 70–73

National Estuarine Research Reserves (NERRs), 273

Native cultures and resource use: marine/coastal foods, 128, 130, 165, 187, 227; in Southern California, 220, 226–27

Natural Bridges State Park, 158

*Naturalist's Rambles on the Devonshire Coast, A* (Gosse), 16

*Neobernaya [Cypraea] spadicea*, 239, 240

*Neorhodomela larix*, 197, *197*

*Neotrypaea [Callianassa] californiensis*, 120

*Nereocystis luetkeana*, 10, 97–98, *97*, 110, 124

NERRs (National Estuarine Research Reserves), 273

*Neverita lewisii*, 120, 228

nitrogen, 51, 174

nomenclature, 70–73

nonnative biota: eucalyptus in California, 181–82; invasives, 84, 122, *146*, 147, 161, 179

*Norrisia norrisii*, 233, 256–57

North American plate, *26*, 82, 113, 118, 121, 142

North Coast. *See* far northern California; Mendocino, Sonoma, and Marin; *specific locations*

northern clingfish, 94, *102*, 103

northern elephant seal, 94, 144, *144*, 154–56, 189

northern kelp crab, 165–66, *165*, 238, *238*

northern sea otter, 188

*Nucella*, 283

nuclear power plant sites and proposals, 113, 252

nudibranchs, 132, 134, 163, 240–42; Hilton's nudibranch, 132–34, *133*; Hopkins rose, 260–61, 266–67, *266*; San Diego dorid, 240, 271, *271*; sea lemon, *88*; Spanish shawl, *241*. *See also* sea slugs

*Numenius americanus, 146*

nutrient cycling, 51–52, 64–65, *65*, 217. *See also* coastal upwelling

nutrient pollution, 51–52, 198

*Nuttallia obscurata*, 122

ocean conditions and processes, 27–33; the coastal upwelling process, 29–30; the Coriolis effect, 27–29, *28*; El Niño, 10, 20, 32–33, 174, 216–17; larval ecology and transport, 30, 57, 85, 106–8, 117, 217; ocean temperatures, 10, 27, 31, 33, 174, 215–17, *216*, 262; the presence of near-shore deep waters, 173–74; salinity levels and variations, 45–46, 91, 94, 110, 143, 147; sea level changes, 20, 21, 22, 76, 78, 108, 145; Southern vs. Northern California, 215–17, *216*; tidal oscillations and cycles, 39–41, 43; tsunamis, 78–79; understanding responses to changes, 9–10; waves

*Phyllospadix. See* surfgrass
phytoplankton, 70, 106-7, 122, 185
*Picea sitchensis*, 106
pickleweeds, 161-62, *162*
Piedras Blancas, 188-89
Pigeon Point, 153-54, *154*; map, *143*
Pillar Point, 153
pine, Bishop, 110, 123
pink abalone, 131
pink volcano barnacle, 106, 199, *199*, 224
pinnipeds, 16-17. *See also* California sea lion; seals
pinto abalone, 131
*Pinus muricata*, 110, 123
pipefish, 83
*Pisaster giganteus*, 229, 268, 283-84, *283*
*Pisaster ochraceus*, 136-39, 164, 203, 229, 258; photos, *86, 137, 138, 152, 230*
*Placida* cf. *dendritica*, *157*, 161
plankton. *See* food webs; phytoplankton; zooplankton
plants: Channel Islands endemics, 226; dodder, 162; eelgrass, 66-67, 90, 95-96, *96*, 103, 123, 168, 190, 275; exotics and invasives, 84, 122, 147, 179, 181-82, *189*; pickleweed, 161-62, *162*; Southern California, 272. *See also* surfgrass; trees and forests; *individual genera and species*
plate tectonics. *See* tectonic processes
*Platichthys stellatus*, 83
*Plocamium pacificum*, 258, 267
plovers, 83, 115, 117, 272
Podicipedidae, 83
Point Arena, 2-3, 112-15
Point Arena-Stornetta Public Lands, 114; map, *107*
Point Cabrillo, 111
Point Conception, 214-16, *216*; map, *173*
Point Dume, 227, 262; map, *215*
Point Lobos, *170-71*, 177; map, *173*

Point Loma, 272-73
Point Pinos, 177
Point Reyes Peninsula, *119*, 120-21, *121*, 123-24; maps, *107, 143*
poison oak, 179
*Polinices lewisii*, 120, 228
*Pollicipes polymerus*, 66, 88, 200-201, 229; photos, *62, 200, 201*
polychaete worms (tube worms), 94, 148, *178*, 205, 224, 233; sandcastle worm, 223-24, 228-29, 233-34, 256, *257*
pompom kelp, *85*
porcelain crabs, *100*, 101, 151, 153
Port of Los Angeles, 236
Portuguese Point, 234, *235*
*Postelsia palmaeformis*, 51, 114, 125-26, *125, 126*
power plant sites and proposed sites, 113, 172-73, 252
predation, 60-64; competition for food, 55; defensive and offensive traits, 63-64; feeding behaviors, 61-63; impacts of predator species losses, 138-39; land-sea predation linkages and their impacts, 64-65, 272. *See also* defensive traits; food webs; offensive traits; *specific life forms*
prickly pear cactus, 272
pride of Madeira, *189*
primary production, 35, 51, 52, 70, 236, 272. *See also* biological productivity; food webs
public coastal access rights, 14-16, 148
public trust doctrine, 14-15
*Pugettia*, 151, 165-66, *165*, 238, *238*
purple encrusting sponges, *207*
purple olive snail, 228
purple-ringed top snail, 70-72
purple sea urchin, 73, 114, 231, 257, 259; photos, *136, 178, 230*; rock-drilling behavior, 229-30, 242; seaweed predation, 10, 135, *178*, 179

purple shore crab, *178*
purple-striped sea nettle, 276-77, *277*
purple varnish clam, 122
*Pusula [Trivia] solandri*, 254-55, *254*
pygmy forests, 110
pygmy mammoth, 22, 226
*Pyrosoma*, 208

raccoons, 64-65, 134
rails, 121
rainfall, 142, 252
*Rallus crepitans*, 121
range shifts, 106, 132, 134, 199, 233
rays, 237
red abalone, *130*, 131, 268-69
red algae (seaweeds), 60, *87*, 101,
    267-68, *269*; black pine, 197, *197*;
    iridescent horn-of-plenty, 94-95, *95*;
    red pepper dulse, 267; salt sacs, 114,
    *115*; sea comb, 258, 267; turfweed or
    sea moss, 193, 194-95, *195*; Turkish
    towel, 112, *112*; Turkish washcloth,
    57, 193, 195-96, *195*, *196*. *See also*
    coralline algae
red pepper dulse, 267
red sea urchin, 73, 135-36, *136*, 231, 242,
    257-58
red-tailed hawk, 90, 179
redwood, coast, 79, 80-81, *80*, 82, 156,
    183
Redwood National Park, 82; map, 77
reproductive strategies, 185. *See also*
    larval ecology; *specific life forms*
research methods and technologies,
    8-10
rhizocephalans, 69, 166
Ricketts, Ed, *Between Pacific Tides*, 6,
    177
river otter, 65, 94
rivers and streams, 5; freshwater
    runoff and ocean salinity, 45-46,
    94, 110; North Coast, 94, 109, 110,
    143; as nutrient-cycling corridors,

65; sediment transport and coastal
    deposition, 5, 64, 117, 217; Southern
    California, 217, 219, 223, 252-53.
    *See also* estuaries and estuarine
    habitats; *specific rivers*
rock crab, 165
rockfish, 176
Rockpile Beach, 258-61, *258*; map, *253*
rockweed, 73, *118*, 127, *127*
rocky habitats: north of Cape Men-
    docino, 84, 87, 93-94; species
    assemblages and, 35, 50; zonation
    in, 68-69, *68*, 229. *See also* head-
    lands; sea stacks; tidepools; *specific
    locations and rock types*
*Rostanga pulchra*, 240
rough keyhole limpet, *204*, 205
Russian Gulch State Park, 110
Russian River, *116*, 117

Sacramento River, 143
*Salicornia*, 161-62, *162*
Salinas de San Pedro, 236-37
salinity level variations, 45-46, 91, 94,
    110, 143, 147
salmon, 46, 65, 83, 91, 121
salt: pickleweed and, 162; salinity level
    variations, 45-46, 91, 94, 110, 143, 147
salt marshes, 147, 236-37; pickleweed,
    161-62, *162*
salt sacs, 114, *115*
San Andreas Fault, 24, 113, 118-19, 120,
    121, 142
sandbars, 31-32, 82, *83*, 84, *116*, 117.
    *See also* estuaries and estuarine
    habitats; lagoons
sandcastle worm, 223-24, 228-29,
    233-34, 256, *257*
sanddab, Pacific, 83
sanderlings, 115, 272
San Diego area, 252-53; Mission Bay,
    217-18
San Diego dorid, 240, 271, *271*

# ABOUT THE AUTHORS

**RYAN P. KELLY** is a professor in the University of Washington's School of Marine and Environmental Affairs, working on topics ranging from marine biology to genetics to environmental law and policy. He has always wanted to be a marine biologist. A native of California, he lives in Seattle and loves the diversity of life along the West Coast. He previously worked at Stanford University and holds degrees from the University of California, Los Angeles (BS), Columbia University (PhD), and UC Berkeley (JD).

**TERRIE KLINGER** is a marine ecologist specializing in nearshore ecosystems of the US West Coast. Drawn to seaweeds and the animals that live among them, she began her studies in California and later expanded her research northward to Washington, British Columbia, and Alaska. She obtained a PhD from the Scripps Institution of Oceanography in San Diego and has been a professor at the University of Washington for more than two decades. Living and teaching in Seattle and Friday Harbor, she is happiest when counting snails on the beach at low tide.

PATRICK J. KRUG is a marine biologist who studies the ecology and evolution of sea slugs, using these colorful animals and their food sources to explore how specialized associations contribute to species diversity in the ocean. Over three decades, he has studied intertidal systems ranging from Californian wetlands to coral reefs to snowy tidepools in Scotland. He holds degrees from Princeton University and the Scripps Institution of Oceanography and is a professor at California State University, Los Angeles.

Raised on the shores of the Pacific Ocean, JOHN J. MEYER's earliest memories are connected to saltwater. He has degrees in environmental studies from the University of California, Santa Barbara (BA) and zoology from University of New Hampshire (MS) and has studied invertebrate ecology along the US West Coast and the deep sea of the Gulf of Maine. He has also worked on ocean policy at local, state, and national levels, which included time as a fellow in the US House of Representatives. Meyer currently is a communications coach and trainer at the University of Washington College of the Environment, helping scientists share their work with the wider world.